RETHINKING A NATION

RETHINKING A NATION

The United States in the 21st Century

Philip Jenkins

First published 2019 by
RED GLOBE PRESS

Red Globe Press in the UK is an imprint of Springer Nature Limited, registered in England, company number 785998, of 4 Crinan Street, London N1 9XW.

Red Globe Press® is a registered trademark in the United States, the United Kingdom, Europe and other countries.

ISBN 978–1–352–00633–9 hardback
ISBN 978–1–352–00617–9 paperback

A catalogue record for this book is available from the British Library.

A catalog record for this book is available from the Library of Congress.

FOR LEILA

Contents

List of Tables

Acknowledgments

My particular thanks go to Rachel Bridgewater, my editor at Red Globe Press, for her support of this project. Thanks also to Kathryn Hume, who read the manuscript and made many useful suggestions; and also to my colleagues and friends at Baylor University's Institute for Studies of Religion.

As always, my main thanks go to my wife, Liz Jenkins.

Introduction

ONLY YESTERDAY

This book concerns a very recent period of US history, so recent that many find it difficult even to view it as history rather than current events. If that is so, then surely it is the proper realm of the journalist rather than the historian. But the idea of writing the immediate past as authentic history does have distinguished precedents. As early as 1931, Frederick Lewis Allen published *Only Yesterday*, a still-valued history of the 1920s. Not only did Allen tell the story of that decade, but he daringly ranged far beyond the conventional political narrative to explore social, cultural, and economic trends. In 1940, he followed that triumph with a parallel history of the 1930s.

Writing any history of "Only Yesterday" has potential pitfalls, as it can be difficult to rise above strictly contemporary concerns and obsessions to arrive at a balanced long-term perspective. When today we write the history of the 1850s or the 1950s (say) we know exactly the topics and individuals that demand to be covered, so that to some extent our narrative framework is preset. We know where the story is going, and the script is already written. That is simply not the case for the most recent era, where we rely on our individual judgments to determine the critical trends, and the key events. Undoubtedly, any such judgments will involve mistakes, which will become all too apparent in later years. The historian may spend far too much time on recent trends that seem so weighty at the time, but which in future years appear trivial, while at the same time missing those that will appear so significant in retrospect. Both types of error are inevitable. Even so, we still value Allen's books as history, and marvel at the richness of the stories he tells and the quality of his analysis. As public servant John W. Gardner wisely observed, "History never looks like history when you are living through it," but history it is, nevertheless.

RETHINKING AND REVOLUTION

With those caveats, we can already identify the years since 2000 as a period of immense significance in American history, at least comparable to any past era in the scale of transformation. We will trace the impact of the 9/11 attacks and the lengthy wars that ensued, and the catastrophic economic crisis of 2008. In their different ways, the elections of 2008 and 2016 were as significant as any in the nation's history. The mid-2010s witnessed an upsurge of wide-ranging activism comparable to that of earlier eras of upheaval like the 1960s. Indeed, many of the insurgent movements and causes that we associate most strongly with the 1960s and with "60s-ism" reached full fruition in these years. Future historians will recall the 2010s as a transformative decade of upheaval.

Repeatedly, we are tempted to invoke the language of "revolution," especially in matters of technology. Among technological changes more or less since 2000, we see the emergence and triumph of social media and artificial intelligence; astonishing breakthroughs in biological science, with their commercial and medical implications; the impact of fracking and new forms of energy extraction; and a near-revolution in military matters. Those advances have revolutionized employment patterns, at a time when regions dependent on the old economic staple industries have faltered.

Social transformations include the overwhelming impact of immigration and radical shifts in the nation's ethnic structure; the decline of traditional industries and working-class communities; and a thorough restructuring of urban life and organization. We trace tectonic shifts in attitudes to gender and sexuality; transformations in American religious life; traumatic debates over historical memory and commemoration; and fundamental shifts in attitudes to climate change. All, in effect, since only yesterday.

I use the theme of "rethinking," in multiple senses. So much of the technological transformation involves new approaches to thinking and the mind. We are still trying to assess the impact on ordinary users, and how they acquire, process, and remember information, how they communicate, and how they interact socially. Those technological innovations demand a "thinking society" – a knowledge economy – which rewards those who contribute the fruits of their education, their insight and creativity. At the same time, in a different sense, we are rethinking fundamental assumptions about social life and identity, in matters of gender, sexuality, and race. Once impregnable concepts of whiteness and masculinity have come under unprecedented assault. Debates over memory imply a new quest for national identity – nothing less than rethinking America.

In approaching these years, I will stress six overarching themes:

The country's ethnic transformation *through the effects of immigration: the growth of Latino and Asian populations in particular, and the move toward a majority–minority nation.*

The pervasive impact of new technologies, *and the industries based on them: social media and mobile technologies; artificial intelligence; biotechnology and pharmaceuticals.*

The growing gulf between old and new Americas: *the divergence between regions and cities based on their ability to respond to new economic structures and social ideologies.*

Revolutions in gender, sexuality, and family: *major advances toward women's equality and full recognition of gay rights and equality; the recognition of transgender rights.*

New forms of racial consciousness and activism: *the revival of black identity movements, and the systematic challenge to white supremacy throughout politics and society, including in constructions of history.*

Globalization and the crisis of US hegemony: *the rise of China to global parity with the US, and the making of a multipolar world; economic globalization.*

An earlier generation might have termed these the megatrends.

Historians of other periods would properly object that, to some extent, such a list of trends would apply to most eras of American history, from the 1790s onward. Technology is a broad term, and a Yankee clipper ship – or indeed an Amish buggy – assumes an array of technologies that were surprising or disruptive in their day. So equally were the innovations of Thomas Edison's time. If you are looking for gender revolutions, you might pay attention to the 1840s, or the 1910s, or other eras. And have not Americans always fought over their history, using commemoration to justify contemporary values and causes? Is today's ethnic transformation any more significant, or more contested, than that underway in 1850 or 1910? Throughout the nation's history, change has been the only constant in American life.

But the pace and volume of such changes varies dramatically over time, and both in terms of scale and speed the accumulated power of transformations since 2000 really has no precedent. That is true above all in matters of information technology, communications and social media, with their multiple impacts on everyday life. We are dealing with a far-reaching change in consciousness.

In the story of immigration, in terms of relative numbers, the influx of newcomers over the past generation was indeed no greater than that of the early twentieth century. Even so, changes in social attitudes and political structures have greatly increased the impact of that phenomenon. The mass immigration of a century ago occurred at a time when American elites had a rock-solid confidence in national identity, to which newcomers were expected to conform and assimilate. Broadly, most immigrants accepted those demands, and accepted the proffered model of Americanism. But no such elite consensus about Americanism exists today, so that ethnic diversification is understood through the lens of multicultural assumptions and ideologies. For many, this contributes to a pervasive sense of change and instability, and a sense of constantly shifting foundations.

The pace of change is also critical. Joseph Stalin once remarked that quantity has a quality of its own, but so in its way does speed. How rapidly trends and movements occur profoundly affects their impact on society, and the degree of disturbance and destabilization they cause. The impact of new technologies would have been enormous enough even if it had been spread over a much longer time period, as opposed to being compressed into 20 years or so. It is scarcely possible today to imagine how many of the electronic resources on which we rely as basic necessities were not available as recently as 2000. Just contemplate a world without social media or Wi-Fi, tweets or texting. In international affairs, many in 2000 imagined a future growth in Chinese power, wealth and even military capabilities, but very few foresaw the precipitous nature of that rise.

In terms of social attitudes, the near-overnight quality of change is exemplified by the idea of same-sex marriage, with all that implies for concepts of the family and "normality." Scarcely accepted even by most liberal opinion as late as 2000, "marriage equality" is today as standard and familiar a principle as racial equality, and as incontestable. In this as in much else, the extremists and radicals of 2000 are today the cultural mainstream, and vice versa. The same remark would apply to all the symbolic commemorations of the old Confederacy – all the statues and flags – which seemed so unassailable as recently as 2012, but which by 2018 had come to bear a horrific stigma. Social and cultural consciousness changed beyond recognition. Besides the word "revolution," we will often have occasion to describe how the "once unthinkable" came to be first tolerable, and then normal, and in such a breathlessly short time span.

THE BOOK

Each of the six overarching themes that I identify was at least present in recognizable form in the Clinton era of the 1990s, which is the subject of Chapter 1. Many of the key decisions that shaped the coming century were taken in these years. The period formulated the agendas for the early 2000s, and established the vocabularies of debate. This is true, for instance, of the roots of the culture wars, the rise of the internet, and the emergence of a new global economic order, with its free trade systems.

In that new century, three years in particular stand out as pivotal moments of change – **2001**, **2008**, and **2016** – and these guide the structure of the book. The first such moment, inevitably, is the assault of September 11, **2001**, which focused the nation's attention on matters of terrorism, warfare and global religious confrontation, and that remained true throughout the Bush presidency. But that justified concern can easily divert our attention from the far-reaching social and scientific changes gaining force in these same years.

Chapters 2 through 7 sketch the large-scale social and economic changes at work in the Bush years, the underlying economic and demographic realities that conditioned political change and social movements. Besides the critical shifts mentioned earlier, I will describe the accompanying financial restructuring. All contributed to the growing divergence between the country's more and less successful regions and social groups, with the richest prizes generally going to the coasts at the expense of the interior. Surging inequalities provoked social and geographical fissures and tensions between old and new Americas, with a traumatic impact on the older white working and middle class.

As we know all too well in retrospect, that financial rethinking proved disastrous, to the point of bringing the whole world to the brink of economic ruin. The scale of that calamity makes **2008** another of the turning-point years, and it cast a long shadow over the following decade. The most alarming period of that crash coincided with an epochal presidential campaign, and ensured the triumph of Barack Obama, the first African American incumbent. Economic, political and social changes thus flowed together to usher in a new and contentious era of reform and social upheaval, which will be the subject of Chapters 8 through 13. Although the Obama administration was often disappointed in its legislative goals, it presided over historic developments in social, cultural, and environmental attitudes. Those movements reached their height between 2014 and 2016, which I have already compared to the turbulent 1960s.

The outcome of the **2016** presidential election shattered liberal hopes about the inevitability of continued social progress, as might have been exemplified by the first woman president. Although interpretations of the election outcome are controversial, contributory factors included attitudes to immigration and to ethnic and racial change, and the growing gulf between more and less successful regions and economies. The speed of change galvanized resentment, and strengthened populist opposition. Together with the crucial role played by social media in shaping the campaign – and arguably the role played by other nations – the 2016 election abundantly illustrates the overarching trends I have outlined above. Chapters 14 and 15 discuss the election itself, and the continuation of those debates through the Trump presidency. But this was anything but a simple period of reaction, as movements of protest and resistance represented a further evolution of the radical upsurge.

FORCES FOR CHANGE

Throughout these years, we will often have cause to stress certain factors and forces that drove and shaped change. As, to varying degrees, these themes run through the whole book, it might be helpful to identify them here. Although these were in no sense new in themselves, or peculiar to this era, they now assumed unprecedented significance in the process of collective rethinking.

(i) Law and Courts

The first of these forces for change is the law, and particularly the work of the courts – above all the US Supreme Court. The US Constitution gives the judicial branch a status fully equal to that of the executive and legislative, and the courts have often advanced or hindered social causes, promoted or stymied official policies. To their critics, such activism can represent a form of meddling, by which courts are actively making law rather than merely interpreting it. Whatever we make of that charge, we will repeatedly witness the decisive role of courts in shaping American society and social consciousness. Even the bitter presidential election contest of 2000 was resolved in the US Supreme Court. Since that date, the same Court has handed down crucial decisions affecting voting rights, private gun ownership, affirmative action, labor unions, patent law, environmental protection, and religious freedom, besides the usual array of cases involving police powers and the rights of suspects or defendants.

In some instances, court activism clearly accelerated the pace of social change, effectively overruling entrenched local opposition. That was most evident in the case of same-sex marriage, where the US Supreme Court decided to treat gay rights as directly analogous to the rights of racial minorities. That likely advanced the marriage equality cause by decades over what might have occurred otherwise through legislative activity alone. Meanwhile, the Court saved Obama's health care reform by refusing to accept legal challenges that many felt were sufficiently well-grounded to pose a real threat.

If Supreme Court activism was not unprecedented, other aspects of legal intervention and influence were new. Since the 1980s, a litigation revolution has transformed attitudes to liability for possible hazards and suffering. Frequent litigation and the fear of its consequences effected fundamental changes in social behavior, in matters such as attitudes to sexual harassment and child protection. Class action suits represent a powerful weapon by which activist groups have transformed corporate behavior in issues concerning harmful substances, medications, or misconduct. To take one key instance, abuse-related lawsuits crippled the once-mighty political power of the Roman Catholic Church. Litigation might yet prove a crucial tool in determining policies toward climate change.

Individual cases and decisions will be described at the appropriate point in the story, but the role of federal (and state) courts in reshaping society must never be forgotten or underestimated.

(ii) Higher Education

Educational issues have always played a paramount role in American politics, particularly at local level. In the modern era, though, higher education has been especially critical, and in ways that would have surprised earlier generations. Universities and colleges have served as dynamos of technological progress and innovation, both through organized research activity and the entrepreneurship of individuals and groups. To take one example of many, Facebook began in 2004 as a social networking service organized by three students at Harvard University. As bastions of the knowledge economy, as engines of growth, universities and colleges contribute mightily to generating national wealth.

Quite apart from the colleges' role in innovation, the concentration of such economic activity has become the indispensable foundation for the prosperity of many cities, large and small. Clusters of universities, colleges, and other institutions are central to the whole process of urban restructuring and rethinking. Globally, the immense prestige of American higher education makes it an essential component of the nation's soft power, symbolized by the legions of foreign students attending US campuses.

The rise of college education fundamentally changed the life experience and worldview of younger Americans. Besides being centers of the knowledge economy, universities and colleges supplied the institutional foundation for cultural liberalism and radicalism, for identity politics and race-based activism. These were key battlefields of the culture wars, and as such, universities have been fruitful fields of litigation in matters of free speech and affirmative action. The combined enrollment for public and private institutions of higher education was 15 million in 2000, peaking at 21 million in 2010–2011, and slightly below this today. Between 1979 and 2009 alone, the number of American men who completed four years of college grew from 20 percent to over 30 percent. The figures for women showed a still more impressive growth, and over the past decade the rates for men and women have become closely comparable. The numbers of both men and women holding advanced degrees grew accordingly.

Shared college experience affected public attitudes in many ways, not least in disseminating liberal and progressive attitudes to race, as well as to sexuality and sexual behavior. If not every student accepted progressive ideologies, most at least learned the vocabulary and the associated mores. The federal Title IX law, which was originally entitled to prevent discrimination against women on campus, became a potent weapon for promoting liberal and feminist attitudes and behaviors in the society at large. The university campus has done much to create much of our present social reality.

(iii) New Media

Throughout American history, "the media" have been indispensable to political change, and that is true whether we are talking of radio and newspapers in the 1930s, or television in the 1960s. The new media of the early twenty-first century carried on this role, particularly through social media. But these novel forms were far from being a simple continuation of previous ones, representing as they did an inconceivably rapid acceleration in the process of gathering and disseminating opinion. They differed from their predecessors in the absence of central control, and the potential they offered for grass-roots organizing and fundraising. They opened the door to a sweeping democratization and decentralization of public opinion. The names of both Black Lives Matter and Me Too began as Twitter hashtags. New media also changed the acceptable limits of public expression and debate, with controversial effects. Conspiracy theories entered a new golden age.

(iv) Celebrities and Popular Culture

No less familiar to all American eras has been the cult of celebrity, of individuals who achieved legendary status for achievements in a variety of fields – show business, cinema, sport, and the military. In the case of military celebrities, that fame has often translated to political office, and Ronald Reagan demonstrated the power of show business fame. But in the past generation, new media forms have led to an unprecedented focus on celebrities and the entertainment world, and a demolition of the wall that traditionally separated entertainment from politics (Ronald Reagan enjoyed a lengthy political career before his 1980 presidential run). In 2003, actor Arnold Schwarzenegger became Governor of California. Donald Trump owed his political success chiefly to his visibility as a reality television star, and some Democrats hoped to oppose him with their own progressive counterpart in talk show host Oprah Winfrey. Moving in the other direction, conservative vice-presidential hopeful Sarah Palin hosted a reality television show. Ex-president Barack Obama contracted to produce shows for the Netflix streaming service.

Beyond producing potential leaders, the cult of celebrity has transformed the working and organization of social movements. The world of show business and Hollywood has always attracted mass attention and devotion, but in recent times that world has become more overtly political. Entertainment and show business have been viewed almost as an unacknowledged branch of government, a "media-politics complex" on the analogy of the older military-industrial complex. Since the turn of the century, talk shows and late-night comedy have become principal vehicles for progressive activism and satire, and the opinions presented there are quoted much more widely than the words of any elected legislator.

By providing famous and venerated faces for social causes, media celebrities have driven change in mainstream society – a linkage powerfully reinforced by social media. #MeToo began as a Hollywood phenomenon before challenging attitudes to sexual behavior in many other areas of society, including politics, business, education, and the churches. Police violence against minorities achieved a sensational new urgency following the public protests by celebrity footballer Colin Kaepernick. Public consciousness of transgender issues was transformed when former sports star Bruce Jenner became Caitlyn, and a television personality in her own right. Through their wide-ranging political and humanitarian activism, film stars like George Clooney and Angelina Jolie exercise global influence with few parallels. More broadly, mass media have been essential to promoting progressive approaches across the cultural spectrum. In turn, such activism has become a primary focus of conservative resentment and counter-organizing.

In earlier eras, American historians drew sharp lines between the "serious" world of politics and the realms of entertainment, mass media, and celebrity culture, which would more properly be consigned to social or cultural history. In the past generation, such a division has become impossible. Popular culture and celebrity culture have been principal arenas of social and political debate, and policymaking. They also undermine the prestige of mainstream politics and politicians.

In his introduction to *Only Yesterday*, Frederick Allen remarked, modestly, that "A contemporary history is bound to be anything but definitive," and he claimed only to be weaving "a pattern which at least masquerades as history." On the other hand, perhaps no history can ever be described as truly definitive, however recent or distant the events concerned. There will always be room for fresh findings and interpretations. What we can say confidently is that the past two decades have been among the most momentous in the American story, and they demand to be described and understood. This book seeks to contribute to that process.

1 Unsettled Accounts

The twentieth century ended with a sense of impending catastrophe. Through the 1990s, commentators on the tech industry warned that computer programs were designed to recognize dates with the years as two-digit numbers, but many of these programs were not equipped to cope with the shift that would occur to the year 2000 – to Y2K. Computers, they claimed, would be so baffled by the date "00" that they would fail, or at best behave unpredictably. At midnight on December 31, 1999, according to this prediction, all major systems would fail simultaneously – energy, transportation, communications, finance – unleashing an apocalypse. As these prophecies evolved and circulated, many Americans prepared for the approaching Y2K disaster, assembling emergency food supplies and weaponry, hoarding cash or gold.

In fact, the Y2K disaster failed to arrive, due in part to the behind-the-scenes interventions of administrators and bureaucrats. The new century began with a pleasing lack of drama, and a collective sense of relief. Outside the specialized worlds of intelligence and law enforcement, few paid attention to stories of the thwarted Millennium Plot organized by al-Qaeda. If this had succeeded, then precisely on January 1, 2000, plotters would have simultaneously targeted tourist sites in the Middle East, hijacked airliners, destroyed a US warship, and inflicted carnage on Los Angeles airport LAX. Thousands would have died in what in retrospect we recognize as a terrifying precursor of the 9/11 attacks.

No era is ever truly new, as each is the inheritor of previous years with all their unresolved conflicts and agendas, so Americans entering the twenty-first century were not conscious of entering a wholly new era. But in retrospect, the US in the 1990s present a complex mixture of the very familiar and the utterly strange, and that is true whether we are looking at issues of culture, politics, the economy – or matters of terrorism. In some areas, we easily recognize the concerns and debates of that world. The Y2K nightmare indicates just how fundamental a part of life computers and the internet had become. In the 1990s, as today, people spoke of the culture war and discussed campus movements for political correctness (indeed, both these terms, "culture war" and "political correctness", were new coinages in those years). Our sense of déjà vu applies to some of the key celebrities of that era, such as Hillary Clinton or Donald Trump. But in many other matters, Americans at that time operated with such very different assumptions that it is hard to believe we are looking back across a mere quarter century. We are at once so close to the 1990s, and so far removed.

The closing years of the twentieth century created agendas that would be addressed in following decades. We still deal with those unsettled accounts.

AFTER THE COLD WAR

In international matters, the early 1990s marked sudden and unexpected transitions. The Cold War ended with the Soviet abandonment of control of Eastern Europe in 1989, and the collapse of the Soviet Union itself following a coup d'état in 1991. In June 1992, the US Strategic Air Command finally stood down, as the US no longer needed to maintain constant vigilance against nuclear assault. This tectonic change allowed the US to reduce arms spending, and shrink military forces. This Peace Dividend contributed powerfully to the prosperity of the following decade, and that in turn redounded to the credit of the then president, Bill Clinton.

For the first time since 1945, that US-Soviet rivalry was no longer the unspoken agenda in so many struggles and rivalries worldwide, which allowed the US a freer hand in conflicts in which Soviet intervention might once have seemed certain. The US intervened forcefully when Iraq invaded Kuwait in 1990, the opening shot in what became a catastrophic phase of Middle Eastern history. Not having to be concerned about a Soviet riposte, the US organized a broad coalition that reconquered Kuwait in early 1991.

Beyond demonstrating US global leadership, the American-led war effort – Operation Desert Storm – provided a coda to the Cold War itself, and a charter for a new military order. At the time, the Iraqis mustered one of the world's largest land armies, and they fought with the classic training, weapons and doctrine of the Soviets, and the Warsaw Pact. They encountered a US-led force in the midst of a revolution in military affairs, which was marked by laser-guided and precision weaponry, smart bombs, stealth technology, and the commonplace use of global positioning, GPS. Iraqi forces were smashed in a ground war lasting just 100 hours. The US suffered fewer than 150 battle deaths, while Iraq might have lost 25,000. This brief war was a traumatic shock for the then-Soviet armed forces, for the Chinese, and for many other conventional forces around the world. The struggle sent the message that any future effort against the US would have to take the form of asymmetric warfare, of guerrilla and unconventional tactics. As was remarked at the time, henceforward there were two ways of fighting the United States: asymmetric, or stupid. But as a few countries realized, perhaps there was also another and riskier alternative, involving the development of independent nuclear weapons.

A NEW WORLD ORDER

The Cold War had so shaped the thinking of all policymakers, East and West, that its passing demanded a fundamental rethinking about what the emerging new world might look like. In 1990, President George H. W. Bush spoke of an emerging New World Order, which as it developed had much in common with the balance of power that had prevailed in nineteenth-century Europe. The new global system would be devoted to peace, at least between the major powers, although combined military action might be needed for humanitarian interventions or the suppression of civil conflict. Local dictators or aggressive states would need to be disarmed or suppressed. An overwhelmingly powerful US faced the temptation to serve as the world's policeman and, more controversially, to help shattered nations rebuild themselves. Those noble goals had very mixed consequences.

US forces intervened in several local crises. An action in Haiti in 1994 exemplified the humanitarian goal, and the US participated in police actions in the Balkans – in Bosnia (1995–1996) and in Kosovo (1999). Kosovo illustrated how a petty rogue state – in this case, Serbia – could be curbed in order to protect its neighbors. But a humanitarian mission went dreadfully wrong in Somalia in 1993, when US forces fought a bloody battle with guerrillas in the streets of Mogadishu. This painful event tainted any talk of nation-building. As a demonstration of asymmetric warfare in action, the affair inspired US enemies, notably Osama bin Laden. Quite as notable as the roster of US actions is the list of situations that seemed to cry out for intervention, but which escaped the full force of US anger because of popular nervousness about both casualties and long-term commitments. In 1994, the US came close to direct action to prevent North Korea acquiring nuclear weapons, but pulled back. US actions against "bandit" states like Iraq and Sudan were confined to missile or bomb attacks, rather than using ground troops, the nightmare of placing "boots on the ground."

Beyond its peaceful goals, the New World Order would be a multipolar, multiplayer system, in which the US coexisted with other leading powers in a spirit of friendly rivalry. The US would exercise its "soft power," a phrase that dates to 1990. US administrations wholeheartedly supported globalization, most strikingly with a free trade agreement with Canada and Mexico. The North American Free Trade Agreement (NAFTA) came into force in 1994. For years, the world's largest economies had combined to form the Group of Seven, G7, which in 1998 became the G8 with the addition of Russia. In 1999, the group became the G20. That emerging economic order faced some severe tests with an East Asian financial crisis in 1997, followed by a Russian meltdown in 1998, but relative stability soon returned.

At every stage, the decade proclaimed the triumph of liberalism, in the European sense of the word – of democracy, free enterprise capitalism, free trade, and globalization. In 1989, political scientist Francis Fukuyama published his essay "The End of History," which in 1992 formed part of the book *The End of History and the Last Man*. Tracing the ideological struggles that had so long riven the world, Fukuyama argued that recent events had ended these conflicts, leaving liberal democracy in unchallenged possession of the field. In that sense, history – as the Hegelian conflict between rival systems – had come to an end. The Soviet collapse effectively removed from political debate not just communism, but also socialism.

TECHNOLOGY AND REVOLUTION

Contributing to the vision of a benevolent new global order was the triumphant march of high technology, which made nonsense of national frontiers. The panic wave associated with Y2K reflected a near-universal recognition of just how central computers had become to every aspect of life.

The internet originated in 1969, but it was only in the 1990s that it entered mass usage. The World Wide Web was developed in 1989, and the first web browser became widely available in 1991. Other browsers followed, notably Mosaic (1993) and Netscape Navigator (1994). Between 1995 and 2000, the number of internet users worldwide grew from 16 million to 360 million. From 1995, mainstream businesses and media outlets began developing websites, which were soon essential to the burgeoning world of e-commerce. Making computers more accessible to ordinary consumers was the spread of the graphical user interface (the windows/icons/mouse model). This had long been used by Apple devices, but it reached a wider public with the coming of Windows 95 (of course, in 1995). That release introduced the much-used browser, Internet Explorer.

Through the decade, historic milestones followed with stunning rapidity, as suggested by the then-new acronyms that today make up the commonplace vocabulary of computer usage. The first SMS message was sent in 1992, and the following year Intel introduced its new Pentium microprocessor. The JPEG format was first released in 1992; the programming language JAVA became available for public use in 1995; in 1996, USB became the standard format for connecting computers and peripheral devices. Short-link radio technology developed during the decade, until in 1997 it was titled Bluetooth. In 1997 too, online thoughts and discussions presented in a "web log" came to be called a blog, the work of a blogger. In 1999, Napster popularized peer-to-peer (P2P) networking, in the process threatening the economic model of the music and entertainment industries. That same year saw the invention of emojis. Cell phone use expanded, as did the personal digital assistants that prefigured later smartphones. Already by 1994, IBM offered consumers a pioneering smartphone.

However good internet resources might be, their usefulness depends on the ease with which they can be accessed. Wi-Fi was invented in 1997. Acknowledging the pivotal role of the internet in coming years, Apple in 1998 introduced its iMac desktop, a pioneering all-in-one machine that abandoned most traditional ports and peripherals. These developments marked a breakthrough in the role of computers in retail and commerce: Amazon, eBay, Google, PayPal, and Netflix all debuted between 1994 and 1998. By the end of the 1990s, the internet was already a vital force in the US stock market, promoting what would prove to be a euphoric investment bubble. But the impact on business and industry was real enough. In 2000, Bill Clinton signed a bill that permitted electronic signatures to be valid for contracts and transactions, a vital step in the development of electronic commerce.

The new tech world had its critics and detractors, as the explosive growth of online pornography raised real concerns about child protection and sexual exploitation. Fortunately for later development, the Communications Decency Act of 1996 avoided heavy restrictions on the emerging Web, and actually established a sense of legal order. The law protected websites from liability for materials posted there by third parties, and that applied both to criminal charges and civil lawsuits. Without such a measure, websites would swiftly have been overwhelmed by legal assaults.

Generally, the lack of limits and restrictions encouraged a sense of techno-optimism, a libertarian vision of a world in which government was largely irrelevant – and in which content was not only freely available but also free of cost. This supported the vision of inevitable globalization, and the victory of free enterprise capitalism.

AGAINST GLOBALIZATION

Of course, that vision had many enemies, both in the United States and around the world. The term "New World Order" was instantly demonized by conspiracy theorists of both Left and Right. The concept was attacked both for undermining national identity and for its celebration of unchecked capital-ism. Globalization attracted far-left protests, and in 1999 a gathering of the World Trade Organization in Seattle sparked extensive rioting. Many protest-ers now defined themselves as anarchists, as the older communist and social-ist labels were now so thoroughly discredited.

Globalization and free trade aroused concern, on nationalistic grounds and due to worries about immigration. Contentious debates over NAFTA focused on fears that companies would move jobs to lower-wage plants overseas through the process of offshoring. In 1992, billionaire entrepreneur H. Ross Perot ran a potent third-party presidential campaign on two critical issues. One was the colossal federal budget deficit that had accumulated during the Reagan era; the other was the menace of free trade and the "giant sucking sound" that Americans would hear as their jobs vanished to lower-income countries like Mexico. He ultimately won 19 percent of the ballot, drawing many independent voters. A prominent contender for the Republican nomi-nation that same year was Patrick Buchanan, who campaigned on culture war issues, but also advocated strict economic nationalism and opposition to immigration. Neither Perot nor Buchanan was successful, and their national-istic approaches were widely mocked at the time. But each in his way foreshad-owed later trends, especially the 2016 campaign that elected Donald Trump to the presidency. Issues of substance apart, Perot's eccentric and irascible character strongly resembled Trump's public image, and Trump consciously drew inspiration from both him and Buchanan. As early as 1999, Trump was floating the idea of a presidential candidacy, perhaps via Perot's Reform Party.

Even at the height of media optimism, by no means all Americans accepted the optimistic narrative of globalization.

TERRORISM

Globally, too, neither history nor ideology showed itself willing simply to fade into oblivion. The bloody wars in Yugoslavia in the 1990s showed how even a European state could be torn apart in the name of nationalism, ethnicity, and religion. In retrospect, the greatest mistake of the End of History rheto-ric was that it defined ideology solely in Western secular terms, and allowed no place for activism motivated by religion. Fukuyama's mentor was political scientist Samuel P. Huntington, who countered his theory with a far-reaching thesis about the historic interaction of great traditions and cultures. In 1996, Huntington's work appeared in book form as *The Clash of Civilizations and the Remaking of World Order*. Although Islam and the West were only two of these mighty civilizations, that rivalry soon attained a central place in public discussion.

The end of the Cold War marked neither the beginning nor the end of international terrorism, but it transformed its ideological content. Since the 1960s, the Soviets and their allies had used terrorist groups as proxies, and had strongly favored secular and Marxist-oriented groups, particularly among Arab factions. The US, in response, supported religious-oriented Islamist groups and movements, often with the assistance of Saudi Arabia. From the late 1980s, the Soviets ended their proxy support for secular Arab revolutionary groups, which declined into irrelevance. Jihadi Islamist groups moved to fill the vacuum, and directed their primary attention against the West. Formed in 1988, al-Qaeda gained a whole new purpose during the Kuwait crisis of 1990 when infidel US forces appeared on the sacred soil of Saudi Arabia, the Land of the Two Holy Places. Islamist terrorists struck repeatedly at US interests, killing hundreds of civilians and military personnel – in Saudi Arabia in 1996, in East Africa in 1998, in Yemen in 2000. Al-Qaeda developed a fascination with multiple simultaneous assaults, and the Millennium Plot of 2000 was an early attempt at achieving maximum global shock. In 1993, Islamists bombed New York City's World Trade Center.

As violence mounted, the Clinton administration failed to respond forcefully, due in part to concerns about any strategy involving boots on the ground. When the United States did launch retaliatory missiles against terrorist facilities, as in Sudan and Afghanistan in 1998, concern about avoiding civilian casualties ensured that the strikes were ineffective. Sophisticated cruise missiles achieved nothing more than "pounding sand," a phrase that neatly symbolized angry futility. Such attacks suggested to al-Qaeda that any future attacks they made would be unlikely to invite any harsher response.

CONSERVATIVES

Through the decade, issues of foreign policy or military affairs made remarkably little impact on US domestic politics. The Soviet Union was finished, the nuclear menace was (presumably) over, and any suggestion that Islamic terrorism might pose a serious danger to the US itself would have been regarded as ridiculous race-based panic-mongering. Unlike every decade since 1945, politicians no longer even had to have a public policy on attitudes to communism, to arms control, or the missile gap. The Cold War abroad gave way to the culture war at home.

Political conservatism remained strong in this post-Cold War world, a fact that seems counter-intuitive given the presidential politics of these years. Democrat Bill Clinton was after all elected to two successive terms, and his chosen successor, Al Gore, came agonizingly close to victory in 2000. But that simple narrative masks a wider drift to the political (and cultural) Right.

On closer examination, the Clinton victories fell far short of political triumph. In 1992, a short but severe recession gravely undermined the incumbent Republican president, George H. W. Bush, and economic distress contributed to the race riots that swept Los Angeles that spring. The situation should have been very favorable for Democrats, as one of Clinton's strategists stressed in identifying his campaign theme: "It's the economy, stupid!" Clinton did indeed win that November, but with a paltry 43 percent of the popular vote – smaller, in fact, than the number who voted for the notoriously unpopular Democratic candidate in 1988, Michael Dukakis. Clinton owed his victory to the large number of votes siphoned away from the Republicans by H. Ross Perot. 1992 was not so much a Democratic wave as a temporary move away from both major parties, and removing that third-party factor shifted the balance powerfully to conservatives and Republicans. In the 1994 midterms, Republicans won spectacular Congressional victories, winning the Senate, and taking the House of Representatives for the first time since 1954. They took a historic 54 House seats, in a total body of 435 Members, besides extensive victories at state level. The new Speaker, Newt Gingrich, became the effective leader of the Republican Right, and a nemesis of the Clintons. The ensuing decade was catastrophic for Democrats at state and local level, marking their worst decade since the 1920s.

Not only did Republicans in general do remarkably well, but so did the party's hard-right-wing factions. Moral and social conservatives gained strongly in the early 1990s. They committed themselves wholeheartedly to the culture war declared by Pat Buchanan in 1992 in a fiery speech that galvanized social conservatives at the Republican National Convention. Buchanan warned that "There is a religious war going on in our country for the soul of America. It is a cultural war, as critical to the kind of nation we will one day be as was the cold war itself." Culture war language epitomized widespread concerns about morality issues such as abortion and homosexuality, easy access to pornography, and the exclusion of religion from public life. Underlying these complaints was the sense that the federal courts had gravely exceeded their proper constitutional role, by imposing social and sexual liberalism upon a reluctant nation. As in the 1980s, the Republicans could count on solid support from evangelical voters, who were mobilized by the Christian Coalition formed by televangelist Pat Robertson. It was in 1994 that the National Rifle

Association adopted the solid right-wing ideology that it has held ever since, abandoning a previous bipartisan stance. The same year brought some harsh new laws directed against illegal immigration, especially California's draconian ballot measure Proposition 187. We are witnessing the birth of the Republican Party as it would exist over the next quarter century.

Already in 1992, Buchanan was singling out Bill's wife Hillary Rodham Clinton as a personification of the culture war, part of the "Clinton and Clinton" team that would promote "radical feminism ... abortion on demand, a litmus test for the Supreme Court, homosexual rights, discrimination against religious schools, women in combat units." For her foes, Hillary Clinton already personified both aggressive feminism and the maternalist state.

CLINTON AND THE CULTURE WARS

This political context shaped much of Bill Clinton's presidency, forcing him to accept centrist or even conservative policies far removed from those favored by liberal activists. In matters of both style and substance, Bill Clinton resembled Ronald Reagan far more than we might expect. Throughout his time in office, Clinton successfully deployed explicitly religious and evangelical rhetoric, making such allusions considerably more often, and more explicitly, than the Republican presidents who preceded and followed him.

On economic issues, Clinton launched a sweeping reform of the welfare system of a kind that would have been quite unacceptable to liberals 20 years previously. His administration was no less conservative in its criminal justice policy. Since the mid-1980s, the Reagan and Bush administrations had been heavily committed to the Drug War, and in 1989 President Bush declared that drugs and specifically crack cocaine were "the gravest domestic threat facing our nation today." Anti-drug zeal continued unchecked under Clinton, as draconian new laws drove the already escalating incarceration rate. The number of inmates held in state and federal prisons combined grew from 773,000 in 1990 to 1.4 million by 2000, and including other institutions, such as county jails, would raise the combined total to around 2 million. The number of imprisoned people roughly doubled during the decade, producing an incarceration rate far higher than other advanced nations.

Throughout the decade, the Clinton administration engaged repeatedly in causes and struggles that would become critical tasks in the Obama years, but in most cases the outcomes were utterly different, as conservatives scored many victories. In 1993, Clinton's attempt to establish a national health care scheme collapsed. The debacle left conservatives still more hostile to Hillary

Clinton, who was a guiding force in the scheme derided as Hillarycare. No more successful was an attempt to allow gays to serve openly in the US military. In 1996, the first stirrings of a move to permit same-sex unions led conservatives to propose a federal law to define marriage as strictly confined to the relationship of one man and one woman. This Defense of Marriage Act, DOMA, was supported by Vice President Al Gore, and it passed both Houses by overwhelming margins: Clinton duly signed it. Underlying the resistance to gay rights advances was the fact that homosexual activity was still criminal in large sections of the country. In 1986, the US Supreme Court had allowed states to prohibit sodomy, which technically criminalized all homosexual acts as well as many acts between consenting heterosexuals. Only at the end of the 1990s did state sodomy laws begin to crumble in parts of the South.

The administration faced a delicate balancing act on another explosive controversy, abortion, which since the 1970s had become a touchstone of political loyalty. Catholics and white evangelicals were generally pro-life, opposed to abortion in all circumstances, while pro-choice feminists favored easy access to the procedure. Repeated surveys showed that most Americans favored neither extreme, and recognized the need for abortion in some circumstances, in the early months of pregnancy. Courts and legislatures agonized over the appropriate limits. These debates mapped the shifting cultural frontier within the Democratic Party, which traditionally drew heavily from white ethnic constituencies in urban and industrial areas, who were strongly Catholic. Anti-abortion sentiment was equally strong among socially conservative Southern Democrats, including Al Gore. At the same time, progressive elements within the party were passionately committed to feminist causes, and those factions were in the ascendant. In 1992, Democrats infuriated Catholic voters by refusing to allow popular pro-life Pennsylvania governor Bob Casey to address the party convention. In retrospect, this was a symbolic moment for the Democratic Party, marking a new emphasis on cultural issues and gender politics rather than traditional economic and class concerns.

The new administration faced the threat of real party schisms over abortion. In 1996, Bill Clinton's solution to the dilemma involved a masterful formula, namely that abortion should be "safe, legal and rare." This favored legal abortion, but recognized that the procedure was a regrettable necessity, to be minimized as far as possible. That formula – inherited by Hillary Clinton – appealed to moderates, but became increasingly untenable with feminist critics. In the long term, the administration's greatest gift to feminist activism was the 1993 nomination of Ruth Bader Ginsburg to the US Supreme Court. Over the next quarter century, she would be a staunch advocate of progressive causes, including abortion rights.

Bill Clinton's centrism did not deter rightist enemies, as conspiracy theories swirled around the president and his wife. In 1998, the sexual relationship between the president and intern Monica Lewinsky sparked an impeachment attempt. This proved too much for a public unsympathetic to extreme right-wing ideologues, and Republicans paid a heavy price in the 1998 midterm elections. Clinton concluded his term in general popularity, and even affection.

GENDER WARS

But if electoral politics leaned so strongly to the Right, issues of gender stirred unprecedented activism and popular anger, diffusing ideas that had previously been confined to radical feminists. Gender conflict drove the culture wars, and, as the feminist adage declared, the personal became political. Successive elections demonstrated a striking gender gap between the parties, as Republicans committed to the culture wars, and Democrats increasingly became the party of women, as well as of racial minorities. In the 1996 presidential contest, Clinton outpolled his rival Bob Dole by 11 points among women voters. For liberals, Hillary Clinton was a symbol of women's aspirations, just as completely as she galvanized men's fear and anger.

The feminist upsurge predated the Clinton election, as a series of incidents sparked feminist outrage. The 1991 nomination of Clarence Thomas to the US Supreme Court publicized complaints about sexual harassment from his former advisor/assistant Anita Hill. The resulting Senate hearings were deeply embarrassing, as Hill faced a de facto trial by a phalanx of conservative white men. This spectacle spread awareness of sexual harassment, and stigmatized behaviors that would once have been regarded as playful or trivial, or even humorous. In the Tailhook affair of 1991, military personnel and veterans were involved in the mass harassment of women at a rowdy event intended to support naval aviation. The same year brought the sensational rape trial of William Kennedy Smith, a member of the Kennedy political dynasty. In 1995, Bob Packwood resigned from the US Senate rather than face expulsion in consequence of extensive charges of sexual harassment and abuse. Issues of rape and sexual violence frequently occupied the news headlines in these years, establishing a vocabulary that has subsequently become a standard part of popular consciousness. It was in 1990 that the new concepts of "sexual predators" and "stalking" entered popular parlance. In this year, Washington State passed the nation's first Sexually Violent Predators law, and California became the first state to criminalize stalking. This decade produced such now-familiar institutions as sex offender registries, with increasingly harsh limitations placed on offenders.

Notorious cases of child abuse promoted awareness of male sexual violence, and the inadequacies of the justice system in confronting what was now portrayed as a lethal social danger. Modern-day perceptions of the danger of "pedophile priests" largely originated in 1992–1993, with charges against a Catholic cleric in Massachusetts. Through the early 1990s, too, the reliability of memory provided one of the hardest fought battlegrounds in debates over abuse and sexual violence. For some, therapists were drawing forth long-concealed memories of brutal abuse suffered by their patients, including acts of ritualistic or Satanic behavior. If these charges were correct (and many critics dissented forcefully), this supplied evidence for the darkest interpretations of sexual danger, and mass patriarchal exploitation. All these trends were abundantly reflected in films, thrillers, TV series, and popular culture. Some of these productions demonstrated striking sympathy for feminist vigilantism against abusers and molesters.

Universities and colleges were critical to the surging conflicts over gender and identity, and the generalized culture wars. The term "political correctness" entered popular consciousness. A series of bestselling exposé books addressed such now-clichéd issues as the sensitivity training required at some colleges, together with campus speech codes, and reported complaints that careers had been destroyed by bogus charges of sexism or racism. The popularity of academic postmodernism provoked demands that curricula should be revised to reduce or eliminate the works of "dead white European males."

ANGRY WHITE MEN

Suggesting the profound gulf that separated the sides in the culture war was the rise at this time of a militant extreme Right. Issues of gender, religion, and morality inspired furious activism and outright political violence. Contrary to the hostile stereotype, the rightists were by no means all "angry white men," and plenty of women leaders emerged, but the Right did unite to defend what were seen as proper traditional values of family and masculinity. Guns in particular served as a symbol of independence, self-reliance, and constitutional values.

Initially, abortion was a primary issue motivating extremism. Explicitly drawing on the tactics of the older civil rights movement, pro-life militants mobilized to shut down abortion clinics through tumultuous protests and mass civil disobedience which deliberately invited arrests. In 1991, thousands were arrested in protests in Wichita, Kansas. Besides the militant organizations there also existed shadowy direct action groups such as the Army of God, which sabotaged and destroyed clinic facilities. Several doctors who performed abortions were assassinated.

But abortion was only one of the driving forces in the new activism. Between 1993 and 1995, right-wing groups formed militia movements that gathered substantial arsenals and engaged in paramilitary training, ostensibly to resist a takeover by forces of communism or the New World Order. At their height, militia groups claimed hundreds of thousands of members, drawn both from rural and declining industrial areas. The Michigan Militia alone claimed several thousand adherents. The far-right found a special cause in the disastrous assault by federal agents on the compound of a religious sect near Waco, TX, which resulted in the deaths of some 80 believers. This appeared to confirm conspiracy theories about the federal threat to civil liberties, to religious freedom, and to gun ownership. In retaliation, in 1995, a far-right cell bombed a federal building in Oklahoma City, killing 168, in what was at that point the largest ever act of terrorism on US soil.

This attack stirred national outrage and did much to discredit the far-right and the militias (although those groups had no direct connection to the event). In an atmosphere of growing prosperity and confidence, the reaction enhanced popular support for Bill Clinton, who appeared as a force for moderation and sanity. The bombing also encouraged law enforcement agencies and mass media to focus their attention in the years that followed to far-right and neo-Nazi terrorists, who became a staple of fictional treatments of crime and violence. In this atmosphere, concerns about Islamist terrorism were commonly seen as overstated or misplaced.

BLACK MOVEMENTS

In 1992, Los Angeles suffered a calamitous race riot in which over 60 perished, an event that activists prefer to recall as an uprising rather than a riot. Unlike many such outbreaks that chiefly targeted police, the Los Angeles riot was marked by brutal attacks based purely on race, targeting white people, Latinos and Asians. The conflict sparked protests in several other black communities. But in marked contrast to developments in the Obama years, we must be struck by the relatively low profile of African American militancy, and of racial conflict, through most of the decade. For some years, culture war issues like abortion seemed at least as likely to incite political violence as did racial protests.

At first sight, the situation in the Clinton years seemed likely to produce a movement recalling the Black Power upsurge of the 1960s, or portending the modern-day Black Lives Matter. The Los Angeles riots taught a bitter lesson about the unresolved problems facing black America, especially in the area of police violence and abuse. Some notorious cases, such as that of Abner Louima, who in 1997 was tortured by police in New York City, inspired fierce local activism. Conspiracy theories circulated widely in black urban communities, claiming for instance that the US government had created AIDS, or initiated the crack cocaine epidemic for its own nefarious purposes. Radical themes reached a wide audience through rap music, and some groups were explicitly political. Public Enemy's landmark album *Fear of a Black Planet* appeared in 1990. But despite these portents, overt activism was scarce. Questions of police violence or discrimination were not prominent in liberal agendas, and few seriously confronted the soaring incarceration rate for minorities.

For many African Americans, the Clinton years proved the virtues of mainstream engagement. The 1990s brought major gains, with many electoral successes. San Francisco mayor Willie Brown and Atlanta's Andrew Young were among the best-known members of a black corporate and political elite. Vernon Jordan was a close companion and frequent advisor to Bill Clinton, who was popular among black Americans. In 1995, the popular General Colin Powell was the first black person ever to be widely favored as a serious presidential contender, and in the Republican cause (Powell was a far more plausible contender than perennial Democratic candidate Jesse Jackson). Although Powell decided not to run, hypothetical polls in 1996 showed him beating Clinton by a wide margin.

Besides such establishment names, a stellar group of black athletes and sports figures became national heroes. Such conspicuous advances supported the argument that black people really could succeed in the political and social mainstream. That in turn raised real concerns about the enormous popularity of hip hop and rap music, and gangster culture. Black figures joined the general outcry against such cultural manifestations, which allegedly incited violence and misogyny, and supported negative stereotypes. Ironically, in light of later developments, one visible figure calling for restraint and respectability was actor Bill Cosby, who would later face serious charges for sexual offenses.

With black political militancy at a low ebb, there was no sense of the imminent rise of a black movement reminiscent of the 1960s.

A NEW WORLD OF MEDIA

Allowing for such differences, modern-day Americans can easily recognize the emerging political concerns of those years. Just as familiar were the means by which issues were debated, as the mass media were transformed to become what we know in the twenty-first century.

Obviously, sensationalism was nothing new in American media, nor was demagoguery. In the 1990s, though, multiple factors combined to reshape the means by which people received news and opinion, and their ability to access extreme and sensational versions of those ideas, commonly expressed in coarse and vulgar terms. The new world made it commonplace to demonize political opponents, and to disseminate conspiracy theories. The relationship between reality and fiction was transformed, making real-life cases and personalities a focus for public concern and debate. Distinctions between news, opinion, entertainment, and celebrity gossip became vanishingly thin, as tabloid values and ethos became commonplace. In an age of prosperity, serious politics gave way to a preference for spectacle and the culture of celebrity. Even before the impact of the internet, the public arena had already changed beyond recognition, transforming what could be talked about in the public realm, and how it was discussed. This new environment created the standards and expectations that users brought with them to the new electronic medium.

Multiple factors created this new world, but a common theme was the reduction or elimination of laws and regulations that would otherwise have limited the expression of views. The repeal of the Fairness Doctrine in 1987 permitted media outlets to broadcast views without offering time to rival positions. An early beneficiary of this was radio talk show host Rush Limbaugh, who became a forceful right-wing voice nationwide through the following decade. Limbaugh's success inspired many imitators, who often expressed views far to the right of the contemporary political spectrum, and who made the Clintons a special target of hostility and ridicule. Talk radio stirred public anger during the various scandals of Clinton's second term. Liberals found a valuable counterweight in television talk shows, in which comedy acquired a trenchant satirical edge. In 1999, Jon Stewart took over as host of *The Daily Show*.

A new focus on reality television took various guises. From 1989, the hugely popular show *Cops* used camcorders to depict real interactions and experiences, and again that inspired many variants and imitators. The same year marked the appearance of *Hard Copy*, a sensational tabloid show with a focus on celebrities, in what in the 1980s had come to be known as "infotainment." A new generation of talk shows drew on (supposedly) ordinary individuals from the real world, who recounted their extravagant or excessive problems and crises before a baying studio audience. The pioneer in tabloid television, from 1991 onward, was Jerry Springer. More sober shows, like that of Oprah Winfrey (from 1986), nevertheless delved into subject matter that would once have been taboo for network television. In the process, these shows turned her and other media figures into popular tribunes, more valued and esteemed than elected political leaders. The proliferation of television channels offered consumers a range of choices far beyond the original three networks. These newer channels were often avowedly partisan. On the right, Fox News (already claiming to be "fair and balanced") was created in 1996, the same year as the liberal MSNBC.

Celebrity court cases became a flagship of the new media order. Only in 1981 did the US Supreme Court reject the argument that televising a trial was a violation of due process, and thereafter, cameras appeared in ever more courtrooms. Recognizing a sizable public interest, Court TV was founded in 1991 (it later became TruTV). Some sensational cases attracted fascinated national audiences, offering much the same attractions as long-running soap operas – or indeed, as gladiatorial combats. By far the most influential case was the 1995 double murder trial of O. J. Simpson. Such cases became vehicles for the exploration of public obsessions about critical issues of the day.

Reality shows continued to blossom into the new century, boosted by the Paris Hilton vehicle *The Simple Life* (2003). Two shows in particular achieved sensational success, namely *The Apprentice* (2004), with Donald Trump; and *Keeping Up with the Kardashians* (2007). The Kardashian show expanded the idea of a celebrity as someone who was famous solely for being famous.

INTO A NEW CENTURY

Particularly given the grim events of following years, the 1990s occupy a fond place in popular memory. As the question has been aptly framed, what did you not like about the 1990s, the peace or the prosperity? Both those elements were in fact prominent themes in the decade, and naturally conditioned people's expectations of what the coming years would bring. In fact, we might usefully survey how informed people in 1999 might reasonably have imagined the near future. Only thus can we understand reactions to what actually happened in the following years.

As in most eras, most in 1999 would have projected the recent past into the near future. World peace seemed secure, with Russia set to play a constructive role as a part of the emerging global community. China would unquestionably be a growing force, but one that would be integrated into that new world, ideally as a democracy. Even in the Middle East, US intervention was nowhere on the horizon, although a strong neo-conservative faction in Washington called for pre-emptive action against a rearming Iraq. Contemplating the global future, the main emerging issues included the poverty of the Global South (a term just coming into use), and the crises of AIDS and international debt. The prospect of climate change loomed larger, with the debate over whether the US would ratify the 1997 Kyoto Protocol to reduce carbon emissions.

Internally, the United States faced the urgent problems of coping with prosperity. The stock market was booming, and the Dow Jones Industrial Average (the "Dow") had swollen from 3,200 at the end of 1992 to 11,722 by the start of 2000. Oil prices bottomed out at 12 dollars a barrel in 1998, down from the 30-dollar levels that had been common in the early 1980s. Allowing for inflation, oil prices in the late 1990s were a quarter of what they had been in the first Reagan term. The Clinton administration encouraged economic progress and confidence by reducing the budget deficit. Inflation and unemployment remained low, while productivity rates soared, eclipsing those of European competitors. It was reasonable to expect that the rate of technological progress would continue.

The US economy was in rude health. Between 1983 and 2007, the US recorded its most prosperous quarter century ever: of a hundred quarters, only four recorded negative growth. Neither debts nor deficits posed any imminent threat in the Clinton years. The surplus for fiscal year 2000 was $237 billion, and that represented the third consecutive year in the black. In late 2000, candidates Al Gore and George W. Bush both planned their policies on the basis of the $4.6 trillion in budget surpluses that the Congressional Budget Office projected for the coming decade (and some experts felt that was over-conservative). The debate was to decide how this largesse might be employed most effectively – should it be used to reduce or eliminate the national debt, to shore up Social Security, cut taxes, or to reward each party's respective political constituencies? Any suggestion of a coming economic crisis seemed as ludicrously inappropriate as threats of Islamist terrorism. Even so, rural and older industrial areas were showing worrying signs of economic distress and social dislocation, a failure to fit into the buoyant New Economy. One symptom of this was the spread of a drug epidemic among white people, in the form of methamphetamines. Those trends portended growing unrest among angry white men, likely in the form of new paramilitary movements.

Such manifestations apart, long political experience suggested that this general prosperity would have potent consequences in the coming presidential elections, where happy and tranquil voters would reward the incumbent party. Matters seemed very promising for Bill Clinton's heir apparent, Al Gore. In the longer run, Hillary Clinton would be a natural successor in 2008. If indeed it was the economy, stupid, then Democrats faced an indefinitely rosy future.

BUSH V. GORE

In reality, the 2000 election produced a shocking outcome. Gore seemed set for victory, and his vice-presidential choice – Joe Lieberman, an Orthodox Jew – actually strengthened his position with conservative Democrats, and many evangelicals. Yet his rival, Texas governor George W. Bush, campaigned well. A prominent businessman, Bush was the son of the previous President, and was heir to a substantial fortune. In 2000, as throughout his career, opponents seriously underplayed his strengths and appeal, and assumed that he owed everything to his wealth and connections. Opponents even used his verbal errors and grammatical lapses to claim, quite seriously, that he was of abnormally low intelligence. Internet memes regularly portrayed him as an infant, a village idiot, or an ape. Those criticisms became standard currency for Democrats and liberals, and media satirists.

But as Bush himself remarked, characteristically, he had been badly misunderestimated. His governorship in Texas had not only been successful, but it had coincided with the virtual extinction of the Democratic Party as a force in statewide politics. Contrary to media orthodoxy, Bush achieved widespread popularity for his close family life, his frankness, and even for the error-prone speeches that seemed to mark his words as untrained, unfeigned, and straight from the heart. Like Donald Trump in later years, this rich businessman exercised a potent anti-elitist appeal. The more liberals mocked him, the less prepared they were to take him seriously, or to challenge him.

Politically, the candidates in 2000 faced a critically different situation from the Clinton years. They did not have to contend with a third-party challenge on the scale of the Perot vote, which had so distorted earlier results: Ross Perot followed his 19 percent of the popular vote in 1992 with 8.4 percent in 1996, which was still far more than the narrow difference separating the two main parties. Even so, the third party that did emerge would exercise an influence far beyond its numbers. This was the Green Party candidacy of veteran environmental activist Ralph Nader, whose supporters were quite confident of a Democratic victory overall but who wished to express a dissent from the Left. Nader would win a mere 2.7 percent of the popular vote, or fewer than 3 million votes, yet even that tiny share proved influential.

On election day, Gore took over 48 percent of the popular vote, outpolling Bush by half a million, and almost matching the best figure Bill Clinton had achieved, in 1996. Yet the election was decided not by the popular vote but by the Electoral College, and everything hinged on a bitterly contested result in elector-rich Florida. Badly designed ballots in some counties had resulted in voters choosing candidates other than they intended, or else leaving their intentions unclear. Democrats insisted on detailed recounts by hand, a lengthy and complex process, which threatened to run past the scheduled meeting date of the Electoral College that December. In the case of *Bush v. Gore*, the US Supreme Court approved the ending of those recounts, in effect deciding the election in Bush's favor (*Bush v. Gore*, 531 U.S. 98 (2000)). Incensed Democratic partisans complained that the whole result would have been quite different without the spoiler role played by Ralph Nader.

The election's outcome proved furiously controversial, and produced charges that the incoming administration was tainted and illegitimate. Some embittered partisans spoke of *Bush v. Gore* as a naked political coup d'état. This foreshadowed the partisan bile of the coming decades, and fostered suspicion about sinister manipulation thwarting the democratic will. This was all the more worrisome because a Gore victory had been so commonly assumed, providing the first of many coming violations of the intuitive and predictable in this new century.

Some of those surprises would make nonsense of the widespread assumptions about continuing peace and prosperity, about globalization and the End of History. In the aftermath of the attacks of September 11, 2001, conservative columnist George F. Will declared that the US over the previous decade had in fact been living through a "holiday from history," a refusal to confront real issues and problems. Although deploying the most modern tactics, Islamist terrorism harked back to a seemingly long-forgotten past, which returned quite unexpectedly to strictly contemporary relevance. The theory of a clash of civilizations became vividly plausible.

2 Wars on Terror

In the last months of 2004, the US Marine Corps added a new battle honor to its long history, with a savage struggle in the Iraqi city of Fallujah. Fallujah was a bastion of the Iraqi insurgent forces that resisted the US-led invasion of their country, and which variously comprised Islamist and nationalist elements, and diehard supporters of the former dictator Saddam Hussein. The city had already been the setting for one battle the previous April, and US Marines now led a second assault, supported by Iraqi and British units. Ultimately, this campaign – Operation Phantom Fury – cost allied forces 100 fatalities, almost all American, besides 600 wounded. The insurgents lost 2,000 dead, and several hundred civilians perished. This six-week-long battle involved urban combat and guerrilla warfare on a scale that the US had not experienced since the height of the Vietnam struggle in 1968. Although Fallujah was a decisive US victory, by no means did it mark the end of combat in a seemingly endless guerrilla war.

In the context of the time, what was most remarkable about Phantom Fury was just how unremarkable it seemed. Today, it only seems natural that US forces should be deeply engaged in fighting in some part of the Islamic world. Such warfare accustomed Americans to the images that featured so regularly in the news media – helicopters patrolling the characteristic landscapes of Islamic cities, lethal car bombs and IEDs (improvised explosive devices), the regular news of troop losses, and video clips of Western hostages being murdered. Such once-exotic names as Fallujah, Ramadi, and Baghdad were now regularly heard, not to mention Kandahar and Kabul. It is difficult to recall how shocking all this would have appeared only a very short time before, when peace and prosperity seemed destined to last into the indefinite future, and when any suggestion of direct military involvement anywhere would have been viewed with horror. By the end of 2004, American attitudes to the outside world had changed inconceivably from what they had been so recently. This was the country's new normal.

Fury at the September 11 attacks led the country into a series of overseas military entanglements. The event ensured that the United States would for the foreseeable future be deeply involved with the Middle East, with terrorism, and with extremist forces within Islam. The response to 9/11 dominated the remainder of the Bush presidency, forcing Americans to debate whether their country could or should maintain the role of a hegemonic global empire.

HOMELAND SECURITY

Rarely in history can a single day be seen as a turning point, a transition between eras, but in the story of the United States September 11, 2001 constituted an obvious pivot. Four teams of hijackers seized control of airliners over US soil, and crashed three of them into highly visible targets, obliterating the World Trade Center in New York City and destroying part of the Pentagon. In all, some 3,000 died. A fourth airliner was intended for the US Capitol building, but the mission was prevented by a courageous rising by the passengers and crew: the flight, United 93, crashed in a field in Pennsylvania. The perpetrators were followers of Osama bin Laden, who was based in the nation of Afghanistan under the protection of the Islamist Taliban movement.

Quite apart from the areas immediately targeted by the terrorist attacks, the events of 9/11 affected the nation as a whole, and transformed Americans' sense of vulnerability. As a precaution, the US shut down all air traffic across the country, leaving many passengers grounded in locations far from their homes. Yet however appalling the attacks, there was a widespread realization of how much worse they might have been, and which other cities might be targeted in future. Commentators speculated about possible attacks by nuclear dirty bombs, and by biological weapons that might wreck the country's food supply. In the weeks following the attacks, a series of anthrax attacks targeted individuals and businesses around the US, leaving several dead, in the so-called Amerithrax case. Although federal agencies concluded that the attacks were the work of a lone scientist within the US, it was natural at the time to imagine an international terrorist connection. For a while, it was not absurd to think that one or more American cities might be laid waste.

The 9/11 attacks had a sweeping impact on American life. Among the most immediate consequences was an upsurge of overt patriotism on a level not witnessed for decades. American flags became a ubiquitous part of the landscape, and in politically progressive cities as well as conservative rural and suburban areas. The new mood was reflected in outspoken support for the US military. Ordinary civilians greeted individual military personnel with thanks for their service, and fliers and banners urged readers to "support our troops." Even those who would long have been hostile to military intervention shared a common vision of the need for direct action against the perpetrators. Days after September 11, the US Congress passed the Authorization for Use of Military Force law, AUMF 2001, which tersely allowed the president "to use all necessary and appropriate force" against groups, organizations, or nations involved with the attack. This brief document came close to giving the administration an open-ended charter for future military ventures, and it was a key moment in the evolution of the imperial presidency.

The new mood was much more favorable to building up domestic defense and bolstering internal security, to what now became known as "homeland security." New laws expanded the powers of surveillance available to intelligence agencies, raising once more the familiar issue of the proper balance between individual rights and public protection. The comprehensive Patriot Act gave federal authorities a lengthy list of new powers in matters of money laundering and border security. Although this Act provided a lightning rod for libertarian protests, it passed with little opposition. Even if they had concerns about such laws, few would have dared vote against a law bearing the full title USA PATRIOT, or in full, the Uniting and Strengthening America by Providing Appropriate Tools Required to Intercept and Obstruct Terrorism Act of 2001. Other laws strengthened border protection, and required educational institutions to provide more information about foreign students. New security concerns had a special impact for ordinary Americans seeking to travel by air, and who found themselves facing intrusive search procedures.

By late 2002, existing security agencies were merged into a new Department of Homeland Security, which among its other responsibilities policed the borders. The Immigration and Customs Enforcement agency – ICE – became operational the following year. The new environment had a harsh impact on the country's two international frontiers, north and south, which now became much more difficult to cross without time-consuming document checks. In 2005, a Real ID Act enhanced the standards required for the identification documents needed to board planes, open bank accounts, and enter government facilities. Such laws placed a special burden on undocumented or illegal immigrants who posed no political risk but who lacked essential evidence of their right to be on US territory. In earlier years, such sweeping changes would assuredly have met fierce resistance from political liberals, but the new patriotic mood gave an enormous advantage to government and law enforcement.

One ugly aspect of the new mood was the wave of xenophobia manifested in attacks and insults against Muslims. There was a tragic irony here, in that many Muslim immigrants had prospered in the US, where their socially conservative values led some to support the Republican Party. Symbolizing the arrival of Muslims as an acknowledged presence in the social landscape, the US Post Office issued a stamp commemorating the Islamic holiday of Eid, with the traditional greeting presented in Arabic writing. This was a powerful symbolic gesture, but the timing was disastrous, as the new stamp appeared at the start of September 2001, just prior to a wave of hate crimes and acts of vandalism against Muslim-owned businesses and mosques. Given the wide-spread popular ignorance about other lands and faiths, extremists targeted not just Muslims but a wide variety of people they believed to fit that label, including Hindus, Sikhs, Middle Eastern Christians, and generally brown-skinned people with origins in the Middle East or South Asia.

AFGHANISTAN

Three days after the attacks, President Bush visited the still smoldering site of the World Trade Center, and addressed rescue workers who were in no mood for political clichés. After the President delivered some remarks through a bullhorn, a worker called out that he could not hear the president, to which Bush responded "I can hear you! The rest of the world hears you! And the people – and the people who knocked these buildings down will hear all of us soon!" The assembled workers roared their approval with a patriotic chant of "U.S.A.! U.S.A.!" It became apparent that Bush was making serious plans to carry the war to the attackers, in Afghanistan or wherever else they might be based. Bush departed fundamentally from the Clinton approach to terrorism, which the new administration saw as sporadic and ill-focused. In contrast, Bush and his advisors sought to reverse what they saw as a decade of appease-ment. Already in the days following 9/11, Bush had spoken of a global war on terrorism, or on terror itself, and the full dimensions of that soon became apparent.

An early response to the 9/11 attacks was a US-led invasion of Afghanistan in order to destroy al-Qaeda. On October 7, 2001, US and allied forces launched air attacks, followed shortly afterwards by a ground invasion, in Operation Enduring Freedom. Meanwhile, the CIA and Special Forces mobilized local factions and militias that were opposed to the Taliban. The initial campaign was successful, and the Taliban regime was overthrown. In December 2001, a new regime was installed, with the hope that it would preside over a stable and peaceful Afghanistan. When President Bush held his State of the Union address in January 2002, he seemed a triumphant conqueror, as his public approval ratings reached heights scarcely witnessed in the history of polling.

However, from its earliest days, the US effort in the region suffered from confused goals. Stunned by the terrorist attacks, most of the American public was happy to contemplate a war that destroyed the perpetrators and their allies, so overthrowing the Taliban seemed a natural step. Yet the administra-tion seemed reluctant to use its own forces or heavy armaments rather than supporting local proxies. Initial victory was only achieved when American forces themselves intervened directly and forcefully. Even then, indecisive use of US forces permitted bin Laden and most of his forces to escape from the fortified cave system of Tora Bora where he had taken refuge. Once the Taliban were removed, the US committed to constructing a new state, a costly and futile exercise in nation-building that would prove controversial at home.

Throughout the military ventures of the next decade, the US faced a serious problem in the inadequate numbers of the post-Cold War armed forces. At the height of the Vietnam War, US forces had 3.5 million active duty personnel, a number that fell to 2 million by 1980, and somewhat below that by 1991. By 2001, the figure was 1.39 million, and even with the commitments in Afghanistan and Iraq the overall total grew little, and never again reached the 1.5 million mark. This was scarcely enough to provide for multiple simultaneous wars and occupations. The scarcity of combat troops forced the US to seek alternative solutions and to make maximum use of high technology and smart weaponry, together with rapid movement by aircraft and helicopters. Also, the US drew heavily on allied forces, whether Western allies from NATO or else local troops. But troop shortages always meant that US commanders would often fall short of the resources they needed to police and control insurgent areas. Nor could these shortfalls be made up by the extensive use of contractor forces or mercenaries, who supplied many thousands of additional personnel to the US efforts in both Afghanistan and Iraq.

As the Taliban regrouped over the following years, Afghan opposition to the occupation became widespread and effective. Resistance became much easier as the US diverted its forces away to other campaigns, and especially the commitment in Iraq in 2003. For the US, Afghanistan became a sideshow in a larger global struggle. Particularly feared by the US and its allies were IEDs, roadside bombs that targeted convoys and individual vehicles. In the invasion year of 2001, just seven US personnel lost their lives in direct consequence of the Afghan war. Fatalities then grew steadily, from 30 in 2002 to over 100 in 2007, and an alarming total of over 1,500 for the four-year period 2009–2012. The cumulative total figure for US personnel lost in Afghanistan reached 1,000 in 2010, and exceeded 2,000 by 2014. That figure did not count allied casualties, especially from such highly committed countries as Great Britain and Canada. By 2015, the total number of Coalition fatalities exceeded 3,400.

Nor were there obvious signs that these sacrifices foreshadowed an early Coalition victory. The Afghan government installed by the Coalition was repeatedly exposed as corrupt and incompetent, and prone to the excesses of tribalism and faction that had sparked Taliban growth in the first place. Large sections of the territory of Afghanistan lay beyond the power of the government, and only with extreme difficulty did US allies retain a foothold there. Making the US position close to impossible, Afghanistan has a long and largely open border with Pakistan, where Islamist causes are widely supported, including by elements of the nation's government and intelligence services. Guerrillas, supplies, and weaponry easily crossed the border into rebel territories. By 2010, Afghanistan had already become the longest war in US history, surpassing Vietnam.

If the United States had fought its recent wars with an army of draftees, as it had in Vietnam, American cities and college campuses would assuredly have witnessed riots and disorder on a par with that of the 1960s. In fact, there were no such protests, and little in the way of an organized anti-war movement. But that lack of protest itself pointed to another conspicuous problem with the US military effort, namely the unprecedented gulf that separated the armed forces from the rest of the population. With the end of the draft in 1973, military service had become increasingly unfamiliar to the mainstream population. The armed forces commonly drew their officers from families with long traditions of service, who almost constituted a distinct military caste. Ordinary soldiers were recruited from poorer and working-class backgrounds, especially from less prosperous parts of the country. In consequence, most middle- and upper-class Americans, and especially those in the prosperous cities, were unlikely to know anyone serving in the military, and thus to be affected by news of deaths and losses. Nor did they stand any risk of being enlisted personally to fight in those conflicts. The proportion of legislators with direct military experience plummeted. For large sections of the educated classes and opinion-makers, war was something that happened to other people.

IRAQ

What initially seemed like an easy victory in Afghanistan segued naturally into another major war, in Iraq. Appalled by the events of 9/11, the administration was determined to prevent any recurrence, and especially an attack involving nuclear, biological or chemical weaponry – the so-called Weapons of Mass Destruction, or WMDs. This fear demanded actions against nations that sponsored terrorism, or were involved in WMD production.

Beyond the danger posed by any particular country, the new atmosphere favored the views of those who had long supported the aggressive projection of US military power against hostile states, in the Middle East and elsewhere. Although many conservatives were troubled by the prospect of overseas adventures and nation-building, others – the so-called neo-conservatives, or neo-cons – strongly supported the muscular interventionist approach. Such views found forceful expression in the writings of Paul Wolfowitz, who had been a hawkish voice within administrations dating back to the 1980s, and who served as Deputy Secretary of Defense under George W. Bush. Other senior officials, such as Vice President Dick Cheney and Defense Secretary Donald Rumsfeld, were outspoken advocates of the neo-conservative position. Since the mid-1990s, Iraq had been the particular target for neo-con rhetoric, on the grounds of its repeated violations of arms control agreements. Very shortly after the September 11 assaults, neo-conservatives were demanding that any upcoming military response should have as its aim not just the destruction of al-Qaeda but the removal of hostile regimes in Iraq and elsewhere.

In his 2002 State of the Union address, President Bush identified as sources of special concern the nations of Iran, Iraq and North Korea, remarking that "states like these and their terrorist allies constitute an Axis of Evil, arming to threaten the peace of the world". That "Axis" phrase recalled the Nazi-led coalition of the Second World War. He singled out Iraq, which:

> continues to flaunt its hostility toward America and to support terror. The Iraqi regime has plotted to develop anthrax and nerve gas and nuclear weapons for over a decade. This is a regime that has already used poison gas to murder thousands of its own citizens ... This is a regime that has something to hide from the civilized world.

Widely reported charges claimed that the Iraqi regime might have directed or assisted in the 9/11 attacks, allegations that were officially denied, but which had a long afterlife.

The Bush administration determined to eliminate the Iraqi regime by armed force, a plan that aroused worldwide controversy. European allies such as France and Germany were especially critical, and the war threat sparked some of the largest popular protests and demonstrations ever recorded. The military build-up was divisive at home, and not just on the familiar left–right spectrum. Adding to the toxic quality of the debate, critics of the pro-war position often charged that it reflected the policies and interests of the state of Israel, which wanted to see the removal of the Saddam regime. Charges of Israeli ties and sympathies – the role of the "Israel Lobby" – sometimes came close to anti-Jewish rhetoric. In October 2002, the US Congress passed a resolution that effectively gave the administration its legal authority for military action. Despite public disquiet, the final vote was overwhelming: the vote in the House was 297–133, and in the Senate 77–23.

The US had no hope of an international coalition on the scale of the successful effort that had driven Iraq from Kuwait in 1991. Despite this, the administration proceeded with its military plans together with a few major allies, notably the British, who joined a "coalition of the willing." On March 20, 2003, the Coalition began an aerial bombardment of Iraq, followed by a ground invasion. At first, the campaign proved successful, and Baghdad fell by April 9. Seeming to confound the worst warnings about the war, the Coalition suffered only 100 fatalities. That victory – that triumph of the American ability to inflict "shock and awe" on its foes – silenced critics at home and abroad. In May, Bush staged a media spectacular when he landed on an aircraft carrier for a celebratory gathering with military personnel, under a banner that proclaimed "Mission Accomplished." Consciously or not, the whole episode recalled the extravagant military boosterism of the 1986 film *Top Gun*. Saddam himself was finally arrested in December 2003, and was executed in 2006. His two sons, the heirs to his regime, had already been killed.

In retrospect, claims of "mission accomplished" seem premature, and rash. The US position soon deteriorated, not least because of the WMD issue. Advocates of war had predicted that overthrowing the Iraqi regime would lead to sensational finds of such weaponry, and indeed, the Coalition did identify substantial quantities of poison gas. Some of that later found its way into Syrian arsenals, others into the hands of the ISIS movement. But there were no finds of nuclear or biological weaponry, and the general reaction was that the administration had simply failed to find the reported WMDs. This gravely undermined the whole rationale for military action.

But whether or not the invasion was justified, few observers would defend the subsequent occupation, which proceeded with little obvious planning. Resemblances to the ongoing debacle in Afghanistan were obvious. In both countries, limited forces were asked to do far too much with inadequate resources, and with a miserably poor political sense of the local context. US forces were utterly insufficient to cope with occupying a country the size of Iraq, and they found themselves with no exit plan. One obvious solution to the occupation dilemma would have been to enlist the older Iraqi security apparatus, the armed forces and police, but here, too, ideology took precedence over pragmatic decision making. US policy harked back to the occupation of Germany after 1945, when the victors had purged Nazi Party supporters or adherents through a rigorous process of Denazification. Viewing Iraq's ruling Ba'ath party in a similar light, the US promptly dissolved the security forces, making what in retrospect looks like the gravest single blunder in the whole story. Many thousands of able-bodied Iraqi veterans were now thrown out of work, with few alternatives but to join the emerging resistance movement. The lack of effective government resulted in a ruinous plunder of the Iraqi upper and middle classes, and threw power into the hands of private armies and militias.

An effective guerrilla war now developed, making nonsense of boasts that the Iraq venture had required little expenditure of American blood. Just counting US forces, rather than the larger coalition, there were almost 500 fatalities during the year of 2003, and a further 3,400 through the three-year period 2004–2007 – a monthly average of over 90 deaths. In April 2004 alone, US forces lost 135 dead, with 137 in November, during Operation Phantom Fury. The monthly total of fatalities still exceeded 100 in October and December 2006. The casualty rate showed no sign of falling, any more than did that in Afghanistan. The US government offered no clear response to the insurgency and, at least in public statements, senior officials failed to acknowledge the seriousness of the insurgent threat.

Iraqi rebels targeted countries and institutions allied with the US, including international agencies and non-governmental organizations (NGOs) in Baghdad itself. The importance of this strategy became apparent as the US increasingly became isolated in Iraq. Insurgents spread their efforts internationally, with terrorist attacks against US allies. A brutal bomb attack on the Madrid subway in March 2004 persuaded the Spanish to leave the Coalition. London was attacked the following year.

PRISONERS AND TORTURE

US prestige and morale were severely affected by scandals involving the maltreatment of captives, from Iraq and Afghanistan as well as the larger global War on Terror. From the US point of view, terrorists were in an anomalous legal position, as they could claim none of the safeguards available either to prisoners of war or common criminals. Such policies had some justification. The Clinton-era policy of treating terrorists as criminals to be prosecuted in court meant in practice that information gained was not efficiently shared between different agencies, and this contributed to the catastrophic intelligence failure of 9/11. Also, a wave of Islamist plots on US soil showed the continuing severity of the terrorist threat.

In the aftermath of 9/11, US authorities took decisions that raised searching questions about the detention, torture and interrogation of captives. In January 2002, the US opened a detention facility for terrorists and suspects at Guantánamo Bay ("Gitmo"), an American enclave in Cuba. As such, it stood outside the jurisdiction of US courts, although this immunity would repeatedly be challenged through the years. Several hundred prisoners were held here indefinitely without trial, and initially even their identities were kept secret. The lack of legal protections offended the American sense of due process. Moreover, denying prisoner of war status was associated with new techniques of intensive interrogation. Some of the questioning did cross the line into what would be recognized as torture, which violated international legal protections. International media portrayed Guantánamo Bay as a US concentration camp. US courts heard several cases arising from the detention policy, and over time the US Supreme Court became increasingly critical of administration policies, rejecting, for instance, the trial of detainees by military commissions.

While the existence of Gitmo was publicly known, other US facilities remained clandestine. Immediately after 9/11, the CIA and other agencies received new operating policies that greatly expanded their discretion in dealing with suspected terrorists, and over the following years US agencies undertook some controversial actions. Some involved so-called extraordinary rendition, the arrest or abduction of suspects in one country, and their transfer to another pro-US state like Egypt or Morocco where they could be held indefinitely and subjected to severe interrogation or torture. Strictly, US agencies were not directly involved in such interrogations, but of course they received the valuable information that was produced. The CIA operated covert prisons and interrogation centers at multiple black sites worldwide, where "ghost detainees" were denied access to courts. The existence of this rendition system was fiercely criticized when it was exposed by US media from 2005 onwards.

In April 2004, charges of abuse were powerfully reinforced when gruesome images came to light of the torture and humiliation of inmates at Iraq's Abu Ghraib prison. Such exposés had a special resonance for European critics, who were already deeply alienated by the Iraq war, as anti-Americanism reached heights not seen since the Vietnam era.

ISLAMIST RESISTANCE

Within Iraq, the Abu Ghraib revelations boosted extreme Sunni Islamist factions that were already gaining influence amidst the general anarchy. Saddam's old Ba'athist regime had been secular in ideology, but even before the invasion it had showed itself ever-more open to Sunni religious piety. The Iraqi population comprises about 55 percent Shia Muslims, and 35 percent Sunni, but under Saddam that Sunni minority held the upper hand.

The establishment of a democratic regime inevitably gave power to the Shia majority, to the horror of Sunnis who now found themselves excluded from what they had come to believe was their natural hegemony. With their political position deteriorating, the Sunni population was driven to greater and more determined militancy. Conflicts between Sunni and Shia militias intensified.

As anti-American resistance grew, former Ba'athists aligned increasingly with Sunni factions, and adopted religious rhetoric. One visible militant was Abu Musab al-Zarqawi, who in 2004 beheaded young American hostage Nick Berg in a videotaped murder that appalled Western viewers. The al-Zarqawi network became an affiliate of al-Qaeda, and was renamed al-Qaeda in Iraq, AQI. Also in 2006, AQI bombed the al-Askari mosque in Samarra, which was highly venerated by Shia Muslims. That atrocity aggravated the ongoing civil war between Sunni and Shia Iraqis, which claimed the lives of perhaps hundreds of thousands of civilians. The democratic government that the occupiers had supported moved ever further in the direction of naked majority rule by the Shia, in close alliance with the Shia nation of Iran. Although US forces killed al-Zarqawi in 2006, his movement became the kernel of the later groups ISIS and Islamic State.

Struggling to defend their own position, Coalition forces left Iraq to degenerate into a disastrous state of anarchy. Although the Iraqi insurgency could never hope to defeat the Coalition on the battlefield, its militants offered an exemplary demonstration of how guerrillas could make a situation intolerable for a much more powerful adversary, a classic example of asymmetric warfare. Iraq did indeed appear ungovernable, a failure that casts a damning light on the Bush administration and its leading figures.

DOMESTIC UNREST

At best, the ongoing wars in both Iraq and Afghanistan were struggling by mid-2004, while the vision of an ignominious defeat in one or both theaters suddenly seemed possible. The national consensus forged by 9/11 was replaced by intense partisanship on both sides. The military crises overseas encouraged rising dissent over domestic issues, to a degree that threatened the Bush presidency.

When Bush took office, he had hoped to win bipartisan appeal for what supporters billed as compassionate conservatism. This involved the generous use of the nation's considerable budget surplus for what would usually be termed liberal goals. A Medicare reform gave the elderly hundreds of billions in additional benefits for assistance in paying for prescriptions. In 2002, the administration again appealed to consensus with its No Child Left Behind Act, which was intended to assist families in low-performing schools. Such a bipartisan strategy was plausible as long as the administration remained popular for its determined foreign policy, but that situation changed with liberal dissent and emerging anti-war activism.

Making heavy use of emerging internet resources, liberals attacked the administration for its failures in Iraq and elsewhere and also created an influential culture of conspiracy theories. At its extremes, critics included a sizable contingent of so-called Truthers, who believed that the administration had deliberately colluded in the 9/11 attacks to promote its political and financial goals. Central to anti-Bush rhetoric were charges of the administration's improper ties to large corporations. Protests about corporate corruption found an early focus in the misdeeds of the Texas-based energy firm Enron, which collapsed in 2001 among exposées of systematic accounting fraud. As the Iraq war developed, liberal critics focused their anger on the Halliburton corporation, which reputedly exercised improper influence over Bush and Vice President Cheney. Halliburton was said to have profited directly both from the Iraq war and from rebuilding schemes in that country. Radical sentiment was exemplified by Michael Moore's comprehensive and mocking assault on Bush and his inner circle in his popular 2004 film *Fahrenheit 9/11*. The film reiterated the view that Bush had stolen the 2000 election, and that he ruled on behalf of a cynical and corrupt oligarchy, a kleptocracy.

Liberal fury was much in evidence during the 2004 election campaign, and found its clearest expression in Vermont Governor Howard Dean. Unlike most mainstream Democrats – including Hillary Clinton and John Kerry – Dean had flatly opposed the Iraq War and the Congressional resolution. He claimed to stand for authentic liberalism, for what he called "the Democratic wing of the Democratic Party." Despite early strength in the primaries, Dean soon fell behind, as Kerry and John Edwards took the lead. Kerry won the nomination, with Edwards as his vice-presidential choice.

In theory, Kerry should have been an attractive candidate in a wartime election, as his Vietnam-era military service gave him excellent patriotic credentials to challenge the misconduct of the current conflicts in Iraq and Afghanistan. However, conservatives challenged the authenticity of his record and the justification for his military decorations, and their charges had some impact. Democrats suffered another blow when CBS news released the seemingly explosive Killian documents that purported to reveal how George W. Bush had used underhand and dishonest means to evade military service during the Vietnam War era. If true, such evidence would have further heightened the contrast with the war hero Kerry. But it soon became apparent that the documents in question were false, and that CBS had failed to check their authenticity, presumably in their zeal to attack the Republican party. This confirmed popular perceptions of liberal media bias.

Despite these problems, Democrats entered the November election with high hopes of a near-certain victory, and perhaps a landslide. In fact, the election was again extremely close, turning as it did on votes in Ohio alone. Renewed rumors about electoral fraud contributed to a corrosive loss of faith in the impartiality of the democratic process. Even so, Bush secured a majority in the popular vote of 50.7 percent to 48.3, becoming the only Republican since 1988 who has achieved such a popular majority. He owed his second term partly to a sense that even his flawed administration was more reliable in the struggle against terrorism and international dangers than the Democrats. Despite all the ongoing doubts and near-disasters, national security was still at the heart of voters' concerns. As we will see, Bush also benefited from the economic situation, during a time of easy credit and soaring real estate prices, and general contentment among consumers and homeowners. At the time, it was not clear just how shaky were the foundations on which that boom was based, and how badly it would crash, producing the crisis of 2008.

THE SECOND TERM

Those rising economic difficulties dominated the second Bush term, from 2005 through 2009. Among the president's rare victories were the appointment of two new Justices of the US Supreme Court, John Roberts and Samuel Alito, who strengthened the conservative wing in that body. Otherwise, the administration faced recurring problems, and it was battered by growing charges of corruption, cronyism, and incompetence. A number of administration officials and aides were prosecuted or tainted by various unrelated scandals and investigations.

Attacks on the administration reached new heights in 2005 when Hurricane Katrina engulfed New Orleans, forcing the city's evacuation. Official agencies at all levels, and of all parties, performed appallingly, while the media exaggerated the crimes and atrocities said to be underway in the ruined city. Yet the federal government assuredly did demonstrate an alarming lack of concern about those displaced by the floods, people who were disproportionately black and poor, and who now found themselves refugees in their own land. However localized the disaster, it highlighted intensifying concern about social inequalities and racial injustice, and about the administration's incompetence.

The Republican Party was already facing serious difficulties long before the financial crash. Economic woes, coupled with despair with the Iraq war, wrought havoc on Republican electoral fortunes in the 2006 midterm elections. The Democrats recaptured both the House of Representatives and the Senate, while Republicans faced a fundamental reversal of the steadily rising fortunes they had experienced over the previous 30 years. The party had squandered much of the goodwill and trust it had received from its response to the terrorist crisis.

THE SURGE

However grim the domestic situation, the administration demonstrated a new political determination that actually succeeded in reversing the spiral of ruin then overtaking Iraq. After the 2006 midterm elections, the administration announced what became known as the Surge, a new commitment of some 30,000 additional personnel directed at key theaters of conflict, in Baghdad and in the province of Anbar. This robust counter-insurgency policy was particularly identified with General David Petraeus, who symbolized a new American will. By October 2007, the number of US forces in Iraq reached an all-time height, of 166,000. The move was largely successful, and Coalition casualties plummeted. After suffering 126 deaths in May 2007, the figure fell to 23 in December.

US military and intelligence officials strove to divide Iraq's Sunni community by persuading more conservative and traditional groups and leaders to resist the Islamist extremists. Traditional and tribal leaders had a growing interest in making peace with the US, as they were all too conscious of the deteriorating Sunni position in a state ruled by Shia Muslims. Apart from stressing quite real ideological distinctions between the factions, the US also engaged in heavy bribery. The resulting scheme involved creating a so-called Sunni Awakening (*Sahwa*), which isolated most lethal rebel factions. By the start of 2008, the US enjoyed a much stronger position than just a couple of years earlier, and had secured such insurgent centers as Ramadi and Fallujah. It was much too early to declare the war won, and between 2009 and 2011 US forces alone lost 260 dead. But successes were sufficiently obvious to raise a simple question: why had these "surge" steps not been taken three years earlier? How many lives would have been saved?

The US was now in a position where it could withdraw from the war with some dignity, as opposed to the undignified scramble that might have occurred in 2006. Under a new president, Barack Obama, the US in 2010 withdrew the bulk of the forces from the country, counting a tally of 4,400 American dead. If this did not constitute a happy ending, it was at least an ending of sorts – although Osama bin Laden remained alive, under Pakistani protection, and terrorist violence continued in Iraq itself. As we will see, though, the after-effects of the Iraq conflict have continued to generate new crises and conflicts across the region.

A GLOBAL WAR ON TERROR

Beyond the direct interventions in Iraq and Afghanistan, the Bush-era War on Terror had a global dimension. After 9/11, the US became actively involved in combatting Islamist radicals around the world, whether in the Middle East, South or South-East Asia, or North Africa, across a region commonly known as the Arc of Crisis. US intervention chiefly took the form of covert warfare and proxy military actions, using US intelligence agencies and Special Forces combined with training local armies. Directing US armed actions around the world were highly active military command units such as Africa Command, or AFRICOM, headquartered at Kelley Barracks, near Stuttgart in Germany. From its base in Tampa, FL, Central Command or CENTCOM directs operations across the Middle East and Central Asia. Also critical, if shadowy, is the Joint Special Operations Command (JSOC), which has overseen many clandestine and unconventional actions around the world.

Although they rarely made much impact in the news media, these interventions were extensive. The American military became adept at the use of airborne drones, firing targeted missiles to assassinate enemy militants. Clandestine warfare tactics won victories in the Philippines, but long-running insurgencies developed elsewhere, most perilously in Yemen. Together, these activities constituted what the administration termed a Global War on Terror, which in many ways recalled the previous century's seemingly endless confrontations with communism. A grim question arose: would the new struggle likewise span several decades?

Military considerations apart, the War on Terror proved ferociously expensive, to a degree that did much to wipe out the nation's former budget surpluses, and it contributed mightily to later financial crises. The exact cost of the twin wars in Iraq and Afghanistan is deeply controversial, but it certainly ran into the trillions of dollars – perhaps 5 trillion overall by 2017, and some authorities suggest still larger numbers. By the end of Bush's term, domestic counter-terrorism efforts were costing perhaps $200 billion each year over and above what they had been at the start of his term.

Hardest of all to gauge is what we might call the question of what might have been. If the September 11 attacks had not occurred, and al-Qaeda had never succeeded in launching a mega-terror attack, then the US would undoubtedly have diverted its attention to other global problems and crises. As it was, the Bush administration paid strikingly little attention to international situations that in later years would become too urgent to ignore, especially in China and Russia, and in North Korea. Although direct US involvement in the Middle East has diminished, those wars still drag on bloodily in various forms.

At the time of the 2000 election, no informed observer thought the country was electing a war president, least of all the eventual winner and incumbent himself. In fact, it is scarcely possible to recall that Bush presidency except in images and speeches related to war and terrorism, such as his stirring appearance at the World Trade Center site, or the horrible realities of the wars themselves. Yet despite the overwhelming significance of those military events, this was only one part of the nation's story in those troubled years. In the first decade of the century, the United States was being thoroughly reshaped and rethought in ways that had little to do with the grueling wars on terror.

3 America's New Faces

In July 2004, the Democratic National Convention met in Boston to nominate John Kerry as presidential candidate, with a keynote address by rising political star Barack Obama. Obama's speech thrilled the convention, and confirmed his image as a potential national leader. He stressed the nation's essential unity, despite its apparent stresses – the unity of Red and Blue states, of different ethnic and racial groups – and above all, presented an optimistic message of hope, and better days to come. The speech had a special resonance at a time when ongoing military crises overseas provoked a mounting sense of despair at home. Yet as Obama recognized, such negative news was only one part of a much larger national story, when most Americans were enjoying great prosperity and participating in headlong technological growth, during an era of incredibly rapid social change and development. To borrow a phrase from Ronald Reagan, the opening years of the twenty-first century felt rather more like Morning in America: it was seed-time.

Obama laid special stress on his mixed ethnic heritage. Born in 1961, he was the son of a Kenyan father and a white American mother. The mother remarried an Indonesian, so that Barack lived some years in that country, and had some early acquaintance with Islam. (His middle name was Hussein.) As he pointed out, even "a kid with a funny name" like himself could still place his hopes in the American Dream. That message resonated at a time when immigrants were flocking to the US in unprecedented numbers, transforming the country's ethnic foundations to a degree that had not been seen for almost a century. And in this era, the new populations were overwhelmingly non-European, people like Obama's own father. More than ever before, the US was becoming a world nation.

AMERICANS BY THE NUMBERS

From its earliest days, the United States has been marked by high rates of demographic growth, mainly fueled by immigration. That model changed in the mid-twentieth century, when immigration restrictions and foreign wars largely closed the borders, and when most of the population growth was domestic. But immigration reform in the 1960s resumed older patterns. The US population swelled substantially, and that trend was in full flood at the

46

turn of the century. The national population grew from 281 million in 2000 to 300 million in 2006, and to 325 million by 2017. The current figure is double the level of the mid-1950s, which represented the height of the post-war baby boom. The modern-day population also stands at 50 percent higher than it was as recently as 1975. By 2050, the US population will likely exceed 430 million. Such growth puts the US in a fundamentally different condition from other advanced nations and economies, giving it an enviable domestic market.

That demographic expansion was anything but equally distributed. Ever since the 1950s, a decisive fact in American life has been the drift away from the north and Midwest to western and southern regions, from the Rustbelt to the Sunbelt. Texas's population today is 37 percent higher than it was as recently as in 2000. In the same short period, Nevada has grown by almost 50 percent, Arizona by 35 percent, Colorado by 30 percent. The prosperity of these southern and western regions is often staggering. If California were a nation, it would be wealthier than France or the United Kingdom, although both those nations are much more populous. By the same standard, an independent Texas would be economically comparable to Brazil or Canada. Conversely, populations in many northern and eastern states have grown little or stagnated. Illinois today has 3 percent more people than it did in 2000, Pennsylvania 4 percent.

These demographic trends had far-reaching political consequences. A 1911 law fixes the membership of the US House of Representatives at 435, but the actual composition of that House shifts every decade on the basis of each new census (and that number helps decide the number of electoral votes each state has in choosing a president). Since the mid-twentieth century, the movement of population – and thus of electoral strength – has overwhelmingly favored the south and west, at the expense of the north-east and Midwest. Since the 1950s, New York has fallen from 43 Representatives to 27, Pennsylvania from 30 to 18, Ohio from 23 to 16. In the same years, Texas grew from 22 Representatives to 36, Florida from 8 to 27, California from 30 to 53. In 1950, the political might of Massachusetts was reflected in its 14 Representatives, while Arizona had just 2: today, the states each have 9 Representatives, and both states carry equal weight in presidential races. The 2020 census will further accelerate these political shifts.

THE BROWNING OF AMERICA

That south- and westward shift accompanied a transformation of ethnic geography by a process some called the Browning of America. Throughout the history of the nation, the "racial" question, for all its complexities, had essentially involved two groups, black and white. In 1930, the nation comprised 110 million white people, 12 million black people, and 600,000 "others", meaning Native Americans and Asians, but not Latinos. Only in 1970 did the US Census attempt to count "Hispanics" as a separate category, and even then the survey methods were not too reliable. Worthwhile figures date only from 1980.

The Otherness of America developed apace after the 1965 Immigration Act repealed the European-biased 1924 measure. In 1970, there were 9.6 million foreign-born Americans, a figure that grew by 1980 to 14 million, or 6.2 percent of the national population. But that growth seems pallid in comparison with developments in the new century, when the scale of change became so visible. Almost 14 million new arrivals were recorded between 2000 and 2010 alone. By 2017, around 45 million residents were foreign-born, or 13.7 percent of the population. That proportion was on similar lines to the previous wave of mass immigration in the early twentieth century, the legendary era that we associate with the millions of east and south Europeans pouring in through New York harbor and Ellis Island. Today, not only were a great many Americans born outside the country, but millions have been in the US for only a decade or less. By 2050, perhaps 20 percent of Americans will be foreign-born. Without that post-1965 immigration, the US population today would not be 325 million but closer to 250 million, a massive disparity.

The new immigrants chiefly stemmed from the Global South – from Africa, Asia and Latin America. Of the foreign-born in 2016, by far the largest contingent came from Mexico, with 11 million residents, a quarter of the whole. Others came from Central America and the Caribbean: El Salvador, Guatemala, Cuba, and the Dominican Republic supplied another 4.5 million combined. Asian countries were the other largest suppliers of migrants, including India (2.4 million), China (2.1 million), the Philippines (1.9 million), Vietnam (1.4 million), and South Korea (1 million). Together, these 10 Latin American and Asian countries accounted for 55 percent of the total foreign-born community. Not counted in the "foreign" statistics are Puerto Ricans, as their homeland is a US possession. Even so, some 5 million Americans claim Puerto Rican origin.

Complicating the statistics are the immigrants who arrived without legal consent or procedures, who were variously known as illegal or undocumented – the latter term is considered more objective and uncontroversial. As an absolute number, the undocumented population reached a peak of around 12 million in 2007, but then fell as jobs became scarcer during the recession that began at that time. Today, the undocumented population is around 11 million, some 3 percent of the overall national total. Controversially for political debates over immigration, perhaps 3.6 million of these "illegals" entered the US as children or teenagers who accompanied their families. They thus grew up in the US, and many had few ties to their original homelands. A law proposed unsuccessfully in 2001, the DREAM Act (for Development, Relief, and Education for Alien Minors) would have granted these individuals residency and protected them from deportation. That name gave rise to the description of "Dreamers," a powerful rhetorical term that suggested that these young people were only seeking the American Dream. Although the DREAM Act failed repeatedly to pass Congress, in 2012, President Obama used his executive powers to introduce a program known as Deferred Action for Childhood Arrivals (DACA), which would assist such individuals to gain permanent status. However, that measure was in turn rejected by the succeeding administration of Donald Trump. Together, Dreamers and the undocumented have played a central role in US political debate over the past two decades.

THE NEW ETHNIC SPECTRUM

The consequences of demographic change and continuing immigration have been dramatic, especially for Latino and Asian populations. (Latinos or Hispanics are officially recognized as a separate category, though they can count as either black or white for the purposes of the census: see Table 3.1.) Asians and Hispanics combined made up 15 percent of the population in 2000, but this share should grow to almost a quarter by 2025, and to a third by 2050.

Table 3.1 America's Changing Ethnic Balance

Racial group	Numbers (millions)	
	2000	*2025*
		(projected)
White	211.0	262.0
Black	35.0	48.0
Hispanic/Latino	35.0	65.0
"Other" includes: *	12.7	28.8
Native American/Alaskan Native	2.5	3.3
Asian/Pacific Islander	10.2	25.5
Total	281.0	338.0

* "Other" groups were not counted separately in 1960.
Note: Numbers in each column add up to more than the total since "Latinos" can be either black or white.

Latino growth has been very marked. In 1970, there were some 9 million Latinos in the US, rising to 35 million by 2000, and 55 million by 2014. Since 2000, Latinos have accounted for over half the nation's entire population increase, and by 2050 some 105 million Americans will claim Latino origin. They will then constitute one of the world's largest Latino societies, more populous than any actual Hispanic nation with the exception of Mexico or Brazil. By 2050, over 65 million Americans will claim Mexican descent. Driving this demographic trend, Latinos are generally younger than longer-established populations.

Asian America also expanded rapidly. Traditionally, the Asian presence in the continental US (outside Hawaii) was largely confined to particular regions, especially the Chinatowns of New York and San Francisco, and the Japanese settlement in California. From the 1960s, Asian immigration swelled mightily. Vietnamese, Koreans and Filipinos added to the East Asian presence, while millions now arrived from the Indian subcontinent. So different are South and East Asians in their cultures and social profiles that the simple term "Asians" is of little use, although it can be objected that the differences between particular nationalities are just as significant. With that limitation in mind, by 2017, 22 million Americans were of (broadly) Asian origin. Asians work in a wide variety of occupations, including smaller retail businesses, but they are especially conspicuous in cities associated with technology industries, and in college towns. Asians have flocked to American universities and colleges as students. A potent stereotype associates Asians of all varieties with learning, high achievement, and professional skills.

Besides those sizable groups were other migrant populations. The US now has a substantial 2.5 million African migrants and their children, a large majority of whom have arrived in the country since the late 1990s. Two to three million Americans claim Arab origin, and the wars and crises of the past two decades have increased that number. The Asian experience points to the high educational and technical skills associated with many immigrant groups. Today, around 30 percent of foreign-born people aged over 25 hold college degrees, and immigrants are especially well represented in such high-skill occupations as computer programmers and physicians. Many of these are indeed Asians, but in terms of postgraduate qualifications, the best-educated immigrant group is in fact Nigerians.

Adding to the nation's diversity was the rapidly expanding population of Native Americans – American Indians – who, like Latinos, were anything but a "new" or immigrant community. Like Latinos also, Native people had become much more likely to assert their identity and distinctiveness, which made them more willing to identify themselves in a census or survey, and moreover they benefited from recent legal changes. Natives, like Latinos, counted as minorities in cases of affirmative action hiring. Where Natives could declare a specific tribal connection, they stood to benefit substantially from the casino and gambling activity that had boomed on reservations since a 1980 Supreme Court decision had legalized such ventures. The number of Native Americans and Alaska Natives grew from half a million in 1960 to over 3 million today, around 1 percent of the population. Another 2 million claim Native status in addition to some other race or ethnicity. Proportions are much higher in particular (mainly western) states, such as Oklahoma, New Mexico, South Dakota, and Alaska.

MAJORITY–MINORITY

American politics in the late twentieth century moved inexorably from a black and white affair to a multicolored reality, initially in certain states, but ultimately through the whole nation. Presently, four states (California, Texas, New Mexico and Hawaii) enjoy majority–minority status, in that non-Latino white people have ceased to form an absolute majority of the population, and other states will soon join the list. Latinos are already the largest single ethnic group in California, while they make up 40 percent of the population of Texas. Already by 2020, non-Latino white people will constitute a minority of the national population aged under 18. By about 2044, the United States as a whole will be a majority–minority nation. As the scale and rapidity of that change has become ever-more apparent, so has its political impact. In different ways, issues of whiteness and white identity have gained unprecedented political significance.

Such figures should, though, be read with some caution, because of the confusion between "minority" and "non-white." In political rhetoric, some activists already speak of the United States as being "40 percent non-white," with all that implies for acknowledging the central role of race and ethnicity in American life. But as noted earlier, the label of Hispanic or Latino can be applied to people of any race, so that our figures include a good number of people who should be counted both as Latino/Hispanic and as white, and millions claim both identities. In Miami-Dade County in 2010, 65 percent of the population were classified as Hispanic/Latino, and a like number report speaking Spanish at home. At the same time, the county was also described as 74 percent white, indicating the large proportion of Latinos who identify as white.

Ethnic diversity is especially apparent in major cities. The Latino population of Los Angeles grew from around a third in 1990 to half of the whole in 2010. Asians made up a further 11 percent of that population, while the figure for non-Hispanic white people had fallen below 30 percent. Overall, around 40 percent of the city's people are foreign-born. Latinos made up 37 percent of the Houston metropolitan area, where 22 percent of the population was foreign-born. Apart from Asians and Latinos, this included a sizable African community, in what has been called the Nigerian capital of the United States. The number of languages known to be spoken in Houston is 145, compared to 220 in Los Angeles.

Newer ethnic communities spread far beyond their older geographical presence, into parts of the country that had long been used to a racial picture based solely on the black–white divide. In the Atlanta metropolitan region, long a classic white/black community, Latinos in 2010 represented 10.4 percent of the population, Asians 4.9 percent. By 2020, Asians and Latinos will together represent some 20 percent of the Atlanta region. The foreign-born population of Boston reached 27 percent by 2014, and continued to grow. Few middle-sized or small cities anywhere in the country lack their substantial Asian or Latino communities. Increasing awareness of the new ethnic presence, the concentration of American media enterprises in southern California means that films and television programs have projected that regional diversity – that majority–minority world – to a national audience. (As yet, such diversity rarely extends to starring roles in those productions.)

PUBLIC LIFE

The very recent character of much of the latest immigration means that newer groups have not yet achieved anything like the political representation that their numbers suggest. Historical precedent suggests that this process can be quite slow, and it took several decades before some white ethnic groups achieved full visibility in national affairs.

Having said that, major progress has been made in the present century in the corporate realm, and above all in the booming high-tech world of these years. Between 2006 and 2010, a quarter of new US startups in technology and engineering were the work of foreign-born entrepreneurs, drawn from a wide variety of regions. Many were white – Russian, Ukrainian, or Israeli. Google co-founder Sergey Brin was born in Moscow, Russia, and he is presently worth some $34 billion. Ukrainian-born entrepreneur Jan Koum reports wealth of over $7 billion. Indian and Chinese entrepreneurs have contributed enormously to tech growth. One early investor in Google was Indian-born Kavitark Ram Shriram, who is now another multi-billionaire. Since 2014,

Microsoft's CEO has been Satya Nadella, who was likewise born in India. From 2006 to 2018, the CEO of PepsiCo was Indian-born Indra Nooyi.

Immigrants have also scored political successes. By 2008, four people of Latino origin sat in the US Senate, which is the same number as today. Two of those Senators – Ted Cruz of Texas and Florida's Marco Rubio – were leading Republican contenders for the presidency in 2016, although both were overwhelmed by the Trump juggernaut. Confounding political stereotypes about Latinos and immigrants generally, both men are strongly conservative. The Congress elected in 2018 included 42 people of Latino origin in both houses, some 8 percent of the whole, which is about half the Latino share of the national population. In 2009, the self-described "wise Latina" Sonia Sotomayor took her place on the US Supreme Court.

Other groups secured their place in state and national leadership. In 2008, Bobby Jindal became the first American of Indian descent to serve as a state governor, in that case of Louisiana. Nikki Haley is a prominent Republican politician, a former governor of South Carolina, and she served as US Ambassador to the United Nations. She was born Nimrata Randhawa, of a Sikh family. Another rising woman politician is Democrat Kamala Harris, who is of mixed Indian (Tamil) and Jamaican origin. In 2016, she was elected US Senator from California, and in 2019 she became a candidate for the US presidency. Several other people of Indian background serve in the House of Representatives. The 2016 election brought a number of other pioneers, including the first Thai American in the Senate, and the first Vietnamese American woman elected to the House of Representatives. In 2018, the first Korean American woman was elected to the House. Increasingly, Latino and Asian political leaders are notable only for the lack of attention that voters pay to their origins.

Minority faiths are also represented in Congress, at a level not far removed from their share of the national population. In 2007, Minnesota's Keith Ellison became the first Muslim to serve in the House of Representatives, and another Muslim member was elected to that body the following year. Two Muslim women followed in 2018, one of whom was of Somali descent. In 2006, two Buddhists were elected.

MIGRATION AND FAITH

In one area of national life, namely religion, ethnic change and diversification had very different effects from what might have been expected. Historically, religious sensitivities had driven much anti-immigration sentiment. During

previous waves of mass immigration, old-stock Americans defined themselves as White Anglo-Saxon Protestants – WASPs – opposed to the influx of
Roman Catholics and Jews. The defense of Protestantism had motivated the
Ku Klux Klan, and the Old Right movements of the mid-twentieth century.
At first sight, the influx of tens of millions of Latino and Asian people might
have been expected to invigorate Catholicism, but also to give unprecedented
strength to non-Christian faiths. The prospect of such diversity excited liberals, and appalled some conservatives.

But although the United States did indeed acquire substantial non-Christian
populations, the numbers are far smaller than anticipated in some circles.
A Muslim population of some 3 million constitutes barely 1 percent of the
national total, and Buddhists, Hindus, and Sikhs represent perhaps 3 or 4 million combined. Even adding Jews would bring the number of Americans following non-Christian religions to at most 13 million, or 4 percent of the whole
population. Compared to many other nations, the proportion of Americans following minority religions is small, making the country strikingly non-diverse
in that respect.

In fact, the main beneficiaries of the great immigration wave were
Christian churches of all shades. A sizable majority of Latino migrants were
indeed Catholic, at least nominally, and they have transformed Roman
Catholic parishes across the country. As old-stock Americans fall away from
Catholic churches, those Latinos will make up an ever-increasing share of the
US Catholic church, and of its leadership. Some have achieved political prominence, as the Catholic commitment to social justice has led many to become
visible activists in matters of immigration. But many other Latinos arrived
as Protestants, usually evangelical or Pentecostal in tone, and those churches
made impressive gains among Latinos the longer those populations settled
in the US. Latinos have become a significant presence among American evangelical churches. If indeed the mid-century US will have a Latino population of
over 100 million, that is encouraging news for evangelicals and Pentecostals
alike.

Christianity was the faith of millions of migrants who came from countries where other religions traditionally held a dominant role. Some 40
percent of Asian Americans are Christian, and Christianity is heavily dominant among groups like Koreans. The great majority of Filipinos are strongly
Catholic. Churches of Asian affiliation proliferate across the country. It
is common to see elegant old churches of some WASP denomination that
have passed into the hands of a flourishing Asian American congregation.
On college campuses, Buddhist groups and societies mainly draw on white
membership, while the booming Christian societies tend to be East Asian.

Christians even represent a majority of the country's Arab Americans. As has so often occurred in past US history, immigrants are likely to cleave faithfully to their churches and religious institutions, where they find a sense of community in their new country, as well as receiving mutual aid and support to face the difficulties of the transition. Far from threatening or undermining American Christianity, recent immigrants have revitalized it. In coming decades, their role within the churches will become ever-more important.

IMMIGRATION DEBATES

Change of this scale, and in such a very short time span, has obviously had sweeping effects. Throughout American history, each new immigrant group has encountered nativism and racism. Usually, a generation or two living on US soil entitles a given migrant group to raise the alarm about some still newer arrivals, and to insist that those newcomers are violating authentic American principles. Liberals today often characterize anti-immigration fervor as being purely racist and xenophobic in tone, a panicked reaction by older White Americans who dread the prospect of living in a multicultural and multi-ethnic society, in a majority–minority nation. But immigration debates today are more nuanced than this picture might suggest, especially when the focus of concern is on undocumented or illegal migrants. Conservatives protest that they seek only the enforcement of laws that are already on the books, but which official agencies evidently fail to use. Debates over the general theme of "immigration" can proceed quite far without addressing crucial issues of definition.

Hostility to immigration runs the full gamut of activism and respectability. A sizable majority of Americans recognizes the importance of immigration through the country's history, and few call for an absolute halt. Meanwhile, only the most radical groups deny the need for at least some restrictions and border controls, and many politically moderate Americans have been disturbed at the pace of change. For decades, some black and Latino groups have feared that excessively generous immigration policies depress wages and opportunities for the poorest by importing cheap labor, and labor unions have wholeheartedly agreed with that perspective. Economists from across the political spectrum still debate the effects of mass immigration on living standards, and especially on working-class wages.

Of themselves, such concerns and qualms are far removed from anti-immigrant prejudice or xenophobia. In his 1995 State of the Union address, Bill Clinton himself addressed the question of illegal/undocumented immigrants in language that would today characterize a member of the political Right, and perhaps the far-right:

> All Americans, not only in the States most heavily affected but in every place in this country, are rightly disturbed by the large numbers of illegal aliens entering our country. The jobs they hold might otherwise be held by citizens or legal immigrants. The public service[s] they use impose burdens on our taxpayers.

Today, both words in the formulation "illegal aliens" would be doubly sensitive for any mainstream politician, and would be suicidal for Democrats. This indicates just how dramatically the politics of immigration have changed over the past quarter century.

CLOSING THE BORDERS?

Concerns about immigration focus on the nation's border with Mexico, which spans over 1,900 miles, longer than the distance separating London from Moscow. That frontier is all but impossible to police effectively without using ruthless and politically unacceptable forms of official violence. Mexican and Central American immigrants have long crossed it illegally, often with the assistance of criminal smuggling organizations. This informal process can be extremely dangerous for the migrants themselves, and the number who die sometimes runs to hundreds each year. Illegal migration angers residents of border states, where landowners often complain of damage and vandalism. The fact of such a relatively open border has become all the more disturbing in an age of terrorism, raising speculative fears that political militants or foreign agents might smuggle weapons of mass destruction into the US homeland.

Alarmingly for conservatives, the process of immigration has shown no signs of ending or slowing. Although the pace of illegal immigration has indeed slowed, that fact has not been widely appreciated, giving the impression of a country that has open borders in all but name. Another endemic grievance concerns migration by refugees, or seekers of political asylum. These numbers are in fact small – around 100,000 refugees admitted annually in the Obama years – but in popular folklore, virtually any foreigner could enter the US by spinning a bogus tale of hardship in some impoverished Third World country. When in 2018 Donald Trump described such nations as "shit-hole" countries, he was accurately if coarsely reflecting a widespread impression prevailing among many Americans.

In this area as in so much else, the 9/11 attacks fundamentally changed the national debate, adding major concerns about national security. Just between 2001 and 2002, the proportion of Americans who felt that immigration was generally a good thing fell substantially, from 62 to 52 percent – although that is still a majority. Fears about open borders sparked the formation of well-armed militia or vigilante groups who undertook to patrol the frontier themselves, and keep out "illegals". The Minuteman Project was formed in 2004, and many smaller groups persisted for years afterwards. The terrorist threat further embittered ethnic relations by stigmatizing Muslims, and also immigrant groups who were wrongly presumed to be Muslim. Most hate crimes targeted property or places of worship, but in 2012 a white supremacist killed six worshipers in a Sikh temple in Oak Creek, Wisconsin. Quite apart from white terrorists or vigilantes, African American militants capitalized on community resentment over the economic power of Korean and other Asian migrants, who ran many local stores and businesses.

ASSIMILATION AND IDENTITY

Some factors in the newest immigration wave made it especially sensitive. A century ago, governments and education authorities had given high priority to ensuring that new arrivals integrated fully, accepting American values and speaking the English language. Making that process easier, difficulties of travel prevented immigrants maintaining too close ties with their homelands, so their families were forced to adapt to American conditions. The success of integration is indicated by the sharp decline of ethnic identification after a couple of generations in the US, so that once-widely spoken languages such as Italian, Yiddish, and Polish have all but vanished among native-born Americans.

But matters were very different in the new social world. Liberal values today favor multiculturalism and the maintenance of other languages and ways of life, while elites are deeply conflicted over the meaning of American values, symbols and historical narratives. This naturally makes them reluctant to impose them on others. It is hard to imagine a contemporary school teaching immigrants about the heroic qualities of such once-idealized figures as Andrew Jackson or Thomas Jefferson, whose reputations have been so compromised by modern racial and cultural sensitivities. Any talk of integration raises the question: integration to what? Meanwhile, cheap air travel allows migrants to stay in close touch with their homelands. That process is particularly easy for Mexican Americans who might live only a few hours drive from their relatives and home communities. Not only has immigration changed the US quite fundamentally, but full integration is a distant prospect.

Far from vanishing, Spanish often seems to be rising to the status of a de facto second language – and in cities like Miami, even a first language. In such communities, Spanish media outlets and radio stations flourish, to the point where it is quite possible for ordinary citizens to live in a wholly Spanish-speaking environment. On some voicemail systems, one of the options requires a caller to "Press One For English." For some conservatives, the popularity of Spanish meant that English-speaking Americans – of whatever race – had become foreigners in their own country. Popular fears were aptly expressed by a mistaken reference made in 1994 by then Vice President Al Gore. Citing the national motto *E pluribus unum*, he translated it not as "Out of many, one," but rather as "Out of one, many," which critics saw as an unintentionally frank avowal of the goals of multiculturalism. That was a recipe not for national harmony, but rather for disunity and fragmentation, and for endemic conflict.

Bilingual education proved a flashpoint for debates over cultural and national identity. Briefly, should children of (say) Latino or Chinese origin be taught in their native languages as well as English, or solely in English? This has long been a critical question, as California alone presently has some 1.4 million English-language learners in its school systems. The issues involved cannot readily be reduced to a struggle over racism or nativism, although such ideas did motivate some English-only advocates. Educational theorists differ over the virtues of the rival approaches, while many immigrant parents favor English immersion as an effective way of equipping their children to cope with their new countries. Controversies over bilingual education have driven political campaigns and referenda. A 1998 vote in California placed English-language learners in English-only classrooms unless their parents signed special waivers. Arizona overwhelmingly approved a similar rule in 2000, Massachusetts in 2002. But debate continued, and opinion has subsequently turned in favor of bilingualism. California reversed its earlier ban in 2017, Massachusetts the following year.

Quite apart from organized movements or campaigns, resentment against immigration – or against immigrants – has never ceased to exist, although the news media have rarely succeeded in registering its scale or vigor. As we will see, that sentiment added powerfully to the 2016 campaign that placed Donald Trump in the White House.

SANCTUARY

Illegal or undocumented newcomers posed special legal challenges. By definition, these had violated federal laws in order to enter and remain in the country. Yet the grounds for sympathy were obvious, and not just for the Dreamers. Many of the undocumented had arrived in the US as refugees from horrendous conditions of war and persecution, notably in Central America during the 1980s. In the overwhelming majority of cases, people who entered the country illegally tended to live very normal lives, working and supporting their families, and generally contributing to the larger community. The conflict of attitudes – between legality and sympathy – posed serious dilemmas for agencies charged with enforcing laws.

Many states and cities wished to assist immigrants by passing laws and regulations regularizing their status. One manifestation of this impulse was the sanctuary movement, which originated as a response to the Central American civil wars. As the name suggests, it began as a mainly symbolic movement sponsored by religious institutions, but in 1985 San Francisco prohibited the use of city funds to assist federal immigration efforts. The movement then spread widely, to cover some 300 cities, states and jurisdictions by 2018, including the whole state of California. Liberal states and cities forbade cooperation with the Immigration and Customs Enforcement agency (ICE), treating it almost as a hostile external presence – as the truly unwelcome alien intruder.

States differed widely on how intrusively they could investigate the legal status of immigrants. Many jurisdictions were reluctant to allow a minor police encounter to expose a person's illegal status, which might lead to serious criminal proceedings or deportation. They were doubly nervous about the prospect of racial profiling, by which police could detain individuals solely on the basis of their apparent ethnicity and demand proof of citizenship or lawful resident status. Accordingly, some states and cities strictly limited the inquiries that police could make during encounters. Meanwhile, other jurisdictions favored a hard-line response. In 2010, an Arizona law permitted local police agencies to enforce immigration laws, under what critics denounced as a draconian "Show me your papers!" measure. (The US Supreme Court limited the operation of this statute in *Arizona v. United States*, 567 U.S. 387 (2012).)

Some states, notably California, have made major steps toward treating illegal arrivals as de facto legal migrants. One crucial issue involves driving licenses, and not just because the ability to drive is so essential to life and work in most areas. Lacking the legal right to drive prevents obtaining insurance, which raises major safety issues on the roads. On the other hand, argued critics, granting such a license abetted illegality. In 1993, California prohibited the issue of licenses to the undocumented, and most states followed. In 2013, however, a new California law required the state to issue licenses to the undocumented, provided they could prove their identity and residence within the state. Over the next five years, 1 million people took advantage of the scheme. But that decision had further consequences, as documents issued by states must be respected by other jurisdictions. Were those other states being deceived into believing that all holders of California credentials were in fact legal residents? At federal level, state licenses traditionally served as acceptable forms of identification, but in the new and harsher security environment, the US government demanded stricter criteria for documents that would allow entry into airports or federal facilities.

Throughout US history, particular regions have often felt so disaffected from federal policy that they have tried to dissent or resist, usually invoking the rhetoric of states' rights and federalism. The immigration issue has aroused passionate challenges to federal authority, but with the crucial difference that the great majority of sanctuary jurisdictions are cities or counties, which cannot claim constitutional grounds for their positions. (California is the only exception to date.) Sanctuary cities thus find themselves in an anomalous legal position, which has led to recurring conflicts with the Trump administration.

RECALLING A LOST WORLD

One of the longest-running American television shows is *The Simpsons*, which has attained the status of a global institution. Early in its history, in 1990, the show introduced a fictionalized Indian (Bengali) character with an unpronounceable name, Apu Nahasapeemapetilon. Fitting precisely into national stereotypes, Apu is an immigrant who runs a convenience store, and his voice is supplied – in exaggerated and parodied form – by a white American actor. Apu's story offers a neat epitome of cultural responses to the immigration phenomenon, as they have evolved during a single generation. Although as a show, *The Simpsons* presents highly liberal and progressive attitudes, its writers in the 1990s had no compunction about what many today regard as a mocking ethnic stereotype. Yet far from taking offense, some informed Indian commentators were happy to welcome Apu as showing that the United States was beginning to take account of its emerging South Asian presence: Apu proved that Indians had arrived. By 2018, powerful new sensibilities had emerged, so that Apu was widely denounced as a racist assault, much as minstrel shows were once used to denigrate black Americans. Indians no longer need to be reassured that they are firmly part of American life, as Apu passed from trailblazer to racist nightmare. In those same years, the portrayals of East Asian, Latino, and Arab characters have likewise changed beyond recognition.

When young people today watch films or television programs from the late twentieth century, they are bemused by the ethnic quality of the American world depicted there. After long struggles for recognition, African American characters were represented quite often in that era, and quite respectfully, but that was not true of many other groups. The American society that modern viewers see portrayed in those older productions is still mainly a black and white affair, without the many shades of race, religion, and ethnicity with which moderns are familiar. There is no sense of the rainbow society that America has become. That visual world reflects the daily experience of the young just as poorly as did mid-twentieth-century productions that censored any suggestion of a black presence. Since the late 1980s, the nation has passed through an ethnic transformation equal to any in its history.

Driving that change has been the stunning prosperity that the nation has experienced, and which has made the US such a magnet for the aspiring and ambitious from around the world. Even more than in matters of immigration, the twenty-first century has been an era of very rapid growth, and of multiple technological revolutions.

4 New Economies, New Media

Apple co-founder Steve Jobs was the leading presenter at the 2007 Macworld gathering in San Francisco. Amidst many technical glitches, he introduced the iPhone, the pioneer of all modern concepts of the smartphone; as he boasted, "Every once in a while, a revolutionary product comes along that changes everything." The new iPhone offered internet access and a GPS (Global Positioning System) connection. The iPhone could send texts and emails, and it also incorporated a music system based on Apple's popular iPod, as well as a convenient camera. Its touch-screen navigation and virtual interface represented a massive departure from earlier systems, which had used miniature keyboards. Little about this device was entirely new, and since 2002, BlackBerry had offered a smartphone including internet access, email, and texting. But the iPhone combined all those elements, together with elegant design, and far superior ease of navigation. It brought these technologies out of the realm of executives and tech enthusiasts, and into the consumer mainstream. Even to describe such a device today may seem ridiculous because smartphones have become so ubiquitous globally. At the time, the whole iPhone concept was so groundbreaking that some critics mocked it as an inevitable failure, but it met a phenomenal new demand. Apple sold 21 million iPhones in 2009, 125 million by 2012, 231 million in 2015. By 2017, the company's revenue was $229 billion, and the following year, Apple became the first publicly traded US company with a market value of $1 trillion. By 2016, the number of smartphones of all types worldwide exceeded 2 billion.

Smartphones and other mobile devices arguably did change everything, opening a new world of social media. By changing people's access to communications and information retrieval, they promoted a democratization of access to information, on a global scale, and instantly. They did it so thoroughly that it became impossible to imagine a world where matters had ever been different, or slower. In its way, the smartphone marked the most important commercial breakthrough since Henry Ford's Model T car a century previously.

In technology as much as in its ethnic and social make-up, the new century began with a fundamental shift in American realities – in the computer world, but also in such fields as biotechnology and pharmaceuticals. It is appropriate that Steve Jobs, the best-known symbol of technological innovation and disruption, was himself the son of a Syrian immigrant to the US.

NEW WORLDS

By far the most significant developments came in the area of information technology, and in new forms of communication. Many aspects of that world were already in place by the end of the twentieth century, and the internet was already a powerful presence in the 1990s. Google, Amazon, and Netflix were already firmly established. Different forms of electronic technology were vital consumption items, including desktop and laptop computers, and video game consoles.

Computers became much faster and easier to use and access. In 1999, Apple's iBook was the first laptop computer to offer Wi-Fi capability. In 2003, Wi-Fi acquired the critical role that we know today when Intel added wireless internet to its newest Centrino chip. Businesses and hotels found it essential to offer Wi-Fi access, which consumers came to regard as a basic necessity or right. Computing speeds accelerated. By 2005, processors were running at 4GHz, almost 70 times the speed of the best chip from a dozen years earlier. Even so, many systems were still slow by modern standards: 3G networking for phones debuted only in 2001, and in 2010 4G brought speeds 10 times faster. 5G systems, which in turn were 10 times faster than 4G, were appearing in 2018. Since 2006, telecom companies have responded to soaring demand for bandwidth by expanding the use of much faster fiber optic communications.

The new century witnessed two radical innovations, namely the revolution in mobile devices and the growth of social media. In the mobile world, ATT introduced texting to mass use when in 2000 it added the feature to cell phones. Meanwhile, the availability of the Sony Walkman since 1979 created a mass public for portable, individual music devices, and that popularized the use of miniature headphones. In 2001, Apple introduced its iPod digital music player, with a user interface that outclassed all existing rivals. After a slow start, the iPod enjoyed great popularity from 2004 onwards, and that in turn popularized the iTunes Store. It was natural to follow this success with a device that incorporated a phone, camera, a music player, and internet access, namely the iPhone. Other companies rushed to compete, as Google brought out its Android operating system, to the horror of Apple and of Jobs personally. In 2011, Apple's Siri became the first modern digital virtual assistant available on a smartphone, the first of many subsequent rivals and competitors.

Besides the devices themselves were the software applications that could be run on them, and the iPhone popularized the word "app." Insatiable public demand for apps spawned a major industry, and countless ambitious start-up firms. Apple's iPad followed in 2010, inspiring other tablet devices. Meanwhile, the electronic world was transformed still further by the rise of cloud computing, a concept popularized by both Google and Amazon from 2006.

One immediate impact of the new technology was the swift removal of the payphones that for generations had been such a familiar aspect of American life and urban geography, and which featured so regularly in culture and fiction. Scarcely reported or lamented at the time, that physical change symbolized a shift in communications and human interactions, and the physical space of cities and streets. Payphones were only one of the artifacts that now became rarities, such as the bank checks that had once been the mainstay of personal finance, the road maps that once helped drivers find their way, or handwritten letters.

Video games constituted another major industry marked by constant development and innovation. Major new products in these years included Microsoft's series of Xbox consoles, introduced in 2001. Between 2005 and 2013, the Xbox 360 sold 77 million units. Its main competitor, Nintendo's Wii, debuted in 2006, and sold over 100 million worldwide. The Xbox Live (2002) brought still further innovations, by introducing online multiplayer gaming to the casual user. Despite frequent legal challenges to games regarded as violent or unsuitable for children, the US Supreme Court decided in 2011 that laws restricting the sale of such items to children violated First Amendment protections (*Brown v. Entertainment Merchants Association*, 564 U.S. 786 (2011)). By 2017, the US video game industry claimed revenues of $37 billion, and provided 220,000 jobs.

SOCIAL MEDIA AND COMMUNITY

The concept of social media involves online communities in which people make contacts and share interests, as users generate content. Social media predated the World Wide Web, and had a long track record in bringing together people seeking sexual contacts. The term "social media" dates from the late 1990s, but the real boom happened after 2000, with a series of new networking websites. The most important included the highly successful Friendster (2002), the name of which recalled the peer-to-peer networking of Napster. LinkedIn followed in 2003, Myspace in 2003, and until 2010 Myspace was the world's largest social networking site. In a different way, shared knowledge was the basis of Wikipedia, which dates from 2001. So fundamental have some of these sites become to shaping popular consciousness that it is difficult to recall just how very new the leading electronic institutions are. Facebook, YouTube, and the microblogging site Twitter all debuted between 2004 and 2006, and the same short period brought Yelp and Reddit. Among many other novelties, Twitter's hashtags debuted in 2007. The upsurge of user-generated content proved immensely influential: in 2006, *Time* magazine named its person of the year as "You."

The process of creation and innovation has continued unchecked ever since. From 2007, smartphones and tablets made it much simpler for people to check and contribute to the networks, to express thoughts through Facebook and Twitter. By 2009, users could judge Facebook content through the new Like button, as constant rating and evaluation became an essential feature of electronic interactions. Much of American life came to consist of constantly evaluating and rating experience, and sharing those views. In 2012, the number of active Facebook users reached a billion, two billion by 2017. By 2017, Twitter had 330 million monthly active users. In 2012, Tinder revolutionized sexual interactions with a social search app that allowed users to like or dislike potential partners by swiping left or right.

It is difficult to exaggerate the disruptive impact of the new social media worlds. In commerce, advertising and retail have been transformed, while much marketing depends on a cohort of powerful "influencers" who owe their celebrity to social media outlets: used in this sense, the word has entered the language largely since 2012. The shift to the electronic world has dealt a fatal blow to many print media outlets. The lodging rental firm Airbnb (2008) has turned the travel industry upside down, and allows ordinary people a previously unsuspected source of income. Twitter created a whole new environment for discussing social issues and mobilizing for causes, for building and destroying reputations. The Twitterverse constitutes a whole new public space. New social media have revolutionized the worlds of political campaigning and participation, for organizing, electioneering, and fundraising. Smartphones changed visual consciousness, as easy access to cameras and video drove a taste for recording any and all actions and behaviors, including those that participants did not wish to be seen. To take one example of many, criminal justice was transformed by the ease with which ordinary individuals could record interactions between police and citizens. The Instagram service dates from 2010, and claimed a billion monthly users by 2018. Snapchat arrived in 2011.

In creating new forms of community, the emerging electronic worlds marked a shift in behavior and consciousness that matched or exceeded any other technological innovation in centuries. The rise of social media and the internet have caused a fundamental reorientation of the way people think and remember, how they organize and retrieve information, on a scale unparalleled at least since the coming of printing six centuries ago. Social media changed such basic behaviors as the means of dating and forming intimate relationships, and profoundly altered concepts of friendship and acquaintance. By removing the need for personal, physical interaction, new media subverted such once basic human concepts as participation and the sense of place, and the whole idea of "being present." Arguably, these trends reduced actual physical participation in events and gatherings, and powerfully encouraged isolation and loneliness.

New technologies often inspire pessimistic responses about the grievous effects they have had on a supposedly superior old world, and social media are no exception. In some instances, though, we can legitimately point to harmful effects, including claims of device addiction. Twitter debates easily escalate into the realm of abuse and paranoia, where contributors post bitter remarks they would never dream of uttering in personal interaction. At its most extreme, hostility advances to the level of personal threats, and the public release of sensitive or embarrassing personal information. Social media exchanges can degenerate into mob rule. Such problems became glaringly apparent during the Gamergate controversy of 2014, which originated as a coordinated series of attacks on women developers in the video game industry. Protected by online anonymity, (male) Gamergaters used their electronic platforms to express vicious misogyny and intolerance, as they threatened their female rivals with violence and rape, and spread slanderous accusations against them. Gamergate demonstrated how the culture war in its most acute and bigoted form had migrated onto the internet.

Of course, such manifestations are only one ugly component of a much larger and generally benevolent phenomenon. So extraordinary are such changes, and so numerous, that it is hard to believe they have occurred in such a brief time, less than two decades.

OTHER TECHNOLOGIES

Besides the internet, other forms of technology played a critical role in the new economies, and some held the prospect of much greater impact in the near future.

Fundamental to the whole mobile world was the wholesale use of GPS. GPS is a navigation system that relies on a network of satellites orbiting the earth, and which allows users to know their precise location. The system was originally developed for military use, but its civilian potential became evident.

In 2000, President Clinton ordered the military to stop scrambling signals so that civilians could use the system fully. Since that time, GPS has revolutionized aviation and transport, navigation and engineering, and is essential to mobile phone use. It is the basis of drone technology, with all that implies for both commerce and military innovation. The collection and mapping of GPS-derived data has created a whole field of Geographical Information Systems (GIS), which has transformed sectors as diverse as policing and the real estate industry, public planning and the provision of public services. GIS mapping has powered social science and research. Since the earliest days of settlement and exploration, American history has been based on ever-more reliable mapping, which new technologies carried forward to unimaginable degrees of precision.

Many of the new technologies uncannily replicated the dreams of science fiction authors and fans through the decades, and other aspects of those speculative worlds now came close to reality. Science fiction had long imagined mobile visual communication through videophones: Skype appeared in 2003, and soon adapted to cell phones. More significant was the steady expansion of robotics in manufacturing, together with machine vision and motion control technologies. Autonomous uncrewed/unmanned vehicles now crisscross the skies in the well-known form of drones, but also flourish in land and underwater forms, deployed by the military and by private industry, and increasingly owned by private hobbyists. Although these were not technically robots, such vehicles matched well with traditional imagery from science fiction. Enhancing the resemblance to fictional robots is the growing use of voice commands to direct the workings of computers of all kinds, including those vehicles. Domotics (home automation) is the emerging science of using the voice to control the home and its smart devices, which together constitute an Internet of Things (IoT).

Several fields of research promise major advances. The most significant is artificial intelligence (AI), by which machines learn through interactions with their environment, and respond appropriately to changing circumstances. AI was built on research dating back to the 1950s, but in a move that attracted global attention in 1997 the computer chess-playing system Deep Blue defeated world chess champion Garry Kasparov. Huge increases in computing power in the new century made rapid progress possible. The number of active projects soared in the mid-2010s, with some spectacular milestones. In 2016, an AI program defeated a world champion of the game of Go, an achievement significantly harder than the chess victory. AI became ever-more important in the work of government and policing, an increasingly dependable tool for image recognition and facial identification.

Another development that apparently harks back to science fiction is virtual reality (VR), computer-generated worlds that simulate real-world experience. Again, there had been high hopes of easily accessible VR in the 1990s, usually in the context of gaming, but again the real leaps forward occurred after 2000. After years of experimentation, the Oculus Rift headset became available in 2016, and hundreds of other companies were pressing forward with their own ventures. Scarcely less important is augmented reality (AR), in which digitally created images and sensations are imposed upon real-world settings, as a powerful tool for visualization. That idea received worldwide publicity in 2016 with the fad for the game Pokémon Go. AR has countless possible applications, in worlds as diverse as architecture, medicine, and – as always in such matters – the military.

Other newer technologies include blockchain, a continuously growing series of blocks or records, secured by cryptography and shared in a peer-to-peer network. This provides a secure and decentralized means of recording transactions between parties. Invented in 2008, blockchain is the basis of digital currencies such as Bitcoin, which some believe will drive a financial revolution.

CORPORATE IMPACT

Some IT corporations have gone on to enjoy gigantic wealth and power, to the point that they dwarf traditional American businesses. In terms of revenue, Apple in 2016 ranked as the world's twelfth largest corporation by revenue, standing alongside such goliaths as Toyota and BP. A listing of the world's largest corporations by market capitalization was headed by Apple, and followed by Alphabet (Google's parent company), Microsoft, Facebook, and Amazon. Other formidable global presences included Intel, Cisco, and Oracle. (Chinese firms like Alibaba and Tencent were fast approaching this exalted status.)

Now, this power has to be put into perspective, in that US high-tech companies exist alongside giant corporations from other sectors, including oil and gas, finance and banking, health care and pharmaceuticals, professional services and retail. But in every case, those other sectors depend entirely for their everyday functioning on electronic systems of a sophistication that would have been unthinkable 20 years ago. Noting the pervasive significance of electronic technologies and related approaches, observers speak of a "techification of industries," which applies to finance, education, and medicine – respectively fintech, edtech, and medtech (healthtec). Other current buzzwords include legaltech and retailtech. Access to mobile devices and to untold resources of data has had its impact in the world of agriculture, which remains a huge US enterprise, and a very significant exporter. In the world of manufacturing, electronic technologies and computers have revolutionized cars and transportation. Today, all major economic enterprises expect that their operations will soon be transformed once more by artificial intelligence.

The triumphant march of the IT companies have created vast personal fortunes, and in the process rewritten American images of wealth. In the new world, the best-known corporate titans tended to be relatively young individuals, often with studious or hippyish images, a dramatic contrast to the staid world of the Fords and Rockefellers. Apart from Steve Jobs, legendary examples included Bill Gates (Microsoft), Jeff Bezos (Amazon), and Mark Zuckerberg (Facebook), but there were plenty of other tech billionaires. Some devoted their wealth to philanthropy, and on an appropriately colossal scale. Launched in 2000, the Bill and Melinda Gates Foundation presently holds $38 billion in assets.

Such dazzling success stories offered potent examples for new entrepreneurs and the venture capitalists who supported them. The gold rush atmosphere inspired an array of start-up companies, concentrated especially in hubs such as the San Francisco Bay area. Each entrepreneur dreamed of building toward creating a public company, through an Initial Public Offering (IPO) that could raise them to the heights of the established stars. Venture capital found its symbolic capital in Silicon Valley, along Sand Hill Road in Menlo Park. "Sand Hill Road" became a metaphor for private equity, just as "Wall Street" represented US business, and "K Street" symbolized Washington lobbyists.

EMPLOYMENT

High technology, broadly defined, was vital to the national job picture, especially when we include tech specialists working in service sectors like banking and financial services. By 2017, 7.3 million Americans worked in high tech. That represents about 4 percent of the US workforce, a larger share than in such traditional fields as construction. Most of these jobs offered high rates of pay, and reinforced the larger trend toward rewarding high educational attainment.

Many millions more had their work and employment defined by mobile technologies. The obvious example is car hire services such as Uber (founded 2009) and Lyft (2012), which assume that users will contact them by smartphone. These are classic examples of the kind of disruption of traditional economic models caused by new technologies. In transforming urban life, such firms have caused untold damage to the older taxi-cab industry. Most basically, they challenge familiar ideas of employment. Notionally, drivers are not employees but independent contractors, who might well work in other areas to maintain their livelihood. They are part of the "gig economy," in which individuals work in short-term and temporary positions or projects (gigs), with nothing like the long-term security of employment seen as normal in earlier decades. That in turn has transformed concepts such as pensions and benefits, not to mention prospects for labor organizing.

Much of the employment generated by the gargantuan new industries was created in countries other than the US. Globalization was fundamental to the operation of corporations that relied on overseas factories to build devices. iPhone manufacture was concentrated in China, but with contributions from factories in other lands, united in efficient interlocking chains. Apart from manufacture, US corporations of all kinds relied on call centers in lower-wage countries around the world. Such enterprises treated national boundaries as largely irrelevant, and favored worldwide interdependence. They also fostered the US–China relationship.

BEYOND IT

Besides electronic technologies, other fields were also advancing fast, and creating substantial industries in their turn. Since the 1970s, information technologies had developed alongside new discoveries in the life sciences, in biotechnology. In the new century, progress in biological sciences continued with many practical real-world applications, especially pharmaceuticals. Advances in genetics were symbolized by the historic project that mapped and identified all the components of the human genome, and which completed its historic achievement in 2003. Another symbolic milestone occurred in 2010, when geneticist Craig Venter announced the creation of a synthetic self-replicating bacterial cell – the world's first synthetic life form. For many reasons, such an achievement aroused controversy, not least that scientists were "playing God." Might such an organism escape into the natural world, or might the new technology be used to create devastating biological weaponry?

But the scientific knowledge on which the new discoveries were based had a broad social and medical impact. Tests and analyses that once demanded the resources of huge laboratories became cheap and simple to perform. The breakthrough in human genomics has changed understandings of diseases and their treatment, while genetic testing allows individuals to be tested for vulnerability to particular diseases. Gene editing techniques permit scientists to change DNA at specific sites, opening new pathways in the development and manufacture of drugs, with a particular focus on cancer. Since the 1990s, also, new understandings of genetics have been applied to altering animals or plants to create genetically modified organisms (GMOs), through a process popularly known as pharming or pharmaceutical farming. (Again, GM products have been controversial, and some products approved in the US are not accepted as exports to other countries.) Both in medicine and agriculture, genome editing techniques often focus on a family of DNA sequences that in 2001 received the acronym CRISPR, for Clustered Regularly Interspaced Short Palindromic Repeats. CRISPR systems edit genes at precise locations, and since 2012 the technology has made revolutionary progress. Most promising, and most troubling, CRISPR potentially allows the modification of the human genome.

The biotechnology industry included over 2,300 public and private companies, with a strong emphasis on patents in the medical and pharmaceutical realms: some 800,000 Americans presently work in the biopharmaceutical industry. Some pharmaceutical and biotechnology companies were corporate giants. From the US, this included Johnson & Johnson, with a 2018 market capitalization of almost $400 billion, followed by Pfizer, AbbVie, Merck and Amgen. As in information technology, funding and venture capital in biotech is heavily concentrated in such key cities as Boston and San Francisco, with San Diego, New York, Seattle and Philadelphia some distance behind. That again powerfully illustrates the coastal nature of the new economies. The US biotech industry accounts for a third of the global market.

Discoveries in genetics reached many fields outside medicine, especially through the use of DNA testing in criminal justice. This remade the process of identifying and tracing subjects, and allowed the drawing of linkages between offenses long thought to have been unconnected. Findings in DNA and genomic sequencing transformed academic disciplines, especially in archaeology and the study of human origins. As these new insights were popularized through television programs and magazine articles, so they attracted public interest and enthusiasm. Private firms offered DNA testing to ordinary people, inspiring a passionate interest in their origins and ancestry, and reshaping views of race and ethnicity. This interest supported a booming consumer industry, as prices dropped and availability increased. By 2017, 12 million people had had their DNA examined by such means.

Quite apart from genetic advances, medicine made enormous strides in these years. Significant innovations since 2000 have included new forms of surgery designed to be minimally invasive to reduce the impact on patients. 3-D printing allows the manufacture of low-cost implants and prosthetics.

Throughout medicine too, the application of IT has transformed every aspect of research and record keeping. The impact of both technological break-throughs and public policy decisions can be traced through multiple indices of health and well-being. In the opening decade or so of the century, deaths from heart disease and stroke plunged by some 40 percent, continuing a fall that began in the late 1970s, while the popularity of smoking fell sharply. Since the late 1990s, new methods of combining multiple drugs have sharply reduced the lethal quality of AIDS, which not long before had been portrayed as a modern-day equivalent of the apocalyptic plagues of the Middle Ages.

MEDIA AND ENTERTAINMENT

New technologies created a world of media and entertainment that would have been quite unrecognizable to Americans of the 1970s. In their various ways, technological changes transformed the cinema industry and the world of television, especially in matters of news. Media and entertainment should properly be considered as another kind of tech industry.

One obvious impact in the world of film was in the form of special effects and the influence of computer-generated imagery (CGI). This made possible illusions inconceivable just a few years previously. Although computer anima-tions dated back to experimental items in the 1960s, they became far more common and innovative at the end of the century. They proved especially suitable for fantasy films that often drew on comic-book superheroes – *Iron Man, Avengers, Batman* – but also from novels such as *Lord of the Rings* and the *Harry Potter* series, and from established science fiction franchises like *Star Wars*. Computer imagery was essential for such popular animated features as *Frozen* or *Toy Story*. When Pixar's *Toy Story* was released in 1995, it was the first-ever computer-animated feature film, and it inaugurated a remark-able era. Each of these films brought near-inevitable sequels and spin-offs, including lucrative merchandising. Together, such films accounted for a siz-able majority of the 30-plus films that have ever grossed over a billion dollars worldwide, and with only a handful of exceptions all were released after 2000. At the head of the list, now approaching $3 billion, is the 2009 science fiction spectacular, *Avatar*. Such productions utterly changed viewers' expectations about what could and should be offered on the screen. They lowered the wall separating cinematic offerings from video games, where comparable visual tricks were commonplace.

This is not to imply that the US film industry turned entirely to block-buster fantasy franchises at the expense of all other work. The years since

2000 have witnessed many substantial productions that observers would rate as equal to the finest and most substantial films ever made by Hollywood. This includes work by such directors as the Coen brothers, Kathryn Bigelow, Darren Aronofsky, David Lynch, Paul Thomas Anderson, Wes Anderson, or Richard Linklater. (That is, of course, a completely subjective list.) Nor does the fact that superhero films aim primarily at young audiences mean that they are necessarily without real artistic qualities; to take one example, Christopher Nolan's *Dark Knight* trilogy (2005–2012) has earned high critical praise. But generally, tech-driven fantasy became an economic mainstay of Hollywood, providing abundant employment for computer specialists as well as for those in the traditional fields of movie-making.

These changes had their impact in the corporate world. By 2017, the US media and entertainment market generated revenue of $632 billion, some 30 percent of the global total. One beneficiary is the Walt Disney entertainment empire, which owns such subsidiaries as Pixar, Lucasfilm and Marvel Studios, including the line of Marvel superheroes. In 2017, the Walt Disney Company reported revenue of $55 billion. But still more successful was the streaming service Netflix, which became a leading producer of original content. Today, the market value of Netflix exceeds that of either Disney or the cable giant Comcast. Between them, Netflix and YouTube account for a quarter of global internet traffic.

In television, technological change resulted in a bewildering diversification of the media and the control and dissemination of news, with traditional media outlets facing near-terminal crisis. Major elements of the change included cable television, with its proliferation of channels, while the internet allowed people to take the further step of watching content without relying on cable, "cutting the cord" forever. Many people abandoned their television sets altogether, watching media mainly on their computers, and often through sites like YouTube. Consequences include the fragmenting and diversification of audiences; and the replacement of unified mass national and regional audiences by niche cultures.

The past two decades have been a flamboyantly creative era for television in the US, and many critics have spoken of these years as marking an authentic Golden Age for that medium. Much of the most experimental and daring activity occurred in the newer cable stations and streaming services, which in turn set the agenda for the traditional networks. One particular cable station – Home Box Office (HBO) – was a key actor in this story. With their freedom from the network censorship standards, cable stations could more freely depict nudity and obscenity, but they could also explore quite radical themes and structures that would once have been thought beyond the pale. A series of critically acclaimed shows made the best television at least equal to highly regarded cinema releases, including what would long have been viewed as art-house productions with strictly minority appeal. Television became a vehicle for cutting-edge culture, and the new shows were essential items in any discussion of contemporary American art and society. As David Lynch observed, "cable television is the new art-house."

Much of the new wave involved shows with gritty themes and very long story arcs, which assumed a committed audience that would pay close attention over a sustained period. These shows were also more adult in their willingness to kill off leading characters and to play with moral ambiguities. They excelled in their extremely high production values and quality writing, and they enlisted some of the finest acting talent available. One pioneering show was *Oz* (HBO, 1997–2003), which featured life in a maximum-security prison, followed by *Six Feet Under* (HBO, 2001–2005). Other major monuments in the new century included the organized crime-themed shows *The Sopranos* (HBO, 1999–2007) and *Boardwalk Empire* (HBO, 2010–2014), and especially *The Wire* (HBO, 2002–2008). With its treatment of poverty, crime, and policing in contemporary Baltimore, *The Wire* became a frequent exhibit in debates over contemporary racial realities in the real world. Crime and drug trafficking provided the theme for series such as *Breaking Bad* (AMC, 2008–2013). *Deadwood* (HBO, 2004–2006) offered a revisionist view of the Western. *Mad Men* (AMC, 2007–2015) traced the American advertising world since the early 1960s. Many insiders in the tech world regard the series *Silicon Valley* (HBO, 2014–present) as excellent commentary on their industry.

One resounding success was the fantasy series *Game of Thrones* (HBO, 2011–present), which constructed a whole pseudo-medieval universe. The show reflected the broad popular interest in fantasy and science fiction that had become so central to the cinema, and of course it drew heavily on sophisticated computer-generated effects. Some innovative series used themes characteristic of progressive science fiction or fantasy literature, with dark and Gothic elements, all supported by elaborate CGI work. With their strong components of magic realism and cultural postmodernism, these new television shows greatly extended the limits of what audiences would once have been thought willing to tolerate. The breakthrough here was David Lynch's series *Twin Peaks* (1990–1991), which in 2017 appeared in a wildly ambitious, and critically vaunted, revival. Also influential were several films by Christopher Nolan, especially *Memento* (2000) and *Inception* (2010), while the works of science fiction writer Philip K. Dick inspired many imitators. Television hosted such acclaimed science fiction series as *Battlestar Galactica* (Sci-Fi channel, 2004–2009), but also went far beyond the limits of that genre.

The "new fantastic" explored such themes as the construction of false identities and memories, the interplay between the supernatural and "regular" life, and the nature of dreams. At every point, the new shows presented seemingly obvious everyday realities as elaborate constructions that were open to subversion, all the more so given the power of the latest technologies. Some successful examples included *Westworld* (HBO, 2016–present) and the cryptic series *Lost* (2004–2010), which was a rare outlier in that it ran on one of the older networks, ABC. Another groundbreaking contribution was the originally British series *Black Mirror* (2011–present), which subsequently ran on Netflix. The series was obsessed with the sinister potential of new technologies.

TROUBLE IN PARADISE

Looking at the sheer volume of technical advances in such a short period, it is easy to speak the language of inevitable progress and constant advance, or triumphalism. Many hoped that this particular technological shift would be more benevolent than earlier industrial revolutions. Surely, they hoped, the fact that so many of the leading figures in the new IT world came from a broadly alternative culture would differentiate them from the nightmare corporate figures of bygone years? Around 2000, Google adopted the motto "Don't be evil." So might not the corporations even be a force for positive change, especially in matters like individual rights, the status of women, and the condition of sexual minorities? But the rapid march of technology, and the juggernaut power of the great corporations, aroused serious concerns and fears even among observers who were by no means hostile to modernity, or to free enterprise. The great corporations are after all private entities intended to make profits for their investors or shareholders, and that interest often conflicted with the public good. Like many past transformations, this one, too, proved destabilizing and divisive.

The clash between public and private interests was evident in the rapidly expanding world of drugs and pharmaceuticals. It became common to describe the dominant businesses here as Big Pharma, a term that recalled the overmighty monopolies of an earlier generation, such as Big Oil. The pharma industry was criticized for promoting and selling new products with little thought of their actual value, while neglecting possible harms. Medical responses to perceived problems and illnesses grew steeply in these years, although the reasons are controversial. Since the 1990s, an ever-increasing number of people, especially children and teenagers, have been diagnosed with conditions that require treatment by drugs and pharmaceutical products.

These include depression and attention deficit hyperactivity disorder (ADHD), for which the recommended treatment involves psychotropic drugs. The use of Ritalin grew by 700 percent during the 1990s. While not denying the reality of these conditions, many critics hold that they have been over-diagnosed, and that drugs have been gravely over-prescribed, to the mutual benefit of doctors and pharmaceutical companies.

Some scandals were particularly damaging, and gave new ammunition to critics of Big Pharma. In 2004, Merck was forced to withdraw its painkiller Vioxx, which had been used by some 20 million Americans, facing charges that the drug raised the risk of heart attacks and strokes. Multiple lawsuits suggested that the company had ignored or underplayed known dangers.

The gravest charges against the drug companies involved the opioid drugs, which from the late twentieth century acquired a vast consumer market, both legal and illegal. In the 1980s, a flawed study claimed that such drugs were unlikely to cause serious addiction problems, and in 1995 that persuaded the Food and Drug Administration (FDA) to approve the drug OxyContin, produced by Purdue Pharma. As so often in previous history, the new drug was marketed as a "safe" alternative to other predecessors that had come to be regarded as dangerous but, in turn, the replacement itself proved to be insidious. In fact, OxyContin was far more addictive than had been claimed, and more vulnerable to abuse. In 1998, the FDA approved a new painkiller based on fentanyl, a substance 50 times more powerful than heroin. Massively over-prescribed, OxyContin and fentanyl-related products were central to the opioid drug crisis, which ruined the lives of millions, and which we will examine in the next chapter. In 2006, Purdue Pharma agreed to pay $600 million for misleading marketing of OxyContin. Even so, by 2012, 259 million opioid prescriptions were written in the US.

The whole opioid affair raised fundamental questions of corporate responsibility, failures of official regulation, and the over-cozy relationship between business and regulators. As we will see, all those issues would surface repeatedly in the financial crises of these same years.

TECH AND INEQUALITY

Both the IT and pharma enterprises raised questions of inequality, a phenomenon that took many forms. Although the gigantic corporations are not actually monopolies – and tech businesses certainly fall as well as rise – firms like Google, Amazon, and Facebook inevitably possess power and influence on a par with the oil or railroad monopolies of a previous industrial revolution. Amazon especially seemed to have unlimited ambitions as a retailer, taking much business that might otherwise have gone to non-electronic bricks and mortar establishments. While many Americans gained much from the new world, plenty of others did not, resulting in inequalities that would inspire protest movements and political dissidence. That is quite apart from concerns about global inequalities and the labor conditions endured by many people overseas who actually manufactured the new products.

Some cities and regions benefited wonderfully from tech-derived wealth, most sensationally in the two respective Bay areas, around San Francisco and Boston (see Chapter 6). By 2017, the nine counties of the San Francisco Bay area had an economy worth $748 billion, in the same league as the Netherlands, and only 18 nations in the world ranked higher. The Bay Area's annual growth rate in the previous few years was double that of the US as a whole. But many other cities had their own interests in the new industries of the knowledge economy, which attracted young and highly educated workforces who spent freely. That growth enhanced the existing gulf with older communities that were not so fortunate, a chasm that became social, cultural and demographic as well as financial. It was all too easy to frame the divisions by a simple formula: Red and Blue states, elite bicoastal America versus "flyover country." That term referred to the large areas of the nation that a traveler flew over while passing from one coast to the other, the assumption being that all economic enterprise, cultural life, and educated opinion was confined to those coasts. Such pat distinctions reflected real grievances and fears.

As we will discuss in Chapter 11, technological advances amplified racial disparities. The tech industries were anything but monolithically white, and they included substantial numbers of South and East Asian personnel. But black and Latino Americans were poorly represented. The urban revival driven by tech-related riches in practice had the effect of expelling poorer minority populations from booming cities. "Tech money" became a major force in redeveloping and gentrifying many older cities, most famously in the San Francisco Bay area. New patterns of economic success placed a high premium on education, and on youth. The rise of technologically sophisticated elites generated hostility from older populations, but it did create a strong spillover effect in terms of luxury consumer goods, leisure industries, and real estate. Together, these trends drove an upsurge in real estate prices in major cities, which further intensified class divisions and resentments. In an age when higher education was the indispensable key to status and success, technological growth reinforced new forms of segregation.

THE END OF PRIVACY?

The IT and social media companies aroused critical concerns involving individual rights, especially in regard to privacy. These firms originated in an era of incomprehensibly rapid change and innovation, and most industry leaders heartily agreed with the maxim credited to Facebook's Mark Zuckerberg, "Move fast and break things." In such an environment, legal and regulatory arrangements appeared tiresome and irrelevant. But as the industry developed, it became apparent that critical problems had not been addressed, or even considered.

All such businesses depend on users providing large amounts of personal information of all kinds, which is used as the basis for advertising. That in turn provides the economic foundations of the operation, and makes it possible to offer a service free of charge. But as the phrase has it, if you are not paying for a service then you are the product. In the language of the business, your data is monetized. Tens of millions of users show little concern at such a trade-off, but the consequences are worrying. Companies know an inordinate amount about their users, including a record of their precise locations at any given moment, a level of surveillance undreamed of by the worst totalitarian regimes in previous history. Corporate mogul Scott McNealy, of Sun Microsystems, dismissed any hope of reversing the situation, saying "You have zero privacy ... Get over it." The question then is whether the corporations could be relied on not to abuse that power, and multiple scandals suggested they cannot.

One epic scandal focused on the relationship between Facebook and the firm Cambridge Analytica. In 2014, researchers persuaded some hundreds of thousands of Facebook users to complete a personality survey. They were then able to access detailed information not just on those particular users but on their friends and contacts, reaching an astonishing 80 million or more. That goldmine of information was acquired by Cambridge Analytica, which sold its consultancy services to various clients, including most notoriously the 2016 election campaign of Donald Trump. This detailed and specific information allowed this campaign (and others around the world) to personalize advertising and influence political decisions. Such cases suggested the grave inadequacy of existing legal structures and sanctions.

Governments and agencies naturally exploit such near-infinite resources of intelligence data. In 2013, former intelligence analyst Edward Snowden revealed that the US National Security Agency (NSA) was gathering mountains of data from internet users worldwide, including those using services like Google and Yahoo, besides mapping cell phones. It was never clear how agencies were using such data, or the legal constraints that might apply. (The acronym for the shadowy NSA was traditionally said to stand for "No Such Agency.") Yet even the fearsome powers of governments and intelligence services are insufficient to prevent the internet being used for large-scale criminal enterprises, including the trade in drugs, pornography and criminal operations via the so-called Dark Web. Apart from internet usage, new technologies enhance official powers of surveillance to levels beyond anything contemplated by George Orwell. New resources include the CCTV cameras that are so ubiquitous in cities; automated license plate recognition, for tracking vehicles; and facial recognition technology.

Finally, the absolute reliance of the modern economy on electronic technology offered new opportunities for the enemies of any society, whether that meant rival states or terrorist groups. Without its IT networks, the United States could not operate the electricity or water supplies on which civilized life depends. Throughout these years, there was repeated evidence of electronic intrusions and small-scale attacks, which were variously traced to Russia, China or North Korea. Presumably, these assaults were not intended to be crippling in their own right, but were rather probing for vulnerabilities in the event of international confrontations. Just how seriously the US military took this threat was apparent in 2009 with the creation of its new Cyber Command, to direct both offensive and defensive operations. Also, the military depend to an alarming degree on its GPS networks, and the satellites on which that relies. This raised the specter of anti-satellite warfare and combat in space – of orbital warfare – as well as cyber-attacks. In 2007, the Chinese alarmed Western observers by launching a ground-based missile that precisely intercepted and destroyed an orbiting satellite. Far from initiating a new order of global peace, the technological revolution opens up scarcely comprehensible new frontiers of warfare.

Looking at the first decade of the twenty-first century, it would be easy to focus on images of violence and warfare, or economic crisis and financial disaster, and the country indeed had its share of disasters. But the pace of technological change in such a very short time also characterizes these years as one of the most effervescent periods of creativity and change in the whole American story.

5 The Crisis of the Old Economy

For much of the twentieth century, the Michigan city of Saginaw was an industrial boomtown typical of many in the Upper Midwest, and it was the vibrant heart of a flourishing Tri-City area. That economic activity relied on several General Motors plants, mainly connected with the Chevrolet brand. In 1979 the corporation employed 26,000 people in the area. In 1968, the city briefly achieved global fame as a quintessential national symbol from a reference in the Simon and Garfunkel song "America." From the 1980s, though, manufacturing activity declined precipitously, leaving the city with the unenviable boast of having one of the fastest-shrinking populations in the US. Saginaw approached 100,000 people in 1960, but that fell to 62,000 in 2000, and just 49,000 by 2016. In 2009, at the depths of the great recession, unemployment peaked at 23.5 percent. The city has suffered badly from crime, violence, collapsing infrastructure, and general urban blight. Similar stories of sharp contraction – if not catastrophe – could be told of many other troubled communities across Michigan, Ohio, Pennsylvania, West Virginia, and Illinois. In the first decade of the twenty-first century, Michigan was the only US state actually to decline in population.

At first glance, America in these years was living through an era of unprecedented prosperity, with an ever-widening range of consumer goods and the unimaginable expansion of electronic resources. The spread of technological innovation coincided with rapid globalization, and both forces in turn drove amazing improvements in productivity. Yet the expansion was patchy and uneven. Some sectors of the economy benefited much more than others, and some regions especially. The growth in national income diverted attention from a decline in living standards and expectations for large sections of the population, including the residents of many Rustbelt cities like Saginaw – or Johnstown, PA, Youngstown, OH, or Charleston, WV. The shift from manufacturing to services and high tech demanded a fundamental rethinking of American concepts of work and prosperity.

WHERE THE JOBS ARE

Beyond the high-tech activity, many traditional manufacturing centers in these years suffered a grim, if not apocalyptic, fate. Since the 1940s, the US economy had created large numbers of high-value jobs, especially in manufacturing, but

80

this trend went into sudden reverse in the late 1970s, with alarming implications for the once-secure middle class. Many familiar American products were now manufactured more cheaply overseas, and free trade agreements such as NAFTA allowed US firms to move employment abroad, through offshoring. The fall in manufacturing jobs became precipitous at the end of the century. In the late 1970s, almost 20 million Americans worked in manufacturing, but that number fell below 18 million by 2000, and to just 12 million by 2010, and that at a time of substantial growth in the overall population. In other words, just in the opening decade of the century some 6 million manufacturing jobs evaporated. In 1950, almost a third of employees worked in factories, compared to 8.5 percent today. Yet falling jobs coincided with increased industrial production, as productivity soared. Between 1990 and 2016, the number of manufacturing jobs fell by 31 percent, but manufacturing output grew by 72 percent. Far fewer people were producing far more goods.

But this was not simply an epochal shift from manufacturing to high tech. Rather, the US was experiencing a pattern of diversification characteristic of a mature post-industrial economy, and a key feature of that was the upsurge in service industries. In 1980, "goods producing" (manufacturing and construction) accounted for 25 percent of gross domestic product, with a further 5 percent in "extraction" (agriculture and mining). By 2010, the combined contribution of those sectors – producing and extraction – had fallen from 30 percent of GDP to 18 percent. "Service producing" during the same decades grew from 70 percent to 82 percent. These sectors were lucrative. In 2015–2016, legal services generated over $290 billion in revenue; management consulting, $250 billion; accounting, $170 billion; architectural services, $73 billion. Each new technical advance generated new business and employment, for instance in the legal fields of intellectual property, patents, and data protection.

The scale of the transition is suggested by the Dow Jones Industrial Average, the "Dow," the most familiar gauge for tracking stock prices. This is based on the prices of 30 large publicly traded companies, which carry special weight for the larger economy. As originally formulated in 1928, the list focused on heavy industry and manufacturing, but over the years economic shifts have caused many older concerns to be replaced by newer enterprises. Even General Motors lost its place in 2009. Today's Dow Jones list leans strongly to other sectors, to technology and communications, health care and pharmaceuticals, finance, retailing, and media. Despite its title, the Industrial Average is no longer very industrial in any conventional sense of manufacturing.

Employment growth in service sectors was also marked. Between 1990 and 2015, employment doubled in educational services, and in health care and social assistance. Professional and business services grew by 81 percent, in financial activities by 23 percent. The banking industry employed 2.2 million in 2007, before the financial crash, the number falling to around 6 million by 2015. Management consulting firms alone employ 1.2 million, accounting firms 1.5 million. In 2016, the US Bureau of Labor Statistics recorded a total of 156 million jobs, of which goods producing (manufacturing, mining, and construction) accounted for some 20 million, with a further 2.35 million in agriculture. But services accounted for 125 million jobs, structured as shown in Table 5.1:

Table 5.1   Service employment by sector in the US, 2016

Sector	Jobs (thousands)
Professional and business services	20,135
State and local government	19,428
Health care and social assistance	19,056
Retail trade	15,820
Leisure and hospitality	15,620
Financial activities	8,285
Other services	6,409
Wholesale trade	5,867
Transportation and warehousing	4,989
Educational services	3,560
Federal government	2,795
Information	2,772
Utilities	556

www.bls.gov/emp/ep_table_201.htm

Such a broad list of sectors and categories masks an enormous range of jobs in terms of pay and status, especially in an area like "health care and social assistance." Even so, many of the newer service jobs differed from their old industrial counterparts in demanding high levels of education, training, experience, and social and analytical skills. Such professional and high-skill positions grew steadily in number from the late twentieth century, while the number of jobs requiring only physical strength remained little changed. Across the system, the better jobs – with growing opportunities and good salaries – demanded educational qualifications, usually college degrees. A degree became not so much a ticket to advancement as a basic qualification for survival. The incomes of workers in jobs requiring skills and education grew impressively, those for manual workers far less. This employment shift particularly benefited women, who found a larger range of positions than hitherto, at better pay. The traditional role of women in health care industries was significant here, as this sector is likely to grow dramatically, partly to serve the needs of a rapidly aging population. When the federal government projects those jobs that are likely to be in demand over the coming decade, there is a strong emphasis on positions in health care and information technology.

As so often in history, the decline of one type of trade or industry coincides with some other kind of activity, which over time makes up for any lost employment. Such a change might well force workers to relocate, commonly elsewhere within a given region or city. On a national level, the loss of manufacturing jobs was offset by the growth in service industries, but these new sources of growth were little consolation to the traditional centers of the industrial economy. Multiple reasons prevented a 50-year-old steelworker or auto worker (say) from taking a position in an insurance office, still less joining a video game start-up. Matters of geography, training, education, and skills all played their part.

RETAIL APOCALYPSE

Other sources of employment proved unreliable, and suffered their own distinctive crises. This was true of the very large retail sector, which today accounts for 16 million workers. The industry has gone through many changes through the years. The traditional image of independently owned stores on urban main streets had by the 1970s given way to chains of stores, often located in burgeoning shopping malls at the edge of a city. For some years, malls became an important social space, especially for young middle-class people. Also growing were the so-called big box stores that sold all manner of goods at a considerable discount. Walmart was the best known of these stores, besides that firm's subsidiary, Sam's Club, and Costco. Walmart remains a massive global concern, with almost 12,000 stores worldwide. During the 1990s, it shifted its main emphasis within the US from the South and Midwest to a national role, and the firm remains a huge employer.

But other forms of retail were not so successful, and that included some of the stars of the late twentieth-century retail scene. Since 2010, many once-successful chains have failed or declared bankruptcy, in the process ruining the fortunes of malls that once depended on them. Even such giants as

Macy's, Sears, and J. C. Penney have closed hundreds of their branches. Since 2015, these trends have become so commonplace, and so painful, as to attract the term "retail apocalypse." Many malls now seem as destined for oblivion as the main streets that they once supplanted. In the process, these widespread business failures further sabotage the employment possibilities for people who no longer find work in factories.

The reasons for the ongoing disaster are not fully understood. Electronic shopping played its part, as Amazon moved from books and music to general retailing. Nor was it easy for most stores to compete with big box concerns like Walmart. But deeper financial forces were at work, which relate to the larger economic disaster that came close to overwhelming the whole economy in 2008. In the booming years before the recession, corporations had engaged in many mergers and acquisitions, which left retail firms with intolerable debt loads. That heavy burden was aggravated by the steep downturn in spending during the recession itself. The full effects of those troubles only became fully apparent after 2010.

Leisure industries advanced solidly in these years, and offered employment in particular regions. Unfairly, perhaps, some of the most vibrant tourist destinations were exactly those cities already booming from high tech and services, such as Boston, New York, and San Francisco. One potent engine for growth was the casino gambling that had been legalized for Indian reservations in the 1980s. Michigan itself has 19 Indian casinos, operated by 14 Native tribes. Other forms of leisure and tourism include theme parks and amusement parks, which had a strong local impact. But like the retail world, leisure could not begin to make up for the job losses from industry, and particularly in the heart of the Rustbelt communities.

THE SHALE GALE

Only one kind of emerging economic enterprise offered major employment opportunities to compensate for the decline of working-class jobs, and that was in oil and gas. This development echoed through the whole economy. New energy sources within the US were exploited in the form of shale gas and oil, which were extracted by fracturing rock with a highly pressurized liquid. This process is known as hydraulic fracturing, or fracking, and in modern terms it implies massive or high-volume fracturing. Although the technique had been used around the world for decades, it became much more common from the late 1990s, when it opened many hitherto inaccessible resources to exploitation – first natural gas, and later oil. In 2000, fracking produced just 2 percent of US oil, but by 2016 the figure reached 50 percent. Beyond that core idea of fracking, US energy companies effectively applied other technologies to maximize output, especially horizontal drilling. In consequence, US oil output is now exceeded only by that of Russia and Saudi Arabia. By 2012, experts were discussing the entrancing prospect of the US being self-sufficient in oil within a couple of decades.

Since the late 1960s, the US had relied heavily on imported energy supplies, leaving its own domestic production to decline. Between 1970 and 2008, domestic oil production fell from 10 million barrels per day (MBD) to just 5, but that latter figure represented a foundation from which future growth would rise. By 2018, US oil production again approached its Nixon-era level of 10 MBD. High levels of domestic production prevented the need for major imports. As late as 2008, US net imports of foreign oil still stood at 12 MBD, but within a decade that figure fell to just 2.5 MBD. All projections suggest significant expansion in the near future, with Texas's Permian Basin alone possibly reaching 7 MBD by about 2022. Presently, the Permian Basin is the world's second most abundant oilfield, lying only behind the Ghawar field in Saudi Arabia.

The oil boom had far-reaching consequences at home and abroad. Through 2014, the resulting production bonanza, the Shale Gale, created boom areas across the country – in Texas, North Dakota, Pennsylvania, Ohio, and elsewhere. The industry was a major employer, especially when we take account of ancillary industries like trucking, construction, and retail. Without those jobs, the nation's unemployment situation following the 2008 slump would have been far worse. New energy supplies raised the seemingly incredible vision of renewing American manufacturing, even in once-blighted Rustbelt industrial cities, and in such seemingly doomed sectors as chemicals, plastics, glass, and steel. The sheer scale of production subverted long-standing warnings that the world would soon reach a maximum level of oil supply, from which it would gradually shrink to near exhaustion – the vision of so-called Peak Oil. The energy industry now spoke instead of the enviable problem of Peak Demand, as the growth of alternative energy supplies made it difficult to sell the new oil riches at adequate price levels.

Besides oil, fracking gave the US vast new wealth in the form of natural gas. After decades of importing liquified natural gas (LNG) the US became a net exporter in 2016, and low-cost American supplies revolutionized global energy markets. The industry surged on the strength of ever-insatiable demand in East Asia and, above all, China. LNG even held environmental promise, as it raised the possibility of altogether replacing coal as a source of energy generation. Although not a wholly clean resource, such a shift would enormously reduce carbon emissions.

As we will see in Chapter 9, this oil boom had immense consequences for international affairs and for US foreign policy. In the late twentieth century, Americans had become grimly familiar with the idea of dependence on foreign oil supplies, with all that implied for reliance on unstable allies in the Middle East. In the new world, the US no longer needed to devote so much effort to cultivating the goodwill of states like Saudi Arabia. Recognizing that prospect, the Saudis tried to use their oil resources to curb and ideally destroy domestic US production, which was highly sensitive to world price levels. Because of the relative difficulty of extracting US domestic oil, the enterprise only became economically worthwhile when worldwide prices stood at or above a particular level. When a barrel of oil cost $100, as it often has in the present century, American producers flourished. But when the price fell below $40, most firms struggled (some regions are more resilient, and the Permian Basin can remain economical with an oil price as low as $25). Much of the recent boom was a consequence of the painfully high prices around 2008, which briefly reached an all-time peak of $145.

In 2014, the Saudis persuaded their colleagues in OPEC (the Organization of the Petroleum Exporting Countries) to increase production with the goal of lowering oil prices to such low levels that US producers would find it impossible to survive. That forced the price of oil down below $40 per barrel, at the extreme limits of what US producers could cope with. While some companies did indeed go under, most survived, and even benefited from a crisis that forced them to develop even more innovative technologies and to slash costs. The crisis had a Darwinian effect in driving the least competitive US ventures into extinction, while ensuring the survival of the fittest and most agile. The Saudi-led effort soon ended, leaving the US energy sector thriving more than ever.

The domestic energy boom had its critics, as community groups worried about the environmental effects of fracking, which can extend to provoking earthquakes. Moreover, as we will see in Chapter 10, ever-more abundant oil was a nightmare for those concerned with the impact on accelerating human-driven climate change. Without the fact of that domestic energy bonanza, though, the economic history of twenty-first-century America would have been unimaginably different, and far more stressful.

THE WORLD OF WORK

That energy sector remained a bright spot in an otherwise worrying employment picture. Quite apart from the decline of manufacturing – or any particular sector – incomes for the working and middle classes were stagnant, to a degree that has puzzled economists. Allowing for inflation, average household incomes did not rise significantly after the 1970s, and remained little affected by the long era of the supposed economic boom. By some estimates, they may even have fallen. Any growth that did occur in incomes was far smaller than the truly impressive advances in productivity.

The lack of improvement in incomes was part of a range of complaints about changes in the world of work and employment, and the pursuit of prosperity. Many of the factory jobs that were lost had carried good pay, solid benefits and reliable pensions, advantages that increasingly seemed like features of a lost dream world. Ever more Americans were in jobs that their parents would have considered inadequate or unworthy, lacking the once-expected job security. Labor leaders and politicians warned of replacing "real" or "decent" jobs with "flipping burgers at McDonald's." Of course, many of the jobs in offices and retail were at least as "real" and desirable as the older factory work, but even those opportunities were not as common as they once were.

The ideal of a lifetime career, probably with a single firm or corporation, gave way to short-term and contract work. This reflected an overwhelming corporate trend toward outsourcing all economic functions not fundamentally connected to a form's core mission. Businesses took to heart the advice of consultant Peter Drucker, that firms should "do what you do best, and outsource the rest." For businesses, that had the advantage of avoiding paying benefits and (particularly) health care costs for full-time employees. Meanwhile, new communications technologies spawned the gig economy, in which workers notionally served as contractors rather than employees, serving firms that owed them no long-term commitment. For workers, that model was impossible to sustain without taking multiple jobs. From a pessimistic perspective, workers ensnared in such an economy of permanent transition and uncertainty constitute a "precarious proletariat" – what has come to be known as the "precariat."

Workers who did remain in the full-time employment of a corporation were increasingly likely to lack the solid pension benefits familiar to their parents. Pensions that were predictable and offered defined benefits had been widely replaced by individual retirement accounts, 401(k)s, which depended on active involvement and decision making by employees themselves. In 2016, 44 percent of private sector workers participated in such a scheme. As workers often failed to fund their accounts adequately, most were woefully unprepared for old age and retirement.

In this respect, as in others, workers in the public sector were much better placed, and usually negotiated contracts that preserved generous benefits and pension rights while resisting lay-offs or dismissals. The problem with that situation was that governments found it ever harder to pay their employees and keep faith with these long-term commitments, especially as the decline of private industry shrank the tax base to negligible proportions. Due in large measure to pension over-commitments and shortfalls, state and city governments faced recurrent fiscal crises which gravely limited their ability to operate. Those economic woes added to a larger problem facing government. At both federal and state level, ideological conflicts between Left and Right generally prevented any substantial government investment in the economy, particularly in improving infrastructure – roads, bridges, airports, or public utilities. Not only could government not replace the wealth creation hitherto undertaken by private industry, but that failure ensured that the conditions of life became ever-more difficult for ordinary citizens in the old industrial states and cities.

While incomes and job security both floundered, middle-class Americans faced higher costs for health care and higher education. Soaring costs for college education from the late 1990s onward threatened the familiar route to upward social mobility. However stereotyped the concept, the American Dream that genuinely had offered prosperity and mobility to millions in earlier decades now seemed increasingly out of reach. Commentators warned of a systematic squeeze on the middle class, a rising crisis.

The long-term decline of manufacturing had multiple effects, which were highly regional in their nature. Some cities were hit hard, including major centers like Detroit, besides mid-size communities like Saginaw or Youngstown. In the Michigan city of Flint, a former bastion of General Motors, collapsing population and rising poverty left a local government struggling to cut costs by seeking a new supply for drinking water. The resulting arrangements left the residents vulnerable to dangerous levels of lead, and the health crisis that developed in 2014 resulted in the declaration of a federal state of emergency. Outside the cities strictly defined were the smaller towns, the rural and semi-rural areas that were home to many working-class people, and who now lost the basis of their livelihoods. Not only did some states boom while others floundered, but gaping disparities of wealth and investment existed within particular states. Some of the cities hit worst by poverty and decline were in California, where other centers were global leaders in economic progress. The resurgence of New York City coincided with the stagnation of upstate New York.

Special factors applied to some regions. Coal-mining had once been a pivotal component of the US economy, but through the years coal had been widely displaced by other energy sources. In recent years, concerns about carbon emissions led to calls to reduce or eliminate the industry. In consequence, coal regions had some of the country's worst unemployment statistics, and the most worrying measures of poverty and social distress. Just how combustible such regional situations and their grievances might be became apparent with the elections of 2016.

MANHOOD AND WHITENESS

Economic change had a special impact on particular sections of society, as defined by gender, race, and class. The swift-fading old industrial world had especially valued male workers, who could earn excellent wages without much formal education. Women certainly worked in those industries, but men attracted the better money, and the greater prestige. The decline of older industries left many men unable to find work they might consider adequate, while opportunities did exist for their wives and daughters. Men were now especially vulnerable to economic downturns, and especially to disasters like the 2008 crash. By 2010, when the national unemployment rate was hovering around 10 percent, some 20 percent of men aged 25–54 were out of work. Such a change could not fail to affect concepts of masculinity, and to undermine deeply held assumptions. The impact was all the greater on middle-aged and older people, again especially men, who found it hard to adapt to the new economic world or to its essential technologies.

Those trends persisted even as the economic figure generally improved. By 2018, the unemployment rate had fallen to a very low figure of around 4 percent, some 6 million people. But the overall statistics also revealed some worrying sub-categories, including 1.3 million long-term unemployed – those out of work for six months or more – and also 400,000 "discouraged" workers, who were not even seeking employment because they believed no jobs existed for them. Millions of other workers were employed part-time, but aspired to full-time regular status. The labor force participation rate fell from 67 percent in 2000 to 63 percent in 2014, and that troubling low level showed little signs of improvement.

Industrial decline hit workers of all races. In the automotive or steel industry, black workers had held well-paying positions that gave them a strong position from which to argue for political and social equality. The decline of the industries, and the cities in which they were based, reduced those workers to the condition of an underclass. But white workers too faced comparable problems, to which they were quite unaccustomed. They responded with concerns about trade and immigration, which they believed made their economic lot far worse. The resulting sense of grievance found expression in many controversies not directly linked to employment, including such issues as gun ownership, and, more generally, threats to gender roles. Over the following decade, the politics of masculinity, and of whiteness, surfaced in unsuspected contexts.

In his 2008 presidential campaign, Barack Obama spoke of declining areas such as these, that had lost their industries and failed to find replacements. Of the inhabitants, he continued, "And it's not surprising then they get bitter, they cling to guns or religion, or antipathy to people who aren't like them, or anti-immigrant sentiment, or anti-trade sentiment, as a way to explain their frustrations." There was much to argue with in his words, and a legitimate argument could be made against free trade and unrestricted immigration of low-wage labor. In terms of their alleged xenophobia and racism, it should be noted that most such areas voted for Obama himself. But Obama was correct to stress the symbolic weight of matters such as guns and religion, and, as so often in US history, faith was bound up with loyalties of class and race. These were the areas that stunned pollsters in 2016 when they voted in such solid masses for Donald Trump, with his drumbeat calls for economic nationalism and a revival of domestic manufacturing. Trump's slogan, Make America Great Again, conjured nostalgia for an old economic order, no less than for bygone social arrangements. In that year, Trump became the first Republican to win Saginaw County since Ronald Reagan in 1984.

LABOR UNIONS

Industrial decline transformed politics at both national and local level. Since the 1930s, the Democratic Party had been closely allied with organized labor, and with the world of heavy industry. Even after industrial decline was well underway at the end of the twentieth century, television advertising would normally show Democratic candidates in hard hats visiting industrial facilities such as steel plants, the source of "real" jobs and work. Such gestures made ever less sense as the shift to services advanced, and whole industries vanished. By 2016, Democratic presidential candidate Hillary Clinton was actively campaigning against the coal industry.

Labor unions hemorrhaged membership. The proportion of American workers who were union members fell from an all-time high of 35 percent in 1954 to 20.1 percent in 1983, and 11 percent in 2016. The nature of those remaining unions also changed, with a historic shift from private to public sector workers, whose jobs generally could not be moved offshore. Even unions that had traditionally served workers in manufacturing now moved their recruitment emphasis to service, to employees in health or education or in leisure and hospitality. The rate of union membership in the public sector is now over 35 percent, compared to just 6.7 percent in the private. Today, the largest labor unions in the US are the National Education Association, the Service Employees International Union, and AFSCME – the American Federation of State, County and Municipal Employees.

As union membership is closely correlated with wages and conditions, collapsing union strength added to middle-class weakness. But the change also had political consequences, as smaller and weaker unions were much less able to fund Democratic political candidates. But just how much further unions might contract depended on political decisions. One effective means of limiting union power was so-called right-to-work laws, which prevented requiring union membership as a condition of employment. In consequence, right-to-work laws tended to reduce the size and power of unions. Historically, such laws were characteristic of more conservative Southern jurisdictions, but they have since spread to 28 states, including even such old industrial heartlands as Indiana (2012), Michigan (2012), and Wisconsin (2015). Although these laws have been fiercely contested in courts, and attracted widespread public protests, they have generally survived challenge. In a potentially crushing 2018 decision targeted specifically at the public sector, *Janus v. AFSCME*, the US Supreme Court ruled that non-union workers who were represented by a union for bargaining purposes could not be required to pay union dues or fees. The weaker unions became through such laws and court decisions, the less able they were to resist the spread of anti-union laws to yet more states.

SIGNS OF CRISIS

Economic crisis coincided with widespread social dislocations that in earlier years had been seen as characterizing only black Americans. Those included symptoms of family fragmentation, with growing numbers of children born outside marriage. Other consequences included high rates of depression and suicide. Former industrial cities and rural white communities also faced grave drug abuse problems strongly recalling those long associated with the black inner city, although the substances involved were now methamphetamine and opioid drugs. Opioids like OxyContin posed a grave danger of addiction, and users easily overdosed. The fact that these crises have coincided so closely with the economic decline does not of itself mean that the one trend caused the other: the opioid crisis might have been brought about by a sudden oversupply that made substances too readily available. But whatever the cause, opioids especially came to symbolize the woes of poor white America. Originally concentrated in Appalachia in the early 2000s, the crisis spread throughout large sections of the country, from New England through the Midwest and the Deep South.

The opioid crisis reached horrifying proportions. By 2011, social costs related to opioid abuse already ran to $55 billion each year, and overdose deaths soon became the nation's leading cause of accidental death. In 2016, some 64,000 Americans died from drug overdoses, of whom 34,000 succumbed to opioids, or some 90 deaths each day. Between 2000 and 2016, deaths from opioid-related overdose grew from 3 to 13 per 100,000 population, approaching the levels of AIDS-related deaths at the worst of that earlier crisis. Fentanyl-related deaths alone grew from the low hundreds in 1999 to over 20,000 by 2016. By way of comparison, the US in that year recorded just 17,000 homicides. Overdose deaths were most common in states that had hitherto symbolized the white working class, including Pennsylvania, Ohio, and West Virginia. Like many declining cities, Saginaw itself was hit hard. As in earlier drug epidemics, consequences were not limited to users themselves but affected their families and communities, producing financial ruin, and leaving children removed from their biological families.

A CRISIS OF THE MIDDLE CLASS?

Economic changes in these years have been so sweeping that, arguably, they represent not a mere downturn or recession but rather a fundamental new direction in American history. But fully granting the reality of industrial decline does not necessarily mean accepting the grimmest and most pessimistic interpretation of larger trends. Much remains to be debated.

According to one powerful and oft-heard narrative, the United States in the late twentieth century moved to economic conditions utterly different from the country's previous history. The incomes of middle- and lower-class Americans stagnated or shrank, and that effective freeze has remained solid up to the present day. Most of the gains in wealth have been secured by the better off, the top 20 percent or so of households, while the very richest subset – the notorious 1 percent – gained vastly. Again according to this interpretation, the rich have become richer while both middle-class and poor people became ever poorer and more demoralized, and that fact reverberates through political life. Repeatedly, government policies have enhanced and accelerated this process of enriching the already wealthy, creating the image of US politics as a game played by and for greedy plutocrats. The decline of the traditional working class even seems to confirm the darkest prophecies offered by the Marxist economic model, which predicted that technological change would scourge skilled workers through a process of immiseration, a reduction to brutal deprivation and endemic crisis.

That model readily supports radical rhetoric, and it directly inspired the Occupy movement that we will encounter in Chapter 8. The language of structural inequality became increasingly popular. In 2013, President Obama declared inequality "the defining challenge of our time." From that perspective, the only solution to inequality would be found in expansive government action, which would redistribute wealth to the poorest while reopening the opportunities that had been so systematically closed in recent decades. Health care reform would be a first stage in such a process. So obvious did this approach seem that liberal strategists wondered at length why such a scheme so often failed to win the mass electoral support of the people who would be the immediate beneficiaries. Again from the liberal point of view, the mystery was just why ordinary people failed to grasp the straightforward class approach but were systematically misled by causes rooted in culture, religion, or race. Why do people so often vote against their real interests?

The emerging inequality debate has revived long-running conflicts between Right and Left, which differ fundamentally in their interpretation of wealth and wealth production. To oversimplify, a left-wing view favors a pie chart approach: in any given society, there is a limited amount of wealth to go round, and this has to be shared in some way. Crudely, the pie is of a fixed size, and a larger portion for one group means a smaller share for some other. As Obama remarked, "I think when you spread the wealth around, it's good for everybody." A conservative view rejects the pie analogy, and assumes instead that the amount of wealth is highly flexible. As long as entrepreneurs are given enough incentives, the pie expands, and overall growth results in larger shares for everyone. Giving credence to that conservative approach, American GDP has indeed swelled solidly through the past few decades, and GDP per capita has actually doubled since 1977.

Assessing debates over inequality and fair shares is by no means an easy task. Economic statistics are notoriously prone to misinterpretation and multiple readings, and that is especially true when dealing with concepts such as family income or household worth. Beyond question, wealthy people benefited mightily from the prosperity of these years, but equally qualified scholars differ greatly on how poorly more modest families performed. Some analyses were indeed pessimistic. But other research produced quite different conclusions by employing a variant form of evidence – using households as units, rather than tax returns – and also by factoring in various forms of payment that people received apart from income. This would include social security or unemployment payments as well as health care contributions from employers. Those alterations might sound trivial, but the consequences were substantial. According to this reading, the incomes of ordinary Americans have not fallen since the 1970s but actually risen, which makes the inequality issue less pressing. In this as in so much else, how we frame the question will decide the answers we obtain.

Moreover, any comparisons between America in (say) 1970 and today are in a sense looking at quite different countries, given the far larger share of new immigrants in the modern nation. New immigrant families always tend to be poorer and less secure than older-established populations, although that does not mean they will long remain in that position. To that extent, the apparent stagnation of incomes is exaggerated.

It is also open to debate how far raw income figures measure quality of life, and the various kinds of opportunity open to people. Nor do they necessarily convey people's sense of well-being, and their perceptions of living standards. Vast strides in technology and medicine mean that people are now living longer and healthier lives than their counterparts did 30 or 40 years before, as suggested for instance by the precipitous decline in deaths from heart attack or stroke. Families are richer than they might have been because so many households now contain two earners, increasing overall income and providing some cushion against a decline in a particular industry. For all the criticisms of globalization, free trade has made abundant goods available at remarkably low prices. The same forces that destroyed American factories have also brought huge volumes of imported products into the country, often to be marketed through the big box retail stores.

We should not minimize the impact of new technologies in computing and smartphones. When an ordinary person today holds a smartphone, she or he has access to transformative technologies that were utterly unavailable to the super-rich in the late 1970s, or even to the most sophisticated corporate laboratories. That gives modern people undreamt-of opportunities in terms of information, communications, education, and entertainment, even if their income is not significantly larger than their parents' might have been a generation before. This is a curious kind of immiseration. Having said that, observers who take a darker view of economic trends naturally minimize the significance of such technological changes, when set aside what they see as the wider losses.

In the late nineteenth century, the German Chancellor Otto von Bismarck offered a much-quoted observation about the rival empire of Russia. Russia, he said, is never as strong as she appears, nor as weak as she appears. For their own ideological ends, commentators naturally highlighted trends that fitted their argument, and extrapolated them to an outrageous degree. The same might be said of the US economy, which it is tempting to report in such starkly contrasting narratives: the explosive growth of cutting-edge technology, but at the same time the ruinous failure of the old manufacturing towns. The best of times coexists bafflingly with the worst of times. In fact, each of those realities has to be considered in a broader national context, and each narrative suffers from popular exaggeration and simplification. What does emerge powerfully is the extraordinary diversity of the US economy, and the range of its sources of wealth. In the twenty-first century, those features were powerfully on display in America's great cities.

6 Cities Reborn

As the former capital of the US automobile industry, Detroit, Michigan, has long symbolized the decline of urban and industrial America. Since 1950, the city's population has declined from about 1.8 million to perhaps 700,000, as many residents withdrew to the suburbs, and businesses left the city. Although causes were many, civic mismanagement and extensive corruption both played their part. Today, large areas of the city are effectively abandoned, with stretches of land reverting to grass. Lacking an adequate tax base, public services operate only sporadically. Detroit represents a process not just of decline but of deurbanization. By 2013, the city was unable to pay its debts and obligations, including pensions, forcing it to declare bankruptcy – in technical language, to seek Chapter 9 protection. Newspapers offered headlines such as "Detroit's Reckoning," "The Motor City Goes Bust," and – from *Time* Magazine – "Is Your City Next?" Debts of $20 billion made this by far the costliest bankruptcy in US history. Some legal maneuvering was required to prevent the forced sale of the world-class collection of the Detroit Institute of Arts. After a thorough financial restructuring, Detroit came out of bankruptcy protection at the end of 2014.

The disaster that overcame Detroit seemed like an obvious sequel to the malaise that had overcome most major US cities from the 1960s onwards – like Saginaw or Johnstown, but on a far larger canvas. Symbolized most famously by New York City, the old metropolitan hearts had lost wealth and population, and entered a swift downward spiral of decay and fiscal catastrophe, endemic poverty and crime. The only economic activities that flourished visibly on the streets were the drug and prostitution rackets that scarcely bothered to conceal themselves. Hard-line criminal justice policies, mass incarceration, and the Drug War further hollowed out old urban minority sections and communities. But from the end of the century, most of America's largest cities entered a remarkable new era of growth and prosperity, even a new flowering, to a degree that would have shocked a time traveler from as recently as 1990. Although the new urban revival did not lack critics, most observers acknowledged the scale of the changes, and their positive qualities.

URBAN RETHINKING

Despite the obvious crises of the mid-twentieth century, at least some American cities flourished and grew, often on a spectacular scale. To some extent, this reflected the steady demographic movement to the south and west that we have already witnessed. In the century or so before the 1960s, American urban centers were concentrated in the north-east and Midwest, and the urban hierarchy was dominated by giants like New York, Chicago, Boston, and Philadelphia. All declined steeply in the 1960s and 1970s, losing people both to the suburbs and to other regions. Other traditional cities suffered just as heavily, including Baltimore, Cleveland, and St. Louis. The great success stories, meanwhile, were to the south and west. Already by 2000, nine of the nation's 15 leading cities were to be found in this Sunbelt region: Los Angeles, San Diego, San Jose, and San Francisco (California); Houston, Dallas, and San Antonio (Texas); Phoenix (Arizona) and Jacksonville (Florida). In 1920, all 10 of the nation's largest cities stood within 500 miles of the Canadian border; today, seven of the leading 10 are within 500 miles of the Mexican border. In the new century, the fastest growing urban areas are all located in the south (in Georgia and Florida), or in the west, in the states of Washington, Arizona, and Nevada.

When tracing urban growth and decline, we have to be careful about how we define cities and urban regions. Throughout modern history, the process of urban growth and decay has been very uneven. Even during the worst years of crisis during the 1970s, ruin afflicted the historic centers of cities while suburbs boomed. So did the burgeoning and even more distant commuter communities known as exurbs, which still belonged within the larger urban complex. Often, these larger metropolitan areas owe their existence to new forms of communication, such as a beltway road system, or the presence of a major airport which becomes the heart of what has been called an aerotropolis. Growing areas attract new office parks and shopping malls, and further spawn thriving residential developments. They are symbolized by the thriving new megachurches that have sprung up far outside the traditional urban cores where older congregations age and fade away.

The growth of urban regions is suggested by the two Texas cities of Dallas and Fort Worth, the centers of which stand some 30 miles apart. Both are surrounded by smaller towns and communities, which progressively coalesced into the larger urban area. The opening of Dallas Fort Worth airport in 1974 marked a rapid expansion for the cities and areas between the two old centers, which were increasingly drawn into one giant urban complex. The present population of Dallas alone is around 1.3 million, that of Fort Worth some 850,000, giving a combined total of 2.15 million. But those cities form part of a larger Dallas-Fort Worth (DFW) region, which contains almost 8 million people. Hypothetically, if "DFW" were a state in its own right, it would be more populous than 37 of the existing states, while covering a larger geographical area than Massachusetts. In Arizona, the city of Phoenix has a population of 1.6 million, but it stands at the heart of a region with a population of 4.7 million. In the north-east and Midwest too, the apparent decline of older cities is misleading to the extent that these figures measure only the core city areas rather than the broader statistical areas to which residents sometimes fled, or which newer populations actively preferred. Even as some inner cities declined or even collapsed, other parts of the same metropolitan region flourished.

But even when we expand our view to the larger metropolitan region, the expansion of the urban south and west is still powerfully obvious. As my unit of analysis of cities here, I will take the combined statistical areas (CSAs), which are defined by their social and economic linkages, as measured for instance by commuting patterns and overlapping media and labor markets. Table 6.1 illustrates the current urban framework using the sprawling CSA

Table 6.1   Urban complexes, 2017

	Combined statistical areas	Population (millions)
1.	New York-Northern New Jersey-Long Island	23.9
2.	Los Angeles-Riverside-Orange County	18.8
3.	Chicago-Gary-Kenosha	9.9
4.	Washington-Baltimore	9.8
5.	San Francisco-Oakland-San Jose	8.8
6.	Boston-Worcester-Lawrence	8.2
7.	Dallas-Fort Worth	7.8
8.	Philadelphia-Wilmington-Atlantic City	7.2
9.	Houston-Galveston-Brazoria	7.1
10.	Miami-Fort Lauderdale-Port St Lucie	6.8
11.	Atlanta	6.6
12.	Detroit-Warren-Ann Arbor	5.3

complexes of core and suburban areas into which traditional cities have evolved, and are continuing to evolve. Employing these rather different units of measurement, we still see that about half the nation's largest urban complexes are to be found in the south and west, and this proportion will only grow in coming years.

Together, this elite category of the 12 largest urban regions accounts for 120 million people, over a third of the national population.

The existence of national frontiers actively understates the growth of southern and western communities. US agencies collect statistics on urban areas within the national territory and not beyond. That means understating the growth of fast-growing metropolitan areas that straddle the border into Mexico, and which should properly be viewed as single regions or (de facto) CSAs. By that measure, San Diego-Tijuana claims some 5 million residents, with a further 3 million in El Paso-Juárez.

The growth in some of these areas in short periods has been dramatic, and was again weighted to the Sunbelt. Just since 2010, the population of the Houston-Galveston-Brazoria area has grown by 16 percent, that of the DFW complex by 15 percent. In the same short period, Miami and Atlanta swelled by 11 percent apiece, and the San Francisco Bay area by 8.4 percent. By way of comparison, among older cities, the statistical area centered in Chicago increased by just 0.6 percent, and that around Philadelphia by a mere 2 percent. Also since 2010, the complexes centered on Detroit, Cleveland, and Pittsburgh have all shrunk in numbers. Although they presently fall a little short of the elite category, other metroplexes will shortly be counted among the leading conglomerations. Since 2010, the Seattle-Tacoma CSA metroplex has grown by 11.5 percent, Denver-Aurora by almost 14 percent. By some projections, the Texas cities of Austin and San Antonio will soon merge into a mega-region at least on the scale of DFW. Inevitably, the west and south will increasingly dominate the map of urban America, with Texas and California playing the lead roles. That fact has immense political, cultural, and ethnic consequences. The booming regions are very diverse ethnically, and the Spanish language is a potent presence.

INNER CITIES

But if the decline of American cities was somewhat exaggerated, many inner cities did indeed suffer dreadfully in the mid- and late twentieth century, to a degree that makes their subsequent revival all the more remarkable. From the 1990s, many cities succeeded in turning their fortunes around in a way that Detroit conspicuously failed to accomplish, making their inner sections as desirable and attractive as they had been at the height of their fortunes.

That revival occurred as cities found successful new economic foundations to replace the industries that had been so critical in earlier decades. As we have seen, new high-tech industries became prominent in some regions, especially in the San Francisco Bay area and around Boston, in Seattle and Austin. But high tech did not preclude growth in other sectors. Besides its huge presence in IT and life sciences, Boston is a key financial center, focused on mutual funds and insurance. Like San Francisco, it supports a thriving tourist industry.

Service industries thrived in other cities historically associated with factories, mills, and heavy industry. Pittsburgh successfully managed the transition from the old city founded on steel and coal to a new emphasis on services, high tech, and medicine, and many firms established their corporate headquarters there. Among other centers, Columbus, OH, is the base for many high-tech ventures, besides such service staples as insurance, banking, food, and medical research. Charlotte, NC, is a banking center, from 1995 to 2017 the nation's second largest after New York City. Just since 1990, Charlotte's population has more than doubled, growing from around 400,000 to 850,000. Nashville, TN, combines a thriving financial sector with health care, tourism, and higher education, and on those diverse foundations the region's population grew by 45 percent between 2000 and 2017.

Many cities found economic strength from universities and colleges as driving forces in economic innovation, prosperity, and employment. As I noted earlier, the student numbers involved are very large, but we also have to factor in those non-students dependent on universities and colleges – faculty, administrators, and staff, not to mention employees of all the stores, cafes, and restaurants, on campus and beyond. In some cases, such institutions were the mainstay enterprises of burgeoning college towns, such as Pennsylvania's State College. But other institutions were central in preserving and reviving older cities, especially those with clusters of higher education institutions. The Boston area has 35 universities, colleges, and community colleges, with dozens more institutions in the larger metropolitan region. Those numbers grow further when we take account of nursing schools, seminaries, and schools of art and design. The Boston Metropolitan area is home to 350,000 students of various kinds. Just counting non-profit institutions, Pittsburgh has 40. Columbus is the home of Ohio State University, which since 2000 alone has grown from 50,000 to 60,000 students, not counting faculty and staff.

Higher education institutions have an extensive impact on their communities. Graduates of particular colleges and universities tend to remain in the area, establishing businesses and startups. Also, universities are associated with specialized research incubators, with hospitals and medical schools. Often, colleges and universities set up operations within a downtown, taking advantage of low property prices in a declining urban area, and restoring its fortunes. Besides their obvious appeal for youth, universities and colleges attract retired people, who enjoy the rich cultural and sporting opportunities, as well as the access to first-class medical facilities.

In the emerging world of education and medicine – of Eds and Meds – universities, medical schools, and medical complexes dominate employment in large cities. The sheer scale of some of these medical enterprises is staggering: Houston's Texas Medical Center employs over 100,000 people. Boston's Massachusetts General Hospital alone employs 25,000. In Philadelphia, Eds and Meds combined account for almost 40 percent of employment.

NEW URBANISMS

Inner cities became much more attractive to new residents, especially to those highly sought-after younger and more affluent groups as well as recent immigrants. It is in fact difficult here to sort cause from effect. Partly, cities became more prosperous, and that fact attracted new residents. Meanwhile, the influx of new residents added to the general prosperity. In either case, we can observe the influence of new approaches to urbanism and urban living, which closely followed the ideas of older theorists such as Jane Jacobs.

In the mid-twentieth century, cities had been hit hard by the vogue for theories of urbanism that emphasized the automobile over pedestrian traffic, and which resulted in large sections of residential or commercial space being demolished in order to build freeways. At the end of the century, not only did cities reject such theories, but they actively tried to reverse them by putting freeway routes underground, and restoring urban streets. The best-known example was Boston's epic Big Dig, a $15 billion project that was completed in 2006 – years late, and hugely over budget. Yet despite the problems, the result restored above-ground space, and allowed easy pedestrian traffic between areas long separated by roads. Dallas's Klyde Warren Park paved over an urban freeway in order to create a deck park, a popular urban green space in the heart of the downtown. New York City triumphantly exploited old industrial space when it transformed an abandoned rail line in the city's heart into the High Line, a green space that became a wildly popular destination for jogging, hiking, and socializing. Opened in 2009, the High Line became a stellar tourist attraction, and a global exemplar of landscape architecture. Again, pedestrians reconquered long inaccessible urban areas.

In other ways too, inner cities became more accessible for urban dwellers, rather than merely being destinations for suburbanites who needed only to find parking spaces. Social trends reinforced urban theory to promote what became known as new urbanism, a vision of prosperous, densely inhabited inner cities with a wide range of retail and entertainment options. The urban ruin of the 1970s and the bitter years of the Drug War era had left large sections of cities impoverished, but that very fact made them affordable for better-off residents willing to improve poorer properties. Those new arrivals, who saw themselves as urban homesteaders, were sometimes in search of bohemian lifestyles, but increasingly they were mainstream workers, business people, or students, attracted by urban values and opportunities. They found many potential dwelling spaces, as old factories and warehouses were partitioned to become apartment or loft space. In an old tobacco center like the Raleigh-Durham complex in North Carolina, imposing old factories and warehouses made splendid restaurants and retail space. Even inner-city Detroit offered many such opportunities.

Cities that might once have been regarded as smokestack industrial monuments were now attractive precisely because of their stock of handsome older buildings crying out for redevelopment. Particularly appealing about urban living was the lack of need for private automobiles or commuting, as cities offered public transport and (often) facilities for bicycles – besides easy walking. These convenient options appealed to those sensitive about environmental issues and the carbon emissions associated with private cars. The eclipse of old industries combined with recent federal regulations to ensure that former "smokestack" communities were as clean as any modern city.

A NEW URBAN LIFE

The revival of some cities was spectacular. In New York City, the transformation accelerated in the 1990s, with professionals moving to hitherto unthinkable areas in lower Manhattan, and then across the East River into the borough of Brooklyn. The main center of gentrification was Williamsburg, which successively attracted artists and creatives, followed by tech professionals, and then those made wealthy by finance. Businesses and services emerged to serve the new residents, and Brooklyn boomed in a way that would have staggered those who remembered the 1970s, when observers were regularly prophesying the city's imminent death. Brooklyn now acquired some of the nation's most chic and fashionable boutiques, bars, and restaurants. From Williamsburg, gentrification has in the past two decades spread through such neighboring communities as Bushwick, Bedford-Stuyvesant (Bed-Stuy), Greenpoint, and Crown Heights. "Brooklyn" has become synonymous with an urban revolution, to the point that each city attempting a comparable process dreams of becoming the "next Brooklyn." Rhetoric apart, many leading cities developed communities on something like the Brooklyn model, where troubled old working-class areas – "gritty" was the common term – re-remerged as centers of fashion and prosperity. Among many other instances, we might look at Ballard in Seattle, Denver's Northside, and lower north Philadelphia.

The new urban landscapes differed markedly from their recent predecessors, and not only in the sharply rising rents and property prices. Younger and wealthier populations had different tastes and needs, and businesses catered to them enthusiastically. We see this in matters of food and drink. The range of cuisines available in cities had already been expanding in the latter years of the previous century, but now extended much further. The ability to find and discuss hitherto exotic varieties of food became an important part of social capital. Meanwhile, the country experienced a widespread transformation in food culture, usually emphasizing locally sourced ingredients. Although the finest restaurants were available only in the largest cities – and to those with the substantial means necessary to afford them – they inspired a wider trend that was imitated in many mid-size and smaller communities.

In their dwellings, clothing, and possessions, new urban dwellers practiced what has been described as an urban retro aesthetic, favoring an idealized bygone world. They had a special taste for goods that claimed an independent or "artisan" quality that set them apart from corporate standardization, whether that meant foods, coffee or beer. Local or regional origins were especially prized, as was the authenticity of "heirloom" vegetables. The upsurge of farmers' markets allowed city dwellers to imagine that they were living in extended villages, close to the land. The word *locavore* was coined in 2005. The same preference supported the growth of community-supported agriculture, through which urbanites subscribed to the produce of particular farms or cooperatives, receiving each week a seasonal basket of fruit and vegetables. Nationally, sales of organic food soared, exceeding $45 billion by 2017, over 5 percent of total food sales. Between 2010 and 2017 alone, the combined total of craft breweries, microbreweries, and brewpubs operating in the US grew from 2,000 to 6,200, and craft beer is now a $24 billion market.

Food trucks began as an essential means by which laborers (often Latino) could obtain a hot meal near out-of-the-way worksites. Originally in fashionable centers like Austin, TX, food trucks increasingly attracted a wealthier clientele, and responded by offering a range of cuisines – Mexican, Vietnamese, Ethiopian, Korean, Thai – the choice depending on the diversity of local populations. Through the years, a series of dishes emerged from the obscurity of ethnic enclaves to achieve broad popularity, initially among knowledgeable foodies and then among a mainstream clientele. Some items migrated from the world of food trucks to become a staple of chain restaurants. Commonly, such tastes spread from immigrant communities in the south and the west, and college campuses were important to their national diffusion. Sushi was already well known by 2000, but the new century brought Vietnamese banh mi, Korean bulgogi, Thailand's pad thai, Hawaiian poke, and Salvadoran pupusas, as well as East Asian drinks like kombucha or bubble tea. The popular television comedy *Portlandia* offered a trenchant satirical commentary about such trends in food and lifestyle as they affected the city of Portland, OR, a hub of hipster chic.

One visible gauge of change was the proliferation of coffee shops, which filled a potent economic need in giving workers and students a "third space" in which they could operate, aside from home and office. This flexibility was made possible by the spread of laptop computers, and the near-universal availability of cell phones. The best-known brand name, Starbucks, began as a single store in Seattle in the 1970s, but from the end of the century began a steep expansion. (The word "barista" appeared in US English only in the 1980s.) By 2017, there were 13,000 Starbucks stores in the US, and a comparable number elsewhere in the world. Apart from such corporate chains, independently owned coffee shops proliferated.

Such shops offered a neat summary of twenty-first-century urban trends. Beyond the fact of the shops themselves, we imagine groups of overwhelmingly younger people, most of whom are examining cell phones, alternating between those mobile devices and their laptops for work purposes. Virtually all of the customers are listening to digital music played through earbuds. Many or most of the patrons bear visible tattoos, a habit that was not common in mainstream populations until the late 1990s. The explosion of tattoo parlors is mainly a post-2000 phenomenon.

The urban transformation acquired a kind of charter in the writings of scholar Richard Florida, notably in his 2002 book *The Rise of the Creative Class*. Florida noted the critical role of "creativity" as a fundamental economic driver, demonstrated by entrepreneurs and workers in the technology industry. High-tech innovation commonly drew freely on the fields of visual art and design, with a strong taste for the fantastic and grotesque. Florida described how such creatives tended to cluster together in particular cities which became very prosperous. Areas with large gay populations, and sizable communities of artists and musicians, were also likely to be centers of growth, innovation, and investment. But all these creative communities were highly mobile, and could decide exactly where they chose to live. They chose the cities they did largely in terms of the values they found there, and the kind of societies they could create. Particularly valued were communities built on education (and so usually blessed with many universities and colleges) but also extremely tolerant in issues of sexuality and lifestyle, and diverse ethnically.

Florida's views not only described contemporary trends, but they influenced state and city governments as to how they could encourage development in their own regions. Cities had long boasted their alternative character through such slogans as "Keep Austin Weird!" (and Portland used its own variant), but in the new world this was not so much a joke as a sound manifesto for economic progress.

CRIME

One critical development in urban life involved not a new presence but rather an absence or a departure, namely the steep and sudden decline in crime rates from the 1990s onward. That made urban living more attractive to middle-class residents, and removed obstacles that might otherwise have posed a fatal obstacle to urban revival. Cities felt safer because they were safer.

Crime, of course, is not exclusively an urban phenomenon, but violent crime in particular has always been a distinctive fact of urban life, and especially of the largest cities. In the mid-twentieth century, rising crime and feral violence had been a major factor driving better-off residents out of the inner cities, and encouraging "white flight." From the 1960s through the 1990s, crime was one of the worst fears assailing city dwellers, and it motivated political campaigns promising law and order. Such fears reached dramatic heights during the drug wars of the 1990s, when respected scholars warned of the arrival of extremely prolific and merciless offenders, the so-called super-predators, who would instigate an unprecedented wave of savagery.

In reality, the past two decades have witnessed a systematic drop in all forms of major criminality and especially violence, and homicide rates offer a powerful illustration. Nationwide, the homicide rate exceeded 10 per 100,000 in 1980, and once more approached that level in 1991. The rate fell to just 5.5 per 100,000 by 2000, and 4.5 by 2014, which represented a return to the relatively peaceful days of the early 1960s. That fall is well illustrated by the experience of New York City, which had long earned notoriety because of its visibility in mass media. In 1990, the city recorded 2,245 murders, compared to fewer than 600 in 2003 which represented the lowest number since 1964. By 2017, the number had fallen below 300, smaller than

London's. Nor was the fall confined to homicides. Violent crimes generally shrank across the nation in these same years.

That decline is not merely a statistical artifact, a new way of counting criminal acts that exaggerates the degree of real change. A similar decline emerges whether we are looking at figures for recorded crimes or arrests, or if we turn to surveys of the general public, asking if they have been the victims of particular offenses. Between 1993 and 2016, the rate for recorded violent crimes fell by about half, a figure that approached three-quarters if we use victimization studies. Victim studies showed a two-thirds decline in property crimes. By all available measures, crime was in free fall. From the standpoint of the late twentieth century, such a change was little short of revolutionary.

But what was the cause? Demography reduced the size of the most crime-prone population, teenagers and young adults, but that trend was not in itself sufficient to account for the shift. Determining other factors is a controversial issue, as no observer wishes to give too much credit to factors they find distasteful or politically unacceptable. Having said that, mass incarceration cannot be ignored (we will discuss this topic more extensively in Chapter 11). From the 1980s, US correctional populations rose sharply, and removed from the streets many urban residents from the ages and social categories most likely to accused of crime. At any given time in the 2010s, the number of incarcerated Americans was usually over 2 million, mainly young and poor people, and such a fact cannot fail to have some impact on crime rates. That comment certainly does not mean accepting or legitimizing the incarceration policies in themselves.

More effective policing was a key factor. From the 1980s, criminologists developed what became known as a "broken window" approach to crime, so that police focused on prompt and severe responses to what might have been regarded as minor or nuisance crimes. That prevented creating a situation in which an area came to be marked by a flagrant disrespect for law, which would in turn permit an upsurge of serious offenses. New technologies allowed the effective targeting of police resources, as GIS materials permitted the identification of potential crime hot spots in urgent need of intervention. New York City integrated these findings into a management approach called CompStat, which established clear lines of command and delegated areas of responsibility, as crime reduction was combined with general improvement in the quality of life. If it was not in fact the sole means of reducing violence, the introduction of CompStat coincided closely with the actual fall in crime rates and it was widely imitated in major cities. That New York City model of broken windows and CompStat found human symbols in the city's mayor at the time, Rudy Giuliani (1994–2001) and Police

Commissioner William Bratton (1994–1996). Bratton went on to serve as Police Chief in Los Angeles (2002–2009).

Reinforcing the general improvement was the massive expansion of surveillance and closed circuit television following the 9/11 attacks. Whatever it might have done for counter-terrorism efforts, the new surveillance apparatus made it difficult to contemplate getting away with regular property crime. Some criminologists point to other and quite surprising explanations for the reduction in criminal behavior, especially to the steep decline of lead additives in the environment from the 1970s onwards. The decline in lead dramatically lowered the occurrence of birth defects and developmental disorders that were associated with anti-social behavior.

The great crime decline was not uniform, and violence rates in some cities stubbornly refused to conform to the new normality. Chicago, notoriously, reported alarming rises in its homicide rate, as did Baltimore, a deterioration commonly blamed on police behavior and priorities. But in most centers, the new environment fundamentally reshaped attitudes to urban living. New urbanites found it all but impossible to comprehend the situation portrayed in films from the 1980s or earlier, where muggings and shootings were assumed to be such a common feature of inner-city life.

THE LIMITS OF GENTRIFICATION

Across the nation, the process of urban gentrification became commonplace, and controversial. By most conventional standards, inner cities were improving massively, becoming far safer, more prosperous, and healthier. Reporting the change, observers commonly spoke of revitalization, but also deployed words like revival, rescue, rebirth, and renaissance, with areas being cleaned up or improved. By implication, the old order in those communities must have involved death, decay, or filth. Matters looked very different from the perspective of the previous local residents, who were predominantly poor and minority, most of whom had nothing to do with crime or drug abuse. They would likely have agreed that their old areas could benefit from improvement and better law enforcement, but not from a wholesale recolonization. After all, the word "gentrification" implies a shift to a higher social class, a gentry, and in an American context that trend often correlated with racial change. The newer residents were not uniformly white, as they included many of the South or East Asians who were well represented in the booming tech industries. Generally, though, gentrification meant a purging of black and Latino residents.

As areas became wealthier, those older minority communities coped in different ways, and some residents did very well indeed, selling their properties for sums that would have been unimaginably high only a few years before. In many instances, though, poorer inhabitants were forced out, and exiled to remote communities cut off from much economic life. As we will see in Chapter 11, many protested the change as a kind of ethnic cleansing. Resentment was all the greater because of the role of intensive policing and incarceration in "cleaning up" areas for redevelopment. With urban land becoming ever-more valuable, developers bought and demolished shabby tenements and hotels that might otherwise have housed poor and marginal people. In their place, they raised luxury apartments and condominiums, while the number of affordable apartments shrank. As the process of change accelerated, so it affected still larger sections of the population, quite distinct from the very poor or the underclass. Gentrification pushed rents to levels far above what could be afforded by ordinary middle-class people, who had to move to new areas far removed from their place of work. This particularly hit aspiring black and Latino middle-class people. In San Francisco, it became all but impossible for middle-class people of any race – for police, teachers, or nurses – to live within many miles of the city where they had their livelihoods. Some activists spoke of a new era of de facto segregation.

In a historic irony, it was the more liberal cities that most thoroughly purged their minority residents. Following their environmental beliefs, cities like San Francisco enforced strict zoning laws and severely restricted new building, especially high-rise structures that could accommodate heavy population density. In consequence, home prices and rents soared as affordable housing became all but unavailable. Between 1980 and 2015, the black population of San Francisco fell from 13 percent to 5 percent, and it continues to shrink. In nearby Oakland, which was long a cultural and political center for black America, a quarter of the black population left between 2001 and 2011 as the city became "Brooklyn By The Bay." In Oakland's new demographic balance, black, white, and Latino populations were almost equal, with Asians not far behind. Los Angeles demonstrates similar patterns. Since the 1980s, the black population of Los Angeles County has fallen from 13 to 8 percent. At the time of writing, activists are mobilizing to prevent what seems like the imminent gentrification of the Crenshaw area, which has for many years been an unassailably black section of that city. Liberal cities like Portland were no more successful in maintaining black population levels. In all these cities, middle-class black communities declined or all but vanished, and black-owned business suffered badly. In contrast, middle-class and immigrant communities flourished in cities like Houston, which lacked zoning laws.

Concern about urban change and gentrification repeatedly sparked bitter conflicts. Sometimes, established local residents struggled to prevent the opening of new businesses that by many standards would signify a major increase in an area's wealth and attractiveness, such as upscale restaurants or art galleries. For many, the prospect of gentrification was a nightmare rather than a vision. In San Francisco again, public anger focused on the tech wealth that allowed many employees to buy expensive homes in the city, while working 40 or 50 miles away in Silicon Valley. Protesters targeted the buses that firms provided to shuttle their employees to and from the city. From this dissident perspective, social changes that seemed so beneficial were in fact destroying communities, benefiting the newly rich at the expense of the poor, and causing displacement and homelessness. Gentrification was presented as opening aggressive new fronts in the ongoing class struggle.

THE NEW URBAN POVERTY

Some years after the triumphant reception of his best-known book, Richard Florida himself offered a perceptive complaint about the harmful consequences of the changes he had championed, and above all the rise of social inequality. While inner cities improved in prosperity and safety, there was also a parallel growth of extremely poor areas in which large proportions of the people suffered from harsh poverty and all its attendant consequences. Those included inferior education, ill health, and lack of access to the transportation that would make it possible to find and hold employment. Although the fracture lines were not explicitly ethnic or racial, such pockets of hard-core poverty tended to be black or Latino. Whereas the gentrified sections boasted such diverse and abundant access to foods of all kinds, these poorer neighborhoods were "food deserts," where it was difficult to find much to eat that was not processed or otherwise unhealthy. In 2011, First Lady Michelle Obama began a campaign to eliminate such deserts.

Not only were such poorer sections profoundly disadvantaged, but the chances of escaping dire poverty were smaller than in previous eras. The fact that education was at such a premium in the new high-tech economy made life difficult for men who in earlier years could have secured excellent jobs with only a high school qualification. Throughout US history, higher education had usually demarcated social elites and aspiring classes, but those geographical divisions now became much more acute. Higher education qualifications came to be one of the best predictors not just of the economic health of a region or city, but increasingly of the quality of its social fabric, and even its physical health. Some cities and metropolitan regions demonstrated their boom status by the very high numbers of graduates among their millennial populations – between 54 and 58 percent in a highly desirable location like Washington DC. At the other end of the spectrum were depressed cities where the comparable figure was below 25 percent. The economic and social schism was powerfully marked not just between regions, but within states. By that educational criterion, some of the nation's most struggling centers were in California itself in such cities as Fresno. In Ohio, Columbus prospered as Youngstown failed.

HOMELESSNESS

Homelessness became a major part of political debate, although the nature of the problem was open to debate, and so, consequently, were any solutions. In the 2010s, homeless populations became much in evidence in cities like San Francisco and Los Angeles, where temporary settlements and even tent cities appeared. Because of the laissez-faire attitudes of police, homeless people engaged in public activities that most ordinary citizens found disturbing or offensive, including using public spaces as sleeping places and toilets. Some of those street people were openly criminal, or assaultive. Although the actual numbers of homeless people are hard to determine, the federal government estimated the 2017 total as 550,000, of which a quarter lived in California, and that state accounted for much of the increase in recent years. Between 2010 and 2017, the number of recorded homeless people in Los Angeles alone grew from 33,000 to 55,000.

From one point of view, the homelessness issue was a direct product of soaring property prices and gentrification, and the destruction of "skid row" accommodation and flophouses. Homeless people were thus portrayed as victims of stark injustice. But other factors came into play, and some were specific to California. In San Francisco, a substantial share of the most visible people who were living on the streets were doing so not because of changes in the property market but rather because of mental illness or substance abuse. In other generations, many of those individuals would have been forcibly confined to psychiatric institutions, but decades of legal cases had made that course difficult to pursue, more so in California than in other jurisdictions.

Also, specific choices by police and courts ensured that homeless people were uniquely visible in San Francisco, where authorities made the conscious decision not to pursue minor quality-of-life offenses. In a sense, this constituted a reversal of the broken windows policing that elsewhere proved so successful. The consequence was that homeless people remained on the streets, fearing no official sanction. Solutions to homelessness thus required rethinking police and judicial attitudes as much as economic arrangements.

For all the undoubted problems and drawbacks, the changes in American cities in these years were widely seen through the lens of improvement, of revitalization, and the media generally presented a narrative of energy and optimism. That was all the more true when urban redevelopment was intimately linked to the technology boom, as was clearly apparent in the twin Bay areas of Boston and San Francisco. But as we have seen, the US economic picture was far broader than these economic snapshots might suggest. Despite the apparent boom, signs of stress and even chaos were accumulating, reaching breaking point in the crisis of 2008.

7 The Crash: 2008

Founded in 1850, the investment bank of Lehman Brothers was long one of America's most prestigious financial firms – by the start of the twenty-first century, the nation's fourth largest. From 1997, Lehman became ever-more heavily involved in the mortgage business, with a special focus on subprime borrowers, those who would not meet the customary criteria of credit worthiness. With its daring use of innovative but risky financial instruments, the firm in effect became a real estate hedge fund rather than a conventional bank. As Lehman's business expanded, so did its vulnerability to any downturn in the real estate market. By 2008, the firm had assets of $680 billion, supported by barely $22 billion of solid capital. Through that year, the likelihood of disaster grew daily as real estate markets plummeted, and a series of attempts to rescue the endangered firm failed. On September 15, Lehman declared the largest bankruptcy in US history, with some $600 billion in assets. The announcement provoked the steepest decline in stock prices since the terrorist attacks of that terrible earlier September, in 2001.

Observers questioned which other financial giants might suffer a comparable fate in the coming days or weeks, and beyond that whether the whole banking system might grind to a halt. Some observers described the 2008 crisis as a convulsive shock at least equal to the 9/11 attacks, and even more severe in its effects. Such a trauma was all the more shocking because it contrasted so sharply with the apparent atmosphere of growth and prosperity in recent years. The more closely we look at those years, though, the less surprising does the economic crisis appear.

CHEAP MONEY

At the turn of the century, the US economy was reshaped by several long-term trends – including the housing boom and the Reagan-era liberation of the finance sector – and each played its part in provoking the global crisis that broke in 2008. Although the crisis had multiple dimensions, two primary causes can be singled out: too much money was available, and the regulations limiting how it could be disposed were too weak. Both the Clinton and Bush administrations must receive blame for the inevitable outcome.

Central to the change was the dramatic economic rise of countries that were projected to become serious rivals of the United States in coming decades. Depending on how we judge its GDP, China either is presently the world's largest economy, or else it will gain that status within the coming decade. (We will return to the strategic and military issues raised by this growth.) At the start of the century, China was building a thriving manufacturing economy founded upon exports, and it was the most popular region for production offshoring. In 2001, the country joined the World Trade Organization. Supporting this growth, China pegged its currency at an unnaturally low rate in order to keep its exports cheap. As people around the world bought Chinese goods, the country acquired an awe-inspiring trade surplus. China in turn invested its money abroad, especially in the United States. In effect, China was supplying Americans with the money that they needed to buy Chinese goods, and Americans showed few qualms about the exchange. So intimate was the relationship that some commentators spoke of "Chimerica."

US financial institutions had to come to terms with a large supply of cash, and faced enormous pressure to lend to a public with a powerful taste for consumer goods and leisure services of all kinds. Government policies strongly encouraged the atmosphere of easy credit and of high risk. Following the collapse of the internet bubble in 2000–2001, and the 2001 terrorist attacks, the US government was desperately anxious to avoid an economic recession. The Federal Reserve Bank – the Fed – pushed interest rates to dramatic lows, encouraging easy credit. The Fed's funds rate sank from 6 percent at the start of 2001 to 1.75 percent by year's end, and to 1 percent by late 2002. That figure in turn decided the prime rate charged by banks to their most favored customers. In 2000, the prime rate stood at 9.5 percent, falling to 4.75 at the start of 2002 and to just 4 by 2003. By keeping its rates low after the immediate crisis had passed, the Fed fueled the credit boom. In retrospect, many commentators saw these Fed decisions as principal drivers of the 2008 crash.

At the same time, the Bush administration pursued a Reaganite program of deep tax cuts, injecting still more money into the economy. Such a policy seemed justifiable, given the existing budget surplus. On strongly partisan lines, Republicans passed two key measures, the Economic Growth and Tax Relief Reconciliation Act (2001) and the Jobs and Growth Tax Relief Reconciliation Act (2003). Despite the high cost of the proposed cuts, conservative economists argued that they would thoroughly pay for themselves in the long term, to the point of eliminating the US national debt.

THE HOUSING MARKET

The cheap money environment had its greatest impact on real estate markets. Administrations of both parties sought to make loans more available to lower-income and minority people wishing to become homeowners. Banks had a long and appalling record of racially discriminatory practices in lending, and it was natural for political leaders to reverse these policies in order to promote a property-owning democracy. Since the 1970s, the goal of ensuring easy credit to low-income borrowers had been promoted by the Community Reinvestment Act, which was frequently revised and updated through the 1990s. The federal government had a powerful say in how banks and lenders operated through the critical organizational and support role played by the Federal National Mortgage Association (Fannie Mae) and the Federal Home Loan Mortgage Corporation (Freddie Mac). Various Clinton-era reforms encouraged Fannie Mae to lower its credit standards for poorer applicants.

Both in economic and political terms, banks and mortgage providers had a powerful incentive to supply credit, and from the turn of the century they significantly reduced the standards that they would previously have demanded. But practices went badly awry. Instead of accepting only the best (prime) customers, banks now expanded their market among what were charitably known as subprime borrowers. As a share of the US mortgage market, subprime loans grew from 7.4 percent in 2002 to over 20 percent between 2004 and 2006, and many of those loans took the criteria for "subprime" to new lows. In scandalous instances, lenders gave money to applicants offering no proof of assets or employment. A semi-serious slang term described NINJA borrowers, with "no income, no job, and no assets," and the word aptly conveys a sense of the fantasy atmosphere in which once-sound financial institutions now found themselves. The rate of mortgage denials collapsed. Studies of mortgage pools indicated serious deficiencies, many acute, in up to half of those examined. Some businesses worked so forcefully to persuade subprime borrowers to accept loans that the term "predatory lending" arose.

The kinds of mortgages being issued changed in crucial ways. The traditional mortgage format used a fixed rate for repayments throughout the life of the loan, so that borrowers knew exactly what they were committing themselves to. Newer mortgages used an adjustable rate format by which the actual amount that borrowers needed to repay depended on interest rates, which could fluctuate wildly over time. At the time, in 2003 or 2004, interest rates stood at a historic and unnatural low point, from which they would clearly rebound. Borrowers were lured into accepting mortgages at what looked like very affordable rates – often, at tempting "teaser" rates – without realizing just how high those repayments could rise when economic circumstances changed, and how swiftly. New homebuyers had little sense of just how vulnerable they were, and how easily they could lose their houses.

The real estate market demonstrated the classic signs of a bubble, with spiraling prices and a common belief that the upward trajectory would never end. This febrile atmosphere encouraged wildly speculative over-building of houses and condominium units that would be impossible to sell in an already over-supplied market. On the good side, this building drove employment in construction, at least temporarily. Many ordinary people took advantage of the boom by house flipping – that is, by buying a property for a short time with the intent of reselling it shortly afterwards at a healthy profit. Banks were happy to lend to these investors (more accurately, speculators) rather than to their traditional core market of homeowners seeking to finance a principal residence. As in previous speculative bubbles, people borrowed heavily to participate in the market, risking sums that they simply could not afford to lose. Seeking quick profits as houses turned over, many middle-class people committed themselves to multiple mortgages. Levels of household debt ballooned. The real estate market became particularly torrid in Sunbelt states like Arizona, Nevada, and Florida, and booming cities like Las Vegas, Miami, and San Diego were acutely affected.

For a while, real estate prices soared nationally, as the median home price grew from $163,000 in 2000 to $223,000 in 2005. In the decade after 1996, the price of the typical house grew by 125 percent. High housing prices had their political impact, as a house is by far the largest single asset that most ordinary people own, and its rising value tends to create a sense of prosperity and well-being. That makes people more satisfied with existing administrations, and less willing to plunge into untested political waters. Together with continuing fears over terrorism, ballooning house prices go far to explaining what some found the surprising re-election of George W. Bush in 2004.

MANAGING RISK

Despite experts' fears about the situation, the general belief in deregulation that had prevailed since the Reagan years discouraged official intervention. It was widely – if not universally – believed that the market itself had developed new financial tools that would allow it to cope with any volatility.

In order to manage risk, businesses developed creative new financial instruments that ultimately posed real dangers to economic stability. The central idea involved packaging mortgages in a form that could be traded as high yield bonds or securities – mortgage-backed securities. They thus became part of the market in derivatives; that is, contracts with a value based on the expected future price movement of an item or commodity. These allowed investors to soften or hedge losses. Although derivatives can be based on any kind of asset, mortgage-based securities now achieved enormous significance. Through collateralized debt obligations (CDOs) and other derivatives, institutions bundled mortgages together into instruments that were sold and traded, thus (ideally) spreading and reducing risk. From the late 1990s, one fast-growing subset of the derivative market involved credit default swaps, an agreement that in essence compensates buyers against a debt default. These contracts in effect were bets on the health of subprime bonds.

Critically for their success, derivatives were strongly favored by the esteemed economist Alan Greenspan, who served as Chairman of the Federal Reserve from 1987 through 2006. As an ardent believer in the free market, Greenspan believed in the necessity of risk-taking as a condition of growth and progress; this could properly be regulated by the ingenuity and innovation of financiers and entrepreneurs themselves. He thus opposed regulating derivatives, and his position and prestige served as a powerful bulwark against change. As he boasted in 2004, "Not only have individual financial institutions become less vulnerable to shocks from underlying risk factors, but also the financial system as a whole has become more resilient."

For advocates like Greenspan, derivatives were an admirable means of giving the market greater flexibility and diversification, but knowledgeable investors worried about their complexity and the heavy exposure of key financial firms. Reading about the complexities of CDOs and derivatives, ordinary consumers of news might assume that only skilled financial experts could understand such highly specialized and technical instruments. The problem was that very few of those alleged experts themselves had any grasp whatever of what they were dealing with. As it was all but impossible to determine the actual value of investments at any given point, companies and institutions invested far beyond their resources, without understanding the scale of the potential liability. In 2003, legendary investor Warren E. Buffett prophetically described derivatives as "financial weapons of mass destruction, carrying dangers that, while now latent, are potentially lethal."

Derivatives were vulnerable to manipulation by firms seeking to maximize profits, ignoring standard rules about conflicts of interest and insider trading. Greenspan underestimated such dangers, believing that enlightened self-interest would ensure that bankers would behave responsibly and ethically, but events proved him badly wrong. Wall Street financial firms entered a period of reckless adventurism, as traders made massively leveraged bets on the market. Between 2002 and 2008, the derivatives market grew from $106 trillion to $531 trillion, a fantastic sum much larger than the size of the entire world economy. In the same years, the market in credit default swaps grew from $2 trillion to over $54 trillion. Those sums involved insuring against defaults, and if such defaults ever did occur financial institutions were committed far beyond what they could possibly cope with, or even comprehend.

For all the concerns, derivatives escaped the kind of scrutiny or regulation that would certainly have been applied in earlier decades. In 2000, Bill Clinton had signed into law a measure preventing these instruments being regulated either as commodities or securities. This gave an advantage to types of investment that in effect became a shadow banking system, yet free of the regulations that guided the "real" banks. In particular, they were not required to maintain adequate capital reserves to withstand crises. Also during that presidency, in 1999, the Financial Services Modernization Act repealed the Depression-era law that had mandated a separation between depository and investment banks. The official hands-off attitude removed an important deterrent to conflicts of interest by those banks.

Through the Bush years, evidence mounted of abuses and outright fraud in property markets. In 2003, the administration sought tighter regulation of Fannie Mae and Freddie Mac, but repeated efforts failed in Congress. Meanwhile, the Securities and Exchange Commission refused to demand that banks should keep more capital reserves as a hedge against disastrous losses. Nor did the private sector exercise any kind of moderation. The key regulators were ratings agencies such as Standard and Poor's or Moody's, which in theory should have used evidence of extensive fraud as a reason to downgrade the mortgage-backed securities peddled by Wall Street firms. Yet agencies failed to respond with any actions that would have soured their over-cozy relationships with those same banks and investment firms. Lacking regulation, financial firms had every incentive to continue giving mortgages, as lending standards continued to decline.

THE CRISIS

As house prices plummeted in 2006–2007, the housing bubble burst. This in turn provoked a national wave of foreclosures and bankruptcies, precipitating a crisis in the subprime market, and threatening to ruin investors. At the end of 2007, the US officially entered a period of recession, and the US stock market began its long-expected period of correction.

Major investment houses found themselves committed to multi-billion dollar rescues of subsidiaries that had plunged dangerously into derivatives. The once-mighty investment firm Bear Stearns had to be saved in early 2008, forcing it into a merger with another giant firm. Other colossi like Lehman Brothers faced their own crisis that September, and Lehman actually was allowed to fail without even the fig leaf disguise of a takeover by another bank. This provoked what was in effect a run on the shadow banking system. The multinational insurance company AIG (American International Group) was predicted to follow Lehman, which would in turn have endangered the survival of Citigroup, Goldman Sachs, and J. P. Morgan. Other key firms like Merrill Lynch, Wachovia, and Washington Mutual all stood on the brink of ruin. These events raised fears that a domino effect would wreck banks and investment firms around the world. Stock markets crashed globally. As banks slashed credit, so businesses and corporations failed. Losses on US-based sub-prime assets probably amounted to a trillion dollars.

By late 2008, the US was facing the worst economic disaster since the horrendous 1930s, and it would have been far graver if not for massive government intervention. According to strict free market doctrine, the problems would ultimately have worked themselves out, leaving inefficient and uncompetitive firms to fail, to the long-term benefit of stronger rivals. But the failure of so many institutions in the short term would have been so extensive as to obliterate the whole financial sector and with that, the whole economy – certainly of the US, and probably of much of the world. The social and political implications of such a disaster did not bear contemplating. A few commentators wrote alarmingly of the imminent end of capitalism. In October, Republican presidential candidate John McCain shocked his party by announcing the suspension of his campaign, and urging both parties to formulate an emergency response to the crisis.

Governments had to take urgent action, and on an unprecedented scale. Among other bailouts, AIG was rescued at a cost of $85 billion. In October 2008, still under the Bush administration, Congress passed a Troubled Asset Relief Program, TARP, which promised the then-staggering sum of $700 billion to rescue failing institutions. The government also took Freddie Mac and Fannie Mae into conservatorship, effectively nationalizing them. Ultimately, the government spent over a trillion dollars in various rescue schemes for the housing and mortgage sectors, as well as bailouts of faltering enterprises including General Motors. In the long term, the cost to the public proved far smaller than these initial figures threatened, and the government even made a profit on the deal. At the time, however, the numbers were staggering.

THE GREAT RECESSION

As in the early 1930s, a financial crisis was linked to a full-scale global recession. Although the financial intervention averted outright catastrophe, it could not prevent economic troubles from growing far worse over the following year. Between October 2007 and March 2009, the Dow Jones index plunged from 14,164 to 6,507, and the S&P500 lost half its value. Officially, the recession that began in December 2007 continued until June 2009, but its effects lingered long after that. Aggravating an already bad situation, oil prices now soared, reaching a historic peak of $145 per barrel in July 2008. High oil prices and tight credit mauled the automobile industry, which had invested so heavily in low fuel economy vehicles like SUVs (sports utility vehicles). America's Big Three auto-makers – General Motors, Ford, and Chrysler – all faced bankruptcy.

The impact on employment was catastrophic. By the end of 2008, the economy had lost 2.6 million jobs, with a special impact on construction. The number of full-time employees fell from a 2007 height of 121 million to a 2010 trough of 111 million, and not until 2015 did it return to pre-crisis levels. The official unemployment rate grew from 4.5 percent in 2007 to 7.2 percent at the end of 2008, and continued to rise. Official unemployment peaked around 10 percent, but critical observers suggest that such figures mask a sizable number of workers who should more properly be included. By some estimates, the "real" unemployment rate by 2011 was close to 17 percent. The number of Americans living in poverty grew from 36 million in 2006 to 46 million in 2011. In reporting the avalanche of disasters, journalists repeatedly noted that a given statistic was the worst of its kind since the 1930s.

The crisis had a predictable effect on real estate and credit markets generally. Between 2006 and 2010, the average price of a house fell by 26 percent – again, a sharper fall than during the worst years of the 1930s. We witness the reversal of all the seemingly positive developments that had been so strongly in evidence at the height of the bubble in 2003–2004. Middle-class homeownership declined steeply, as some 9 million Americans lost their homes. The regions worst affected were exactly those that had boomed so promisingly in the earlier period, especially in Florida, Nevada, and California. Americans lost some $6 trillion in housing wealth. Far from being excessively generous with prospective borrowers, financial institutions now so tightened their lending standards as to shut out many creditworthy customers who would once have been warmly welcomed. Small businesses were harshly penalized.

Foreclosures now became painfully commonplace. By 2010, 2.21 percent of all households were in some stage of foreclosure, compared to just 0.58 percent in 2006. The great majority of these actions affected people who were already financially stressed, and who perhaps were losing the only home they could ever have hoped to own. However unpopular the banks were for their behavior during the crisis itself, their subsequent actions over foreclosures deeply aggravated the situation, and gave ammunition to political critics. In 2010, media reports showed that banks had improperly sent out many thousands of foreclosure notices, based on dubious information collected in affidavits that were signed automatically without verification – so-called robo-signings. The resulting public scandal forced several major banks to suspend foreclosure proceedings, and some paid substantial settlements. Even if homeowners did not actually suffer foreclosure, millions found themselves owing more on their mortgages than the actual free market value of their homes, leaving them "underwater," so that they could not contemplate selling.

Economists commonly argue that the depth of a recession is proportionate to the strength of the recovery that follows it, so that a harsh recession like that of 2007–2009 should in theory have been followed by a powerful boom, an era of rapid expansion and a return of optimism. In this instance, that certainly did not occur. Although the recession ended in mid-2009, growth rates proved sluggish through the Obama years, disappointing hopes of an easy or thorough recovery. Between 2009 and 2016, the US recorded annual growth of little more than 2.1 percent annually, rather than the 4 or 5 percent that might have restored the economy to pre-crash levels.

Following so closely upon the real estate crash, the new crisis accelerated the decline of an already troubled working and middle class, and it sabotaged many retirement schemes. The crisis proved especially damaging to younger people and the generation of millennials, those born since 1981. The systematic decline of incomes and opportunities reinforced and substantially increased the already large wealth gap between generations, and the effects of that shock still reverberated a decade later.

Difficult to quantify are the psychological effects that the crisis had on ordinary people, the impact on the attitudes and beliefs of consumers, workers or investors. Since the Reagan years, most Americans had become thoroughly accustomed to growth and progress, with the exception of the brief recession of the early 1990s. Everyone knew as an obvious fact that house prices were on a permanently upward trajectory, as were stock prices, incomes, and job numbers. Few people under 40 actually remembered a serious and prolonged bear market. The crisis of 2008 transformed all those assumptions, introducing a new element of doubt, insecurity, and pessimism. In terms of work and pensions, many people had grudgingly accepted the shift from defined pensions to 401(k)s tied to the stock market, as these were regularly producing impressive returns. Matters were very different in an era of plunging stock prices and shrinking retirement nest eggs. That in turn had its political consequences, raising deep concerns about globalization and inequality – not to mention the competence and integrity of ruling elites. People feeling poorer and pessimistic about the future are unlikely to vote for an existing administration or a party that represents the status quo, making it all but certain that the coming election of November 2008 would result in a Democratic triumph.

A CRISIS OF CAPITALISM?

Quite apart from its direct economic effects, the crisis forced a reconsideration of long-running debates over the proper scope and function of the state in economic life, of the need for the state to regulate businesses and corporations. Journalistic and official investigations made it obvious that the crisis had not simply occurred without warning, and that the disasters should long have been foreseen. The crisis arose not simply from bad luck or poor judgment, but rather from repeated violations of laws by leading figures in finance and business, and some had engaged in gross criminality. Particularly common was the habit of placing mortgages that banks knew to be questionable into securitized pools. To varying degrees, such charges tainted all the giant banks. Calls for sweeping criminal investigations came not only from radical politicians but from quite moderate figures. In fact, very few bankers actually faced prison terms, and senior executives in deeply compromised firms continued to receive multi-million dollar bonuses. As the crisis produced so few convictions or penalties, the question arose whether criminal laws ever applied to the reckless super-rich who had inflicted such havoc.

The fact that the state had intervened so massively to save banks and businesses led many to argue that the rescued firms had special obligations to the public and the larger community, but events like the 2010 foreclosure crisis showed no signs of any improvement in attitudes. For the many critics of TARP, the government had actually spent those vast sums to rescue the bankers rather than the banks. In 2010, a third of those questioned believed that the bank bailout had been improper or unnecessary, and protesters called for bailout funds to be diverted to indebted homeowners rather than rapacious financiers.

In reinforcing the need for effective regulation, the disaster undermined uncritical support for unregulated free enterprise capitalism, especially in banking and finance. Through the debate over TARP, advocates of a bailout had repeatedly declared that the businesses involved were simply "too big to fail," that their collapse would irreparably damage the nation at large. One riposte to that was that if they were too big to fail, then they were too big to be allowed to exist. They should thus be cut back significantly. That argument laid the foundation for a new wave of anti-trust and anti-monopoly intervention, recalling the older Progressive era. Politically, too, the crisis opened the door to a new willingness to accept expansive government intervention in the economy, offering liberals their greatest opportunity since the 1960s. After decades in which conservative supply-side economics maintained its supremacy, Keynesian thought became respectable once more. Economist Paul Krugman quoted the saying that "There are no atheists in foxholes, and there are no libertarians in financial crises." Libertarianism, in this view, was a luxury for times of special prosperity.

DEBTS AND DEFICITS

But if the crisis opened the door to an expansive role for government, it also placed strict limitations on what a government might feasibly hope to achieve. With its trillion-dollar rescues, the sharp decline of the US tax base, and the terrifying expense of the ongoing overseas wars, the financial crisis focused attention on the underlying issues of debts and deficits. In an age when the state had to respond to so many demands at home and abroad, when debts and deficits were persistent nightmares, some observers feared that the national government might reach a breaking point at which it could no longer fulfill its essential functions. Throughout these years, debts and deficits were among the most explosive issues dividing the parties. However urgent the calls for government intervention in many areas – for instance, in upgrading the national infrastructure, in rebuilding roads and bridges – any administration has to confront the almost inconceivable scale of America's national debt.

These debt problems were rooted in earlier historical eras. Some pressing issues could be traced back to Franklin Roosevelt's New Deal and Lyndon Johnson's Great Society, which wrote expensive social programs into law – entitlement schemes such as Social Security and Medicare/Medicaid. On the conservative side, the Reagan administration cut tax rates, while not shrinking the size of the state or tackling rising entitlements. Federal revenues were systematically reduced, at a time of booming defense spending. Matters improved in the Clinton years, but deficits and debts grew at a dizzying pace in the Bush era. The main gauge is the closely watched figure for the national debt – technically, the Total Public Debt Outstanding – although that figure does not take account of other forms of indebtedness, by states, cities, and municipalities. Between 2000 and 2008, the national debt doubled, growing from $5.6 trillion to $11.3 trillion, and the figure approached $22 trillion by 2018. Although the rate of growth slowed somewhat after 2014, the trend is still clear.

Since 2008, total federal debt has grown from 68 percent of the country's GDP to around 105 percent. Each year, a sizable and increasing share of the budget must be allotted merely to keeping up payments on the debt. Soon the federal government will be spending more just on debt interest repayments than on the combined figures for education, housing, energy, transportation, and environmental protection. The debt problem forces the US government to be highly sensitive to the needs of creditors, and foreign governments now hold $6.3 trillion in US treasury securities. Historically, European nations held the largest share of these securities, but China supplanted the United Kingdom as the second biggest holder in 2007. Presently, by far the two largest creditors are China and Japan, each of which holds over a trillion dollars.

Nor is there an easy or obvious solution to the debt problem, even if governments strove to reduce deficits in the near term. Through the years, politicians have promised to cut the US budget and reduce the size of the state, but they have soon found that such a task is all but impossible, legally as well as politically. US governments are legally committed to paying for expensive and popular social programs that seem immune to cutting. The United States must pay the cost of Social Security, Medicare/Medicaid and other mandated programs, besides debt interest payments. By 2016, 65 percent of the US budget was pledged to such mandatory spending. The cost of entitlement programs rises along with the growing number of older people in the national population. Current estimates suggest that Medicare will be technically insolvent by 2026, and Social Security by 2034.

By some projections, by 2040 or so various forms of mandatory spending will actually exceed total government revenue. In that circumstance, the United States could not set its finances right even if it eliminated all other government spending, including defense, and a ruinous national default would be conceivable. The only alternative would be to print money and inflate the currency, with all the dreadful consequences that implies. Governments would face the politically lethal choice between ruthless cuts on spending on popular programs or raising taxes to crushing levels. Whether governments chose to emphasize taxes or spending cuts, any debates on such basic economic questions would involve toxic conflicts over the inter-linked politics of class, gender, and especially race. Controversies over wealth transfers and welfare inevitably spark charges of a racial assault on black and minority communities.

Although issues of debts and deficits are normally framed in terms of federal spending and the US government, states and cities face their own particular crises. As we have seen, pension issues have been a significant driver of such over-commitments, but the wider 2008 crash caused serious damage in particular areas. The total cost of unfunded state pension liabilities rose from below $300 billion in 2004 to approach $1 trillion by 2013, and $1.4 trillion by 2017. Levels of underfunding are critically serious in spendthrift states like Illinois, Connecticut, and Kentucky. Unlike the federal government, states are forbidden from running deficits, so that any shortfall must be made up by other and often quite desperate means. Several states have faced endemic fiscal crises, over and above the national debt problem.

The economic crash thus made it all but certain that Democrats would win the presidency in 2008. It also ensured that any new administration would have to contend with severe structural problems, and that almost anything it did to address these issues would stir ferocious opposition. Both long- and short-term economic trends laid the foundation for vicious partisanship in the coming years.

8 The Obama Years

Barack Obama inspired very high expectations. In 2008, artist Shepard Fairey designed a stylized portrait of Obama that featured the word "Hope," which became one of the best-known political posters in modern American history. Although it was created several months before the financial crash, the message of hope gained new significance as the economy plunged. Recalling the image of Che Guevara that had adorned so many student apartments and dorm rooms in the 1960s, the Hope poster was displayed without irony by millions of Americans, especially among the young. It appealed to those who might have described themselves as too cynical for political dreams. Although the image is often described as "iconic," it often bore a greater resemblance to an actual religious icon than a mere poster. As we will see, religious imagery and expectations followed the candidate. At Obama's inauguration in 2009, megachurch pastor Rick Warren declared that "We celebrate a hinge point of history with the inauguration of our first African American president of the United States. ... And we know today that Dr. King and a great cloud of witnesses are shouting in heaven." For his supporters, Obama's election was a time of unlimited potential, and even a chance to remodel American society in a way that had not been done since the New Deal of the 1930s.

THE 2008 ELECTION

Although Democrats were strongly favored to win the presidency in 2008, it was not obvious what directions that future administration would take. The obvious candidate was Hillary Clinton, who enjoyed enviable financial resources together with the support of the Democratic Party apparatus and who benefited from fond memories of the her husband's presidency. But as would again occur in 2016, she faced a challenge from more progressive-minded rivals.

Obama himself had an unconventional background in many ways, with his immigrant father and cosmopolitan origins. He entered an academic career and taught constitutional law at the University of Chicago. He first emerged as a political figure to watch in 2004 with his keynote address at the Democratic National Convention, and he cemented this popularity with a bestselling 2006 book, *The Audacity of Hope*. Ironically, in light of conflicts that ensued during his time in office, he owed much of his original appeal to framing what aspired to be a bipartisan message. Even so, his experience with national politics was limited to a brief term in the US Senate representing Illinois. His overseas background exposed him to conspiracy-minded charges that he had in fact been born outside the United States, which according to some interpretations would make him ineligible for the presidency. Alternatively, he was rumored to have a Muslim past. However often rejected, such charges – by Birthers and Muslim theorists alike – simmered in the popular imagination.

At first, the Obama candidacy seemed like a hopeless enterprise given the overwhelming strength of the candidate known by friend and foe alike simply as "Hillary." But Obama was a formidable campaigner. He mobilized vast and exuberant bands of followers, not just among the expected liberals, but also among young adults and ethnic minorities who had not hitherto been much interested in electoral politics, as new voters registered in huge numbers. His campaign made extensive and imaginative use of social media. At the same time, Clinton's overconfidence led her to commit errors, and she made impolitic remarks that demanded explanation and backtracking. The ensuing Obama–Clinton contest revealed striking and unsuspected gaps between generations and classes as much as races, with Clinton appealing to older and traditional-minded working-class voters, while Obama won the support of the young and better educated. Many who recalled the horrors of segregation and the travails of the civil rights movement saw an Obama presidency as a resolution of the hopes and fears of that time. In retrospect, the Clinton constituency in the primaries – older, whiter, and poorer – curiously prefigures the Trump supporters of 2016.

Obama was regularly described as a charismatic figure, which is a subjective term: supporters might find a particular individual charismatic or inspiring for reasons that opponents fail to comprehend. If followers extolled Obama's speeches as magnificent political rhetoric, foes scorned them as overblown and arrogant. In 2008, supporters dominated the debate, and enthusiastic liberals spoke of the candidate in terms that were frankly religious or messianic. Some presented Obama as a figure of destiny, subject to a special guidance, a man who occupied a superior plane, with his candidacy regularly described as an event of biblical proportions. Even mainstream supporters found him such an overwhelming favorite that they could understand no reason that anyone might oppose him, except for crude racism. That divided perception did much to poison party relations in the coming years.

Witnessing the contest, it was easy to forget what an astonishing commentary it was on the degree of social change in recent decades: an African American man was in competition with a (white) woman candidate. On the other side, the Republicans nominated highly decorated war hero John McCain, who chose a woman as his vice president, namely Alaska governor Sarah Palin, a conservative firebrand.

OBAMA AS PRESIDENT

The Democratic victory was overwhelming. Ultimately, some 130 million Americans cast votes in 2008, compared with 100 million or fewer in most elections during the 1990s. Obama received almost 70 million votes, almost 53 percent of the popular vote, compared with the 50 million that had put George W. Bush in the White House in 2000. That support assisted broader Democratic victories down the ballot, giving the Party strong majorities in both houses of Congress. For a critical year, the Democrats enjoyed a Senate majority sufficient to withstand filibuster threats, but that situation soon ended, leaving many administration efforts to perish in a hostile Congress. Throughout his two terms, Obama's legislative accomplishments fell far short of his original ambitions.

Democrats returned to power in Washington with a great deal of pent-up demand for new social legislation, and they gained some mighty victories. These followed the classic New Deal pattern of sweeping federal laws, bolstered by new and reinforced regulatory agencies. In 2009, Congress passed an ambitious economic stimulus measure advertised as a counter to the recession and budgeted at over $700 billion. The administration passed a historic financial regulation law, the Wall Street Reform and Consumer Protection Act, which sought to prevent a near-cataclysm like that of 2008. This so-called Dodd–Frank law regulated the financial services industry, and curbed abusive lending and mortgage practices by banks. A new Consumer Financial Protection Bureau had jurisdiction over a wide range of financial institutions, including banks, mortgage providers, security firms, debt collectors, and foreclosure agencies. Generous government assistance helped save the auto industry from collapse, although it emerged with far fewer jobs than before the crisis. Among other social reforms, a measure passed in 2010 ended the "Don't Ask, Don't Tell" system that had prevented openly gay and lesbian individuals from serving in the US armed forces.

Most historic was the passage in 2010 of systematic health care reform, a goal that liberals had been seeking since the time of Franklin Roosevelt.

This Patient Protection and Affordable Care Act was commonly known as Obamacare. Although the complex new law did not offer state-funded single-payer universal care on European lines, Obamacare did aspire to cover all Americans within a decade. Among its main principles, the law created a mandate for every individual to have health insurance, and individuals who could not afford premiums would receive government subsidies. That idea borrowed from a pioneering scheme enacted in Massachusetts in 2006 and associated with the Republican then-governor, Mitt Romney. The new federal law created a system of insurance exchanges that allowed consumers to shop among a variety of options offered by various companies. States could operate their own exchanges, while the federal government created its own system for those living in states that chose not to operate such a scheme.

For its advocates, the hard-won law was a sensible compromise that should have attracted bipartisan support. It reflected a remarkable willingness to tolerate government intervention and even social democratic solutions, and it can be seen as a form of wealth transfer to the poorest citizens. At the same time, the mandate idea had its roots in a Republican-supported state initiative. Private enterprise would benefit, as insurance companies would recruit millions of new clients.

Yet the health care law proved bitterly divisive, not least because of the partisan way in which it was passed, without any Republican support. The measure also attracted legal opposition because of the questionable constitutionality of the mandate system. To the surprise of conservatives, the US Supreme Court upheld the measure in 2012, with Chief Justice John Roberts supporting its legitimacy. In the view of the court majority, the taxing power that the Constitution granted Congress permitted the law to enact and enforce the mandate and thus the requirement to buy insurance (*National Federation of Independent Business v. Sebelius*, 567 U.S. 519 (2012)). For several years thereafter, conservatives made the law the target of repeated repeal efforts, and sought wherever possible to limit the new system's scope and effectiveness.

In many ways, the health law fell short of expectations. The system depended on a web-based application system, which failed catastrophically in its early months. Over time, many insurance companies dropped out of the scheme, leaving few available options for prospective buyers of health policies. Also, such opportunities varied widely according to one's state of residence. Having said that, the law did indeed cause a substantial reduction in the number of Americans who lacked insurance coverage, from 16 percent of the population in 2010 to 9 percent in 2017. That was a decline of 20 million individuals who by definition were among the poorest and least privileged.

For the law's advocates, such a statistic fully justified the measure and all its difficulties – and, arguably, in itself validated the whole Obama presidency.

Hoping to secure his achievements, Obama also succeeded in placing two new Justices on the US Supreme Court. Respectively, these were Sonia Sotomayor, the court's first Latina, and Elena Kagan. Both women were strongly liberal in judicial philosophy.

THE ECONOMY STRUGGLES

While the administration faced discontent on many fronts, economic issues remained paramount. Initially, Obama and his advisors had hoped to set the economy right as a first stage in the quest for even more ambitious liberal reforms, but this was far too optimistic. Unemployment remained stubbornly high throughout both of Obama's presidential terms, and there was no sign of a return to the old high-wage middle-class economy. As we have seen, the crisis of foreclosures and underwater mortgages was still very much alive in 2010. Millions of voters expressed growing concern about increased state intervention and soaring deficits, which were running at over a trillion dollars each year between 2009 and 2011. Matters would have been far worse if not for the luxury of the country's new energy wealth.

Recent defeats provoked a restructuring of the Republican Party, and a revival of both populist and conservative views. The party's ideological right found a figurehead in Sarah Palin, who adopted a strongly populist message. Uniting all currents of opposition was the administration's free spending, and the calls being made for still more expansive programs to solve the continuing economic crisis. One suggested scheme involved offering government assistance to failing "underwater" mortgage holders. But as critics pointed out, that would divert taxpayer money to those who had taken excessive or imprudent loans, while offering nothing to the prudent and solvent. That mortgage issue proved uniquely inflammatory.

Opposition coalesced as the Tea Party movement, the name being taken from an acronym – TEA, or Taxed Enough Already? The name commemorated the Boston Tea Party of 1773, an earlier protest against over-extended government and unjust taxation. The group thus placed itself in an old-established American model of anti-state populism. The Tea Party became a national force, pushing for the election of candidates committed to a firmly conservative and populist agenda, rather than the despised moderates and compromisers, who were merely RINOs – Republicans in Name Only. Although inspired by fiscal concerns, the group was committed to moral conservative issues, notably opposition to abortion and (increasingly) to the rapidly expanding scope of gay rights. The Tea Party favored immigration reform, restricting new immigration, and demanding a firmer line against undocumented workers.

From 2009 through 2012, the Tea Party was the most vocal and aggressive face of anti-Obama opposition. The movement attracted intense journalistic attention, and liberals commonly presented the movement as being racist and near-fascist. These themes reached new heights in 2011 when a gunman in Tucson, Arizona, tried to assassinate Democratic Representative Gabrielle Giffords in an attack that killed several bystanders. The attacker was mentally disturbed and had no discernible political motivations, but media reported the crime as a manifestation of ultra-Right terrorism, which they linked to conservative groups. In fact, charges of fascist extremism were wildly exaggerated. Many of the Tea Party's concerns were widely held – about the deficit and the burden of taxation, but more generally about the unstoppable growth of the state. Like many counterparts on the Left, right-wing activists were appalled at the falling hopes and expectations of ordinary Americans, and alarmed at the threat of steep national decline.

Just how deep popular discontent ran was evident in the 2010 midterm elections, when Democrats lost the House of Representatives in one of America's worst electoral massacres since the 1930s. Republicans gained 63 House seats, and made huge gains at state levels, in an election that demonstrated profound disenchantment with the soaring hopes initially stirred by Obama's election. Tea Party support enabled the victory of dozens of conservative Republican candidates nationwide. So heavy was the defeat as to raise grave questions about the claims commonly made for Obama's election as the beginning of a new era, a revived New Deal.

PARTISANS

Multiple structural changes enhanced Republican electoral strength both in the short and long term. Although commentators often focus on presidential and congressional successes, organization at state politics is vital, not least because state governments shape electoral districts. Since the Reagan era, Republicans had developed their state parties, to which grass-roots organizations like the Tea Party were a valuable addition. In populous Texas, for instance, no Democrat had been elected to statewide office since 1994. Through the Obama years, Republicans won sweeping victories in governorships in many regions, and dominated state legislatures. Those Republican state authorities extensively reshaped electoral boundaries to their own advantage, in some cases to the extent of gerrymandering.

Democrats faced multiple structural disadvantages, notably the long-term decline of the labor unions that had so long been critical to funding that party and to mobilizing the vote. Also, Republican politicians have long expressed concern about the extent of voter fraud, and legal changes at state level have required prospective voters to offer proof of their identity and their right to cast a ballot. In practice such laws deter less-educated minority voters of all races, who are far more likely to vote Democrat. Republicans also benefited from the decision by the US Supreme Court in the case of *Citizens United* (*Citizens United v. FEC* 558 U.S. 310 (2010)), which considerably expanded the ability of organizations to contribute to election campaigns. In practice, the main beneficiaries were corporations, and this too favored Republicans.

This helped future victories, but also promoted the choice of more extreme and ideologically minded candidates. If Republicans in Texas (say) were guaranteed to win in the general election, then everything depended on the choice of candidate in the primaries. Those contests tended to attract harder-line partisans, and electoral turnout was low, favoring the choice of strongly rightist candidates. Democrats experienced a similar phenomenon in California, where elections regularly produced solid liberal loyalists. This encouraged partisan polarization nationwide.

OCCUPY

Successes on the political Right provoked a reaction on the Left. The conservative state politicians newly elected in 2010 tried to enact multiple reforms targeted at reducing the power of public sector workers. This included cutting benefits, and curbing workers' right to take industrial action. Most notably in Wisconsin, these measures stirred mass demonstrations and popular organization, and revived hopes of a new labor activism that could combat the Tea Party. Continued grievances about foreclosures further inspired public resentment against banks and corporate institutions.

In 2011, insurgent leftist populism found a new face with the Occupy movement, which began with a campaign to Occupy Wall Street. Protesters set up encampments in order to present their demands, which were a wide-ranging condemnation of large-scale corporate and financial institutions and the ways in which these supposedly subverted democracy. The movement's greatest achievement was in bringing the inequality issue onto the center stage of American political life and thus influencing electoral debate. According to the movement's slogans, the country was in the malevolent hands of the top 1 percent of the population, the super-rich, who were the great gainers of recent social and taxation policies, and it was incumbent on reformers to regain power for the 99 percent. The original Wall Street movement was widely imitated around the nation and the world, and it received staunch support and favorable publicity from media outlets. Some sections were much more radical than others, and in California some campaigns were overtly anarchist. Occupy remained a major phenomenon until it faded during 2012.

Far less publicized than Occupy, left-wing and strongly liberal groups won real successes in particular regions and especially cities, which strongly resisted the larger conservative trend. In 2013, New York City elected a passionately liberal mayor in Bill de Blasio, in a 72 percent landslide. But Democrats – and usually progressives – dominated most major urban areas. Not only did a Texas metropolis like Houston elect Democratic mayors, but the incumbent from 2010 to 2016 was the popular Annise Parker, a lesbian.

THE SECOND TERM

The national conservative resurgence buoyed Republican hopes for the coming presidential election, and a swift end to the Obama era. Continuing partisan conflict and Tea Party militancy sparked a governmental crisis in 2011, when the White House resisted Republican demands for cuts in the national deficit, bringing the US perilously close to defaulting on its international debts. Obama himself continued to infuriate conservatives, not least with a 2012 speech in which he reportedly said that "If you've got a business – you didn't build that!", and that the government role must be duly acknowledged. Although the words were taken out of context, they seemingly proved the president's loathing of private enterprise.

Several strongly conservative candidates emerged to challenge Obama in 2012, although the eventual nominee was the more moderate Mitt Romney. Even so, Romney had several drawbacks. He was not a charismatic figure, and his wealthy background made him the perfect symbol of the uncaring plutocrat: he seemed to incarnate the "1 percent" personally. In remarks intended for a private audience, he undiplomatically condemned Democratic votes as the 47 or 48 percent of people "who are dependent upon government, who believe that they are victims, who believe the government has a responsibility to care for them, who believe that they are entitled to health care, to food, to housing, to you-name-it." Moreover, his Mormon faith made him suspect to the evangelicals who were such a core component of the Republican electorate.

Obama defeated Romney by 4 percentage points in the popular vote, somewhat less than his 2008 victory, but still a convincing majority of 66 million votes to 61 million.

This result encouraged Republicans to rethink how they might cope with the multi-ethnic and multicultural nature of the emerging new America. Some hoped to cultivate more socially conservative and entrepreneurial elements in those newer communities, although that might mean adopting a softer line on immigration issues. However, traditional conservative messages were again prominent in 2014, when Republicans again triumphed in the midterm elections, winning the US Senate as well as the House. This election, like that of 2010, made a poor case for the virtues of political moderation in campaigning.

These electoral pressures made Obama's second term far more difficult and conflict-ridden than might have been expected from the optimistic days of 2009. Obama supporters pointed proudly to the lack of significant scandals during his whole tenure, and the president himself remained personally untouched by the customary range of political sins. His administration, though, was the focus of numerous charges and investigations, which might well have developed into serious scandals if the media had not been so overwhelmingly supportive of the administration. One early instance involved generous government subsidies and loan guarantees to green energy companies, some of which collapsed amidst charges of fraud and official deception. More serious was a sting operation titled Fast and Furious, by which US federal agencies had permitted weapons to flow across the Mexican border – "gunwalking" – in the hope of tracking and apprehending major drug dealers. Most of the weapons vanished from view and the scheme's net effect was to increase the arsenals of the drug cartels. Congressional committees pursued the investigation to the point of holding the US Attorney General, Eric Holder, in contempt of Congress. Federal agencies were also attacked for using their powers against political opponents – of weaponizing them against conservative critics. In 2013, the Internal Revenue Service was the main target of such charges, and of ever-widening investigations. Throughout the second term, as we will see, Congressional committees investigated the terror attack in Benghazi in 2012, and the alleged misconduct of then Secretary of State, Hillary Clinton.

CONGRESSIONAL DIVISIONS

Through much of his time in office, Obama faced robust Congressional opposition to virtually all of his policies, and to the appointments that he tried to make. That situation provoked a far-reaching crisis in the Senate. Through the twentieth century, Senate rules made negotiation and exchange essential on key issues, by demanding super-majorities for some key decisions. If a minority party vigorously opposed a nominee for the US Cabinet or the federal bench, then it could delay confirmation by means of a filibuster. Debate could be closed by a majority of 60 votes (the process of cloture), which was all but impossible to achieve without at least some crossover support from the minority. Moderates and swing votes were thus essential. For years, frustrated majority parties had from time to time contemplated reforming this system by applying a simple majority, of 51 votes rather than 60. Although this was superficially attractive, its consequences for Congressional life and interactions were so extreme that the reform was known as the nuclear option, a weapon so destructive that ideally it would never be used.

When Democrats controlled the Senate from 2007 through 2015, they become increasingly angry at what they saw as Republican obstructionism, and in 2013 Majority leader Harry Reid "went nuclear." He introduced the simple majority vote for most nominations, although retaining the 60 vote cut-off for Supreme Court appointments. This made it much harder to resist nominees, and more broadly it reduced the need for compromise and consensus-building. It severely weakened the minority party. But as we will see in Chapter 15, the problem with Reid's policy became apparent not long afterwards, when Republicans became the majority and were able to push through many appointments in the Trump years that would not otherwise have been possible. As with changes in elections, invoking the nuclear option enhanced partisan polarization, both in Congress and in the country at large.

Reid's error was to assume that the then-existing partisan balance in the legislature would remain constant in the future. As political friction grew, Republicans in their turn made exactly the same mistake, as they changed the grounds on which House committees investigated the administration. The House Oversight Committee used the powerful device of subpoenas to force administrations to reveal information, and before the 1990s these were usually issued with the joint consent of majority and minority parties. In 1997, Republicans began issuing unilateral subpoenas with the authority of the majority party alone, and the committee extensively used that power to investigate and harass the Clinton administration. In 2015, the Republican-controlled House extended that power to some 14 committees, all of which received the power to launch aggressive challenges to the Obama administration: the Benghazi investigation was the most damaging and enduring example. Like the nuclear option in the Senate, unilateral subpoenas gravely reduced the potential for bipartisan cooperation. The change also had unintended consequences when the Democrats won the House in 2018, and deployed the new power in their own partisan interest.

EXECUTIVE ACTION

Repeated failures and defeats in Congress frustrated Obama's reform efforts on most fronts, while forcing him to push forward change through ambitious executive actions that bypassed Congress altogether. While he was by no means the first president to pursue such means, he did so on a very large scale, and in the process he reinforced a marked trend in the shifting balance between the different branches of government. Between 2009 and 2016, the number of significant new regulations finalized by the Obama administration was more than 50 percent larger than the total created during the eight-year presidency of George W. Bush.

These decisions pushed the boundaries of constitutional government. Most ambitiously, in 2014 the administration used an executive order to shield several million illegal/undocumented immigrants from deportation, giving them the right to regularize their status in the US. This policy raised serious questions of constitutionality, and the Supreme Court overturned the immigration order, in one of several defeats that the administration suffered at the hands of the judicial branch. The administration also implemented controversial new policies through the acts of agencies that were part of the executive branch. We will explore such actions in later chapters, but repeatedly they promoted policies in matters of gender rights or the environment that would never have stood a chance of passage in Congress. After 2014, Obama did not have to face future electoral contests, and felt at greater liberty to promote his goals through executive orders, and that tendency became even stronger in his "lame duck" months after November 2016. Such orders raised troubling precedents for future administrations, which might similarly deploy executive privilege for whatever causes they believe to be critically important.

The magnitude of the difficulties Obama faced with Congress was suggested by his attempt to nominate a new member of the Supreme Court in 2016, to replace the powerful conservative Antonin Scalia. He selected respected judge Merrick Garland, who in less embittered times might have been considered a non-controversial consensus figure. However, the Senate took the unusual step of refusing to allow the nomination to proceed to a vote, denying the president a third Court appointment. That decision then offered a rare opportunity to the incoming president, who would prove to be Republican Donald Trump.

TOWARD PEACE?

In 2009, the Obama administration had hoped to concentrate its efforts on domestic reforms within the US, while withdrawing from what it saw as the excessive interventionism and militarism of the Bush years. Apart from Obama's personal inclinations, the base constituencies of the Democratic Party were strongly anti-war and anti-militarist. Realistically too, America had been weakened by the two wars, by the 2008 crash and the ensuing recession. The new president sought to lead a peaceful and magnanimous administration, creating high hopes worldwide. In 2009, he was awarded the Nobel Peace Prize, in a decision that was perhaps premature.

The upsurge in domestic energy supplies gave Obama a far freer hand in international affairs than his predecessors, as the US gained new leeway in relations with many regions, especially the Middle East. In the late twentieth century, the US and other Western countries relied massively on imported oil supplies, and thus faced constant concern that rising prices would cause economic dislocation and even full-scale depression. The oil cartel, OPEC, enjoyed immense power in global affairs. Some countries in particular flourished on the strength of their estimated supplies of crude oil, but also how easily accessible those supplies might be. Most prolific of all were Middle Eastern nations as Saudi Arabia, Iraq, and Kuwait, which promised to retain healthy supplies long after most other regions had exhausted their own. Conflicts in the Middle East always threatened to disrupt supplies or raise prices. Meanwhile, high oil prices gave added power to energy-rich nations like the Soviet Union and Iran that were deadly enemies of the United States. But the expansion of domestic oil and gas resources fundamentally transformed American economic expectations, giving the country exactly the kind of independence that it could only have dreamed of in the decade following the cataclysmic OPEC crisis of 1973–1974. Reduced dependence on foreign oil meant that the US could in theory afford to ignore the chaos in oil supply resulting from political convulsions in Iraq and elsewhere. For the first time in decades, non-intervention became a practical possibility.

One illustration of Obama's foreign policy priorities was his outreach to the stubbornly communist regime in Cuba, which had been a source of friction with the US since the early 1960s. Obama wished to end what he saw as outdated tensions and prejudices in order to overcome a pattern of endless confrontation. He began negotiations that most earlier administrations would have found unthinkable, and in 2014 relations were finally normalized. In 2016, the president himself visited the island.

Obama also pursued the globalization and free trade agenda that was so strongly identified with the Clinton era. While NAFTA remained a cornerstone of US policy, the administration pursued other ambitious international agreements, including a Transatlantic Trade and Investment Partnership (TTIP) between the United States and the European Union; and a Trans-Pacific Partnership trade deal (TPP) with the nations of the Pacific Rim. Both proved contentious, and not only with conservative opponents of globalization. Labor groups and many liberal Democrats were strongly opposed, in what should have been a warning sign of rising popular discontent with free trade assumptions. The administration signed the Trans-Pacific agreement in early 2016, but it was never ratified, and the incoming President Trump withdrew from the pact.

Obama wished to see US foreign policy focus on peaceful cooperation and the removal of unnecessary borders, with the defusing of old enmities. Yet throughout his time in office, long-standing conflicts and confrontations continued and often deteriorated, forcing the administration to pay far more attention to foreign affairs than it ever planned. Assessing the foreign policy of these years is a delicate matter. Many observers certainly felt that the Bush administration had been too willing to intervene overseas, so that it was blamed for an irresponsible "cowboy" approach. Others, though, and by no means only extreme conservatives, argued that Obama-era restraint created as many problems worldwide as had earlier the taste for interventionism. Commentators criticized Obama-era foreign policy for its reluctance to name and identify Islamist enemies, to acknowledge them as part of a common ideological cause, and to recognize the gravity of the threat they posed. Especially in his second term, Obama experienced embarrassing setbacks.

TERRORISM AND JIHAD

In 2009, the new administration attempted to end the charged rhetoric of a Global War on Terror, preferring the less charged language of Overseas Contingency Operations to be undertaken by US forces as need arose. But that verbal change could not conceal striking continuities from earlier administrations and their policies. The US Secretary of State during Obama's first term was Hillary Clinton, who was in turn succeeded by John Kerry, the former Democratic presidential candidate in 2004. As Senators, both had actually voted in favor of the Iraq war in 2002. As Secretaries of State, both drew heavily on the diplomatic and intelligence establishment, and neither favored a dangerously swift change in US policy.

The main legacies of the War on Terror were the twin wars in Iraq and Afghanistan, and the camp at Guantánamo Bay. Despite many hopes and promises, the incoming Democrats did not close the now-notorious Guantánamo prison. The new administration was just as willing as its predecessors to invoke national security privileges in order to avoid the exposure of sensitive intelligence information in trials.

Far from ending the grueling war in Afghanistan, the US escalated that involvement, and extended attacks into neighboring Pakistan, often against the will of that country's government. One such assault, in 2011, finally took the life of terrorist leader Osama bin Laden. The new administration also continued the drone campaign that had proved highly successful in targeting militant leaders. The US had first used military drones during the Balkan conflicts of the 1990s, and deployed them to fire missiles early in the Afghan war. Their great virtue was that precision attacks could take out specific leaders and armed groups, in a campaign that took a heavy toll on the morale of Islamist militants. Liberal and anti-war critics complained that attacks based on shaky intelligence often killed innocent bystanders, and the casualties from such collateral damage continued to mount.

Despite these concerns, the Obama administration actually extended the scale of the drone war to new battlefields in areas where Islamists and al-Qaeda fighters were most active, including in such failed states as Somalia and Yemen. In 2011, a US drone assassinated the strident al-Qaeda propagandist Anwar al-Awlaki in Yemen. But al-Awlaki was a US citizen, who according to critics was executed without formal charge or due process. Others argued that he was killed while acting as a combatant against the US. Although the rhetoric of the War on Terror was now officially rejected, the concept seemed to be fully operational.

WITHDRAWING FROM IRAQ

However determined the administration was in some respects, in many situations it appeared indecisive to the point of creating a dangerous power vacuum, notably in Iraq and Syria. Repeatedly, the Islamic world posed the most serious problems for Obama-era foreign policy.

The most urgent situation concerned Iraq, where Obama conspicuously did reverse the earlier policies that had so appalled liberals and had stirred support for Democrats. In 2010, US forces were formally withdrawn, although a good number remained in advisory roles. This decision fulfilled campaign promises, and it fitted well with the administration's distaste for war and intervention. The problem was that removing US troops also diminished the country's influence over Iraq's domestic affairs. The country's prime minister was Nouri al-Maliki, who represented Iraq's sizable Shia minority, and who was allied to the neighboring Shia power of Iran. Without US troops at hand, al-Maliki abandoned any pretense of running a non-sectarian government, and that bias appalled Iraq's Sunni minority. In protest against government repression and persecution, many Sunnis turned to the extreme militant movement that we have already encountered in a previous chapter, and which in 2013 took the name of ISIS, or the Islamic State in Iraq and al-Shams [the Levant].

ISIS won many successes. In 2014, the movement made vital territorial gains in northern Iraq, taking the long-contested centers of Ramadi and Fallujah, and then seized the regional capital of Mosul. They then took the historic step of proclaiming a new Caliphate. ISIS thus placed itself in the succession of Muslim political/religious regimes that dated back to the years immediately following the Prophet Muhammad in the seventh century, but which had been dismantled with the collapse of the Ottoman Empire in the 1920s. The Islamic State engaged in savage violence against all other religious and ethnic groups, massacring and expelling Christians and members of the Yazidi minority. It enslaved its enemies on a large scale, taking women captives for sexual purposes. The group terrorized potential enemies by public beheadings, stonings, tortures, and crucifixions. As chaos overwhelmed northern Iraq and eastern Syria in 2014, the Caliphate became a powerful ideological inspiration for terrorists worldwide. Tens of thousands traveled to the Islamic State for indoctrination and training.

Despite the medieval rhetoric of the Caliphate, and its barbarous acts, the movement deployed the most modern technology, including social media, and proved expert at manipulating public opinion worldwide. It murdered many Western hostages in gruesome videos circulated around the world. Those videos showed hostages clad in orange garb, in deliberate parody of the characteristic uniforms of Islamist prisoners in Guantánamo. Such atrocities naturally appalled Westerners, and many Muslims, but they had a powerful effect in radicalizing and recruiting young followers, and demonstrated that the Islamic State could act with impunity. The West, it seemed, could do nothing.

In the presidential campaign of 2016, Donald Trump described President Obama and Hillary Clinton as the co-founders of ISIS, a statement that was justly attacked as ridiculous hyperbole. But a case could legitimately be made that the explosive growth of that movement had been made possible by a too-rapid withdrawal from Iraq, and the subsequent US refusal to deploy its vast military resources to crush the dangerous presence of ISIS. Meanwhile, the US abstention from the Syrian war prevented that country achieving any kind of stability, so that Islamist factions could gain widespread power and influence. Meanwhile, Obama and administration officials underplayed and underestimated the rising threat. Although the president made the remark before the full horrors of ISIS became apparent, he was roundly criticized for declaring that the group was a "jayvee" or junior varsity (JV) team, trivializing the movement by comparing it to a minor high school sports operation.

Lacking major US involvement, the process of containing and then destroying the Islamic State was protracted. US personnel participated at many levels, supplying air support and intelligence as well as Special Forces activity. Most of the direct combat, though, was pursued by US allies and proxies, especially the Iraqis, but also by the Kurdish people who hoped to obtain an independent state in the region. On occasion, the US engaged in delicate and largely clandestine coordination with its Iranian rivals, who shared a common interest in uprooting the Islamic State. Not until the end of 2017 was the Islamic State driven from its two main centers of Mosul and Raqqa (Syria).

THE AGE OF INDECISION

The ongoing disaster in Iraq merged seamlessly into a larger regional crisis, which provoked the collapse of state systems across much of the Middle East. In 2011, a so-called Arab Spring movement provoked popular risings against long-entrenched governments and dictatorships across the Middle East. Western observers hoped that the outcome would be an upsurge of democracy, but in practice Islamists benefited mightily. One early theater of conflict was in Libya, which since the 1970s had been ruled by Muammar Qaddafi, a deadly enemy of the US. In 2011, US and allied forces intervened to support rebel movements, and Qaddafi was overthrown and killed, like Saddam before him. But Western forces failed to carry through on military intervention after the initial assault, and Libya descended into anarchy. The country suffered a de facto partition, becoming a failed state, as Islamist forces and affiliates of the Islamic State gained influence. As had become apparent in Afghanistan and Iraq, Americans were adept at destroying governments and destabilizing countries, but not at bringing any kind of improved order. Critics wryly complained that US foreign policy seemed to be based on Mark Zuckerberg's dictum, "Move fast and break things."

Libya illustrated the administration's persistent qualms about accurately identifying the Islamist forces challenging the US. In 2012, a group of al-Qaeda guerrillas attacked the US embassy in Benghazi, killing the ambassador and several other Americans. At first, the administration falsely suggested that the attack might have grown out of spontaneous anti-American protest, minimizing charges of organized Islamist plotting. Meanwhile, it was faulted for failing to intervene promptly to defend its personnel on the ground. For this and other reasons, the Benghazi attack provoked acrimony in the United States, chiefly directed at the honesty and competence of Secretary of State Clinton. That in turn spawned venomous Congressional hearings, which lasted for several years.

Syria likewise proved deeply divisive for the administration. In the tumultuous year of 2011, an insurrection broke out against the dictatorial regime headed by the Assad family, and its current president Bashar al-Assad. Initially, the rebellion included a great many elements, including proponents of liberal democracy, but increasingly Islamist forces took the lead. Sunni Muslim forces were heavily engaged in a struggle against the Assad regime, which found its support among non-Sunni Muslims, and indeed non-Muslim groups. Many of the anti-Assad opposition groups were militant Islamists and jihadis, and some were affiliated to al-Qaeda. All sides committed horrible atrocities. Syria descended into chaos, with its territory ruled by multiple competing armies and militias. The bloody civil war claimed hundreds of thousands of lives, and forced millions of Syrians to become refugees, many fleeing to Europe.

US policy toward this spiraling crisis was chaotic and inept. The US tried to sponsor and train armed factions that it found most sympathetic ideologically, but this effort proved disastrous. The expenditure of vast sums of US money failed to produce any but the tiniest armed rebel group. While not wishing to engage directly to defeat the Assad regime, the US tried to prevent the Syrian government using its most effective weapons, of air power and chemical armaments. Matters reached a head in September 2013 when the administration warned that further use of chemical weapons would provoke US retaliation and a bombing campaign. When Syrian forces actually did use those weapons, the path to US intervention seemed clear, and in September President Obama announced his intention to give a speech that was widely expected to rally public support for his action. The prospect of intervention horrified critics, who feared new military actions in the Middle East coming so soon after the Iraq debacle.

That September speech was a critical turning point in the history of the administration. To widespread bemusement, Obama withdrew the imminent threat of military action, although saying generally that the West might act in the future. Instead, he supported a Russian scheme to take control of the weapons of mass destruction, in what looked like a face-saving climbdown.

In effect, Obama was declaring that the US would abstain from further interventions in the region. That sent a troubling message to various powers who now saw little cause to fear the US, and the consequences would soon be apparent – in Syria and Iraq, but also in the Ukraine and the Korean peninsula.

The situation in Syria remained desperate, as multiple external forces intervened, chiefly to support the regime. The Russians deployed substantial military power, as did the Iranians and their Lebanese proxies the Hizbullah, or Party of God. US acquiescence in Russian involvement was surprising in light of the decades-long US efforts to exclude Soviet forces from the region during the Cold War. After 2013, however, the Russians were deeply involved in air and ground missions, using both regular troops and contract forces or mercenaries. Russian forces engaged in combat with US-supported militias and guerrilla groups, and even sometimes with US personnel. In 2016, Russian air power proved decisive in helping the regime capture the rebel bastion of Aleppo. In this battle and many others, both the Russians and the Syrian government were widely denounced for their violence against civilians, but the absence of US forces made it difficult for Western countries to do anything other than (frequently) issue formal protests. Incredible as this would have seemed at the start of the crisis, the Assad family remains in power at the time of writing.

TERRORISM AT HOME

Inspired by the successes of the Islamic State, jihadi terrorism became commonplace in many Western countries. This ended any hopes that US actions against al-Qaeda might have destroyed the phenomenon. Particularly frightening was the new tactic of leaderless resistance, in which ordinary believers carried out violent acts without any direction from a military command, and thus making their actions all but impossible to predict. Such attacks became endemic across Western Europe, where Islamic State claimed responsibility for numerous attacks and massacres.

The US too suffered several such blows, including the murder of 13 soldiers at Fort Hood, in Texas (2009), and the slaughter of 15 civilians by a married couple in San Bernardino, CA (2015). Many lesser lone-wolf attacks claimed lives around the nation, commonly killing two or three victims in each incident. The 2013 bombing of the Boston Marathon was followed by an intense police pursuit of the two perpetrators, with terrifying firefights in and around the city. For some hours, the entire city was under a state of lockdown, with residents ordered to remain in their homes.

In 2016, an attacker killed 49 in a gay nightclub in Orlando, FL, the largest terror incident on US soil since 9/11. As evidence about the shooter's motivations came to light, it became clear that he had been inspired by Islamist extremism, and by sympathy for ISIS: this was indeed terrorism in its classic sense. Initially, however, that orientation was not so obvious, allowing a great deal of speculation and partisan rhetoric. The response to that catastrophe thus encapsulated the ideological divisions within a thoroughly polarized US. Conservatives interpreted the act as a straightforward manifestation of Islamist terrorism, and contextualized it with other Islamist violence around the globe, suggesting a global clash of faiths and cultures. Orlando was thus part of the same story as Fort Hood, San Bernardino, Boston, and the rest, a common Islamist movement affiliated to groups like al-Qaeda or the Islamic State. Commonly, the perpetrators openly espoused those movements, or had closely followed their activities and propaganda. The enemy was thus easily identifiable, and should be publicly acknowledged as such. Some on the extreme right went still further, and saw the enemy not as jihadi extremism, but as Islam itself.

The administration, and much of the news media, strove desperately to avoid any such reading either of the Orlando attack or of other comparable incidents. Instead, they compared the actions to other non-ideological mass murders, and strove to minimize claims of international connections. Their motives for minimizing the political dimensions were complex. Most important, Obama had no wish to return to the Bush-era image of the US locked in a death struggle against a worldwide terrorist conspiracy, a full-scale clash of civilizations. Nor did the administration wish to face pressure to act more overtly and aggressively against the Islamic State in its home territories. Domestically, it was vital to avoid stirring hostility or bigotry against Muslims, and against immigrants more generally. It was thus in the administration's interests to avoid linking domestic attacks to international struggles. In the case of Orlando, politicians and media downplayed the Islamist motivations, and suggested instead that the crime demonstrated the evils of anti-gay religious bigotry, and also proved the need for new forms of gun control. An avowed Islamist attack thus spurred a public outcry against Christian conservatives.

In foreign policy matters, the Obama administration naturally devoted much of its attention to the Middle East and the Islamic world and to terrorism threats, and in this it followed all its predecessors since the time of Jimmy Carter. But Obama shared his predecessors' concern with other issues that were arguably even more critical to national interests. Another attack like 9/11 would cause massive casualties and profoundly damage national interests. But other rivals possessed weaponry that could potentially destroy much of the US homeland, and even devastate the planet. Besides nuclear weapons, that menace included biological arms, and cyber weapons now had the potential to wreck an adversary's society and economy. In these international encounters too, the Obama administration enjoyed mixed success. This was partly a consequence of the divided government in Washington and the country's partisan schisms, but Obama often showed a lack of decisiveness that encouraged foreign rivals. The consequences are still open to intense (and highly partisan) debate.

9 America in the World

Stuxnet was an alarming and highly destructive new computer worm identified by IT experts in 2010. Although the worm caused widespread damage, it particularly aimed at devices that automated electromechanical processes. The principal target was the centrifuges that were at the heart of Iran's uranium enrichment program, through which the country sought to develop nuclear weapons. Unlike most such worms or viruses, this particular example came not from malicious civilian hackers but from a government or intelligence agency, and the chief suspects were the United States and Israel, presumably working in cooperation. As an example of cyber-warfare, Stuxnet represented a whole new clandestine front in international struggles. It also demonstrated the extreme concern that the worm's inventors had in preventing the further spread of advanced weapons of mass destruction.

Through Obama's presidency the US had to confront nuclear nightmares, focused especially on the military and geopolitical ambitions of Iran and North Korea. But these years also witnessed the revival of concerns and rivalries that seemed to have vanished, or gone underground, since the 1980s. The administration had to navigate relations with two other states that could claim superpower status, namely Russia and China. The United States faced not just a new era of Great Power politics but a disturbing revival of Cold War tensions and fears, even a new world disorder. During the Obama years, both Russia and China made significant gains in power and status, at the expense of US primacy.

NUCLEAR FEARS

US tensions with aspiring nuclear states had deep historical roots. Through the late twentieth century, many nations had flirted with the possibility of gaining nuclear arms, and at least eight had succeeded (South Africa voluntarily renounced its weapon after the fall of the white minority regime in 1994). Several of the aspiring nations were avowed enemies of the United States and of Israel, and were closely associated with promoting international terrorism. They were also notorious violators of human rights. Some were associated with apocalyptic ideologies that made it highly likely that they would actually use their nuclear arms rather than merely holding them in reserve as a last desperate measure of self-defense. This group included North Korea, Iran, Iraq, Libya, and Syria, and the prospect of any of these countries gaining nuclear arms was troubling. The threat became acute following 9/11, with the prospect of a "bandit country" supplying such weaponry to a terrorist ally or proxy, for use against Washington DC or New York. Particularly worrying was the vision of a dirty bomb, which would release large amounts of radioactivity. It was the nightmare prospect of Iraq sharing its alleged weapons of mass destruction that persuaded so many moderate Americans to support the 2003 invasion of that country.

If such a country threatened to go nuclear, then the US and its allies had three options. The first was direct military intervention, but the US experience with Iraq showed how unreliable intelligence reports could be in assessing weapons capabilities. That made it all but impossible to be sure that military action would totally destroy all targets. Moreover, any attack threatened to detonate a major conventional war, and even without going nuclear a middle-ranking power like Iran or North Korea could pose a dreadful threat to its neighbors, or potentially to the US itself. Over time, aspiring nuclear nations built their installations deeper and deeper underground, making them probably immune from air attack. Military approaches also ran other dangers. Even discussing such an attack encourages the potential target country to seek the means to defend itself and deter attack, and strengthens the arguments of hardliners in that regime who urge against compromise or diplomatic discussions. Finally, a pre-emptive attack on any nation runs the risk of violating international law and uniting the international community against any aggressor.

The second option was diplomatic, to pressure or persuade a nation to renounce its weapons. New opportunities arose following the 9/11 events, when the US made common cause with a number of "bandits" who likewise loathed al-Qaeda. New diplomatic openings persuaded Libya to renounce its nuclear program in 2003. Even Iran announced its willingness to consider a wide-ranging rapprochement, a kind of Grand Bargain with the US. But diplomacy, too, faced many difficulties, as few countries were prepared to tolerate the kind of intrusive monitoring that was demanded to ensure that they were keeping to agreements. It was often difficult to tell when a nation was engaged in a legitimate pursuit of peaceful nuclear power, and when that was merely a cover for building weapons.

If preventive measures failed, then the last option was containment, or learning to live with new nuclear powers. Such an approach could succeed, even with nations that appeared subject to few constraints such as China in the late 1960s. But it remained open to question how much latitude could be extended to nations like North Korea or Iran.

IRAN

Iran illustrates the US dilemma. Ever since that nation's Islamic revolution of 1979, Iran has been a persistent enemy of the United States, and had sponsored acts of terrorism and violence around the world, usually through proxy forces such as the Lebanese Hizbullah. The Iranian leadership was motivated by revolutionary Islamist ideology with a strong apocalyptic and messianic bent. For Western observers, this made it likely that Iran might not only develop so-called doomsday weapons, but would actually use them against its enemies. The country's leaders made extremely hostile and confrontational remarks about the state of Israel, challenging its right to exist. In 2005, the country's president Ahmedinejad denied the historical reality of the Holocaust, crossing a rhetorical red line that alarmed Western governments. Since the 1980s, also, Iran had been pursuing nuclear weaponry. Iran freely admitted using nuclear reactors for peaceful purposes, but by the end of the century the country was pursuing a nuclear enrichment program that would give it the capacity to produce bombs. Both the US and Israel repeatedly declared their refusal to contemplate Iran gaining nuclear status, and intervened by means of irregular actions, sabotage, and cyber-warfare.

US hostility to Iran gained new vigor after the seemingly easy conquest of Iraq in 2003. If Iraq could be overthrown so swiftly, then what about the other members of the so-called Axis? In the mood of elation following the fall of Baghdad, US neo-conservatives speculated whether, as its next step, the Third Army should turn left or right: that is, should the newly victorious American units conquer Syria next, or Iran? In retrospect, such wild overconfidence seems dangerously naïve. A bloody stalemate tied up US forces in Iraq for several years, in a conflict that greatly strengthened the Iranian position as a regional power. Iran supplied the unconventional weapons, and the tactical skills, that killed so many Americans during the Iraqi guerrilla war. Iran, meanwhile, spread its influence over much of Iraq, Syria, and Lebanon, and also had its proxies and allies in Afghanistan and Yemen. From some perspectives, the US intervention in Afghanistan and Iraq might ironically be portrayed as the war to found an Iranian regional empire.

Despite its hostility to armed actions, the Obama administration made clear that Iran's nuclear enrichment program must cease, and Stuxnet represented a forceful intervention. Several years of negotiations followed between Iran and the so-called P5+1 group that included the US, Russia, China, and the leading nations of Europe. In 2015, the two sides agreed on a Joint Comprehensive Plan of Action, under which Iran would eliminate its stockpile of enriched uranium and massively reduce its facilities to produce more.

An inspection regime was agreed, and in exchange long-running international sanctions would be lifted.

Although that agreement was not technically a treaty requiring approval by the US Senate, it did face numerous challenges. Through the summer of 2015, the Iran deal was vigorously debated in the US media and political world, creating one of the liveliest and most contentious foreign policy battles since the controversy over the invasion of Iraq in 2003. Supporters presented the Plan as the only means of averting war, while critics warned of the risk that, based on past experience, Iran would inevitably violate any restraints imposed on it. Advocates of Israel warned that Obama had naïvely fallen into a trap. Although the deal might limit Iran in the short term, the deal left the country too much leeway to rebuild its arms program as and when it chose. Significantly, in terms of emerging diplomatic alignments, Saudi Arabia wholly shared Israeli concerns about Iranian power. Even so, the Iran deal survived and the sanctions were lifted.

Yet what seemed like a major achievement was blighted by subsequent charges of Iranian misbehavior and treaty violations. Assessing such claims is difficult as they were usually based on intelligence information, and different parties and interests made wildly conflicting allegations. From one perspective, the Obama administration was determined to ignore even blatant evidence that contradicted its policies. Alternatively, hawks and extreme Right Israeli interests were seeking to destabilize a crucially significant agreement. The debate persisted into the Trump administration.

NORTH KOREA

Another recurrent site of nuclear crisis was on the Korean peninsula. The degree of danger this area posed to international security is remarkable given the size of the adversary. North Korea is an extremely poor country with a population of just 25 million, living under a brutal and often delusional communist dictatorship. But its nuclear ambitions demand special attention because of the extraordinary conduct of the regime through the years. Untouched by successive waves of global détente, the regime has repeatedly tried to foment wars through acts of terrorism, sabotage, and assassination. It has been deeply involved in organized criminality and drug trafficking, and has abducted foreign citizens. The regime has frequently declared its goals of reuniting the whole peninsula, which would mean conquering the flourishing democratic state of South Korea, a close US ally. Such rash and aggressive conduct suggests strongly that if the North Korean regime had nuclear weaponry and missile technology, it might well attack its neighbors, or the United States itself.

North Korean aspirations to obtain a nuclear weapon date back at least to the 1980s. So serious was the perceived threat that in 1994 the Clinton administration seriously debated launching a pre-emptive attack. This option was rejected in favor of a negotiated agreement under which the North Koreans agreed to freeze their military nuclear efforts in exchange for oil supplies, economic cooperation, and assistance in building new reactors that lacked military capacity. Notionally, this would be a prelude to North Korean nuclear disarmament. Although North Korean research and development efforts continued, Clinton-era officials continue to believe that the agreement was justified in terms of buying time.

Tensions grew again in the new century when President Bush included North Korea in the Axis of Evil. Meanwhile, the country was pressing ahead with both its nuclear program and missile technology, although on a clandestine basis. A nuclear test in 2006 was only a limited success, and the same was true of an attempted missile launch in 2009. It was, though, in 2009 – at the time that the Obama administration was replacing George W. Bush – that North Korea made its most determined and brazen efforts to gain advanced weaponry. Previous international agreements were repudiated as the remaining inspectors were expelled. More nuclear tests followed, and the new weapons achieved serious yields. In 2015, the country claimed the ability to hit US targets with nuclear-armed missiles, and possibly even with fusion weapons or hydrogen bombs. Although these claims initially met skepticism, the country was far better armed in 2017 than it had been a decade earlier.

At home and abroad, North Korean propaganda has for decades spoken of war as an always imminent reality, and so far this has been empty rhetoric, presumably intended to unify the regime's own population. Even so, the country might someday launch a real attack that in theory could destroy one or more great US cities, presumably on the West Coast. In response, some alarmed experts proposed reviving urban civil defense plans that had been moribund since the worst years of the Cold War.

Obama faced a near-impossible situation. In conventional terms alone, North Korea remains one of the world's best-armed nations, so that any preemptive attack would spark a war that would engulf South Korea and possibly Japan. Millions assuredly would die. Nor was there serious evidence that North Korea would observe any likely diplomatic agreement, any more than it had in the past. It should also be said that, because of the nature of covert warfare, we do not know exactly what, if anything, US agencies might have done to sabotage or slow North Korean military research, likely by electronic warfare actions on the lines of Stuxnet. Such interventions might have been far more effective than we will ever know, and might even have been responsible for repeated failures in the country's nuclear tests. But with all those caveats, the fact remains that at the end of the Obama presidency North Korea was a much more dangerous and better-armed foe than it had been when he took office. That has to be counted as a serious failure.

Apart from an overt nuclear attack, North Korea has been highly active in electronic attacks, the cyber-warfare that potentially could pose such a damaging threat to an adversary. Such an attack might, for instance, take out the critical systems on which a modern nation depends for survival, including power supplies. Increasingly popular as a weapon in the arsenal of advanced states, this kind of clandestine warfare has the added advantage that it is difficult to assign blame with certainty, making retaliation difficult. Cyber-warfare is eminently deniable. Also, its legal status is hazy, so that it is never quite clear when a given attack might cross the line to become an overt act of war.

Among the attacks commonly blamed on North Korea was a 2014 assault on Sony Pictures, after the studio threatened to show a film about an imaginary assassination of that country's leader. To the firm's embarrassment, large quantities of internal documents were leaked. In 2017, North Korea was probably responsible for the WannaCry ransomware attack, which overwhelmed corporate and government computers in many countries (although, in fairness, it should be said that the tools that permitted the creation of such cyberweapons were probably of US design before they were purloined). In turn, the US has certainly struck at North Korea. It remains open to question whether other incidents involving the failure or collapse of electronic systems in the US might in fact have been attributable to rival nations which were testing their resources in preparation for a larger assault in future. Besides North Korea, those potential adversary nations would include both Russia and China.

RUSSIA

However much the US feared the prospect of a rogue state coming into possession of a few nuclear warheads, the prospect of conflict with either Russia and China would be infinitely more perilous. The danger of armed conflict with either or both seemed negligible in the Clinton years, but during the 2010s the prospect became very real. Particularly from 2013 onward, the growth of international threats forced the US administration to give high priority to foreign affairs, and to military challenges, to a far greater degree than President Obama ever wished.

After the collapse of the old Soviet Union, the successor state of Russia struggled to find a political and cultural identity. Initially, many hoped that the country would evolve into an advanced democracy aligned with the West, and in 1997 Russia joined the G7 club of leading economies. Soon, though, conservative and nationalist Russians sought to reverse the collapse of the old USSR, and to reclaim the lost territories of what in effect had been a Russian empire. From 1999, the country was led by Vladimir Putin, whose regime became increasingly dictatorial and militaristic, and was allied to a network of corrupt and extremely wealthy oligarchs. Putin was frank in his ambitions to regain a Russian hold over the former territories of the USSR. In 2008, Russia fought a war with the former Soviet republic of Georgia. Beyond the old USSR, Russian ambitions extended into Eastern Europe and the Baltic region.

Despite these troubling signs, Obama remained skeptical, even mocking. In a 2012 candidates' debate with Mitt Romney, Obama derided his rival for describing Russia rather than al-Qaeda as the great geopolitical threat to the US. He continued, tellingly, "And the 1980s are now calling to ask for their foreign policy back – because the Cold War has been over for 20 years." Although Obama's scornful put-down earned media praise, in retrospect it is difficult to contest Romney's analysis. Obama was slow to confront new global realities. His relaxed attitude to potential Russian expansion underlies his otherwise baffling acceptance of that country's powerful new position in Syria.

Putin's expansionism reached new heights in 2014 when Russian forces occupied portions of Ukraine, a former Soviet republic that had become a sovereign state. Russia then formally annexed the Crimean peninsula, with its critical naval facilities. In order to deter a concerted reaction by other states, the Russian venture used innovative tactics of deception. Instead of deploying the Russian army and navy, activism notionally stemmed from ethnic Russian groups within Ukraine. They formed parties, movements, and militias, and these were supported by mysterious and well-armed paramilitary units. In reality, the whole operation was obviously directed and organized by Russia, and the shadowy combatants were Russian military forces. But that thin subterfuge gave Russia enough deniability that the West could not accuse them directly of invasion, and thus threaten military retaliation. Russian actions on the ground were powerfully supported in cyberspace, by ruinous electronic attacks on Ukraine, and by the overwhelming deployment of internet propaganda and fake news. The combination of cyber-warfare, conventional military actions, and paramilitary dirty tricks constitutes what has come to be called hybrid warfare.

The US and Europe responded to the Ukraine conflict with sanctions, while the country was suspended from the G8 (it formally withdrew in 2017). But in practice, these restrained measures in the face of aggression sent a powerful message to the Russian government. Europeans feared other Russian assaults in future, particularly in the Baltic states. Like Ukraine, these nations had once been part of the Soviet Union, and they too contained restive Russian minorities who might appeal to Moscow for help.

The US had one powerful weapon in its dealings with Russia, but deploying it involved serious economic dilemmas. Briefly, should the US cooperate with its Saudi allies to promote low oil prices worldwide? If prices were kept unnaturally low, this would be ruinous for oil-dependent nations like Russia and Iran, which would be forced to come to the bargaining table on US terms, and such a policy had undermined the old Soviet Union in the 1980s. But low prices also threatened to make the extraction of US shale oil resources uneconomical, thus threatening the country's own energy boom. The Obama administration tended to a low price strategy, despite the domestic harm that (briefly) resulted.

US/Russian tensions grew acutely in the latter stages of the Obama administration, particularly in consequence of the mounting crisis in Syria. Observers feared that air forces of the two nations might accidentally become involved in combat, provoking a global crisis and a large-scale military confrontation. Similar fears surrounded the growing military tensions in the Baltic. NATO and the Western powers showed their political resolve by organizing military exercises and war games, which met similar activity from the Russians, and the prospect of accidental encounters became troubling. The Russians spoke publicly of their intention to use nuclear weapons against European nations if war erupted.

Renewed global tensions had a direct impact on US domestic politics. Fearing further US attempts to undermine their power, particularly in Ukraine, the Russians organized a major internet campaign to destabilize and discredit their enemies. Although these efforts affected Europe, the main target was the US, where online armies of "trolls" or propagandists sowed dissent, confusion, and outright paranoia. In 2015, US military forces organized major domestic exercises under the title Jade Helm. Russian propagandists encouraged the belief that this exercise was a prelude to a military coup in the US, or perhaps the confiscation of private firearms. This campaign was so successful in provoking right-wing opinion and activism that Texas activated its State Guard to monitor the exercise.

By their nature, such clandestine actions are difficult to interpret precisely, but in light of what we have subsequently learned about Russian goals and tactics we must reconsider the origins of some earlier episodes. In 2013, Edward Snowden created a global scandal when he exposed large quantities of intelligence data in a case that exposed the surveillance capabilities of

Western intelligence agencies (see Chapter 4). At the time Snowden was widely regarded as a libertarian hero, even a patriot, but the affair was a phenomenal boon to Russian propaganda and Snowden took refuge in Moscow, where he still lives. The intelligence context of the whole affair remains controversial.

Russian efforts reached a height in the US presidential election of 2016, when propaganda sought to discredit the US electoral system and to undermine Hillary Clinton. As we will see, allegations of direct ties between the Trump campaign and the Russians have proved toxic in US politics since 2016. If the Russians were trying to sow dissension in the American political world, they have succeeded amply.

CHINA

Potentially, the greatest military rival of the United States is China. Future historians will likely regard the economic rise of China as the most significant theme of the twenty-first century, and that economic might will inevitably be reflected in growing political and military power. As China grew economically, its leaders became increasingly assertive in international affairs. This activism involved pressing expansive Chinese claims to what the government saw as its proper historical boundaries, which included rule over Tibet and Taiwan, and the country sternly rejected any challenges to its sovereignty. China condemned any assertions of independence by Taiwan, which became very isolated in global affairs. Since 2000, China has projected its economic and diplomatic power far afield with ambitious schemes for trade and investment in Africa and across Central Asia. If only in commercial terms, this is the beginning of a new informal empire.

None of those policies necessarily involved military aggression, and China has generally kept a low military profile. Over time, though, any rising economic power will acquire the means to defend and project its interests. Western countries have actually welcomed Chinese involvement in international affairs as the country fulfills its proper and legitimate role in maintaining the global order. During the Global War on Terror the US found common cause with China, which faces its own peril of Islamist extremism and separatism in its outlying regions. Chinese warships joined international navies in suppressing piracy off the coasts of East Africa, and the country has developed naval bases in East Africa and the Indian Ocean.

In some situations, the new Chinese self-confidence raised dangers of international conflict. The Taiwan issue is so perilous because the Chinese regard the question as a matter of internal affairs, of regaining a rebellious province, so that outside powers would have no right to intervene. China has repeatedly stated that it would view any official declaration of Taiwanese independence as an act of war, and Chinese armed forces have conspicuously displayed their armed power to deter any such action. Such demonstrations take the form of military exercises, in which the Chinese fire missiles in disputed areas. Repeatedly, the US has demonstrated its own willingness to use force to defend Taiwan, and in 1996, President Clinton sent two aircraft carrier battle groups to the region in a crushing display of naval power. At this time – unlike today – the US enjoyed such an overwhelming advantage in military power that China could easily be deterred.

In the present century, the Chinese government has become much more assertive in its claims. The main thrust of expansion is into the South China Sea, a region of vast economic significance, through which passes a large proportion of global trade. As in the Taiwan case, China justifies its policies not in terms of overseas expansion but as a reassertion of its natural boundaries, which had been weakened during the long years of Western meddling and domestic chaos. Despite strong international opposition, and contrary to several legal rulings, China claims virtually the whole sea as its territorial waters, using a map dating back to pre-communist times that asserted Chinese control within a so-called Nine Dash Line. Apart from stirring conflict with the United States, Chinese policies are also a grievance for other regional powers, including Vietnam, the Philippines, Malaysia, Indonesia, and Taiwan. Those ambitions were expressed more aggressively following the ascendancy of Chinese leader Xi Jinping, who became General Secretary of the Communist Party in 2012, and president in 2013. As in the case of Russia's Putin, Xi subsequently centralized authority in his own person, with a growing cult of personality. And as in Russia's case, this development disappointed US hopes that China might evolve to resemble the advanced and democratic Western powers.

Beyond merely claiming the sea, in Xi's time China has confirmed its power by building and occupying numerous artificial islands, fortifying some, and building airstrips and bunkers. If these islands are in fact Chinese territory, then that nation would claim control of a 12-mile boundary around each one, so that the US and other nations in the region would face a fait accompli. Quite separately, China has declared separate claims in the East China Sea, which threatens bitter rivalry with Japan and South Korea. Many observers fear that these various nautical claims could inspire future regional wars, or even a global conflagration. Supporting these Chinese efforts has been a dramatic rise in popular patriotism and militarism, stimulated by official propaganda. In Chinese social media, potential confrontations with the United States arouse fiery expressions of patriotic enthusiasm.

PIVOT TO ASIA

All US presidents since Bill Clinton have sought to respond appropriately to the rise of China. Since the 1980s, US observers had spoken of the twenty-first century as an era dominated by Pacific concerns, usually with a focus on Japan as the key engine of growth. China's success powerfully reinforced that approach, and in 2011 Hillary Clinton wrote perceptively of "America's Pacific Century." She also described a major theme in US policy as a Pivot to Asia, and this idea became a centerpiece of the administration's foreign and economic policy.

But the US has also reacted to China's military expansion. The Bush administration increased the number of submarines in the Pacific and developed port facilities in allied nations like Singapore. Under Obama, the switch to Asian concerns involved a "strategic pivot," under which 60 percent of US warships would by 2020 operate in the Pacific. The US also built up its system of alliances with regional powers equally concerned about Chinese might. Apart from such long-standing allies as Japan and Australia, the US also cultivated its former enemy, Vietnam. For the Chinese, this strategic pivot looked uncomfortably like a policy to contain their nation and to constrain its legitimate interests.

In Obama's second term, tensions over the South China Sea became acute as the US sought to balance diplomatic and military policies. Under international law, most of the regions in the South China Sea claimed by China are in fact international waters through which foreign ships and aircraft can pass freely. The Chinese, in their turn, regard such transits as violations of their territory. They make forceful diplomatic protests, and in some instances Chinese warships directly confront intruders. On several occasions, the US Navy has sailed warships through disputed waters as deliberate efforts to establish the principle of free navigation: these were thus Freedom of Navigation Operations (FONOPs). From the administration's perspective, such operations adequately made their point and reaffirmed international law. Critics, however, condemned them as over-cautious and falling lamentably short of the decisive force needed, and they denounced Obama for appeasement.

The prospect of confrontations with the Chinese gave a new significance to US naval power. At the height of the Reagan-era Cold War, the US had approached a 600-ship navy, a formidable number that had shrunk progressively after the supposed End of History in the 1990s. By the time Obama was elected the navy had just 275 ships, even though that reduced navy faced a range of demanding challenges – against the Russians, Iranians, and, increasingly, the Chinese. At the core of the US fleet were weapon systems with few rivals on the planet, most spectacularly the 10 massive Nimitz-class aircraft carriers with their attendant battle groups. But the Chinese were contemplating a future in which they might challenge and defeat even those behemoths. Beyond being a long-standing nuclear power, China has extremely sophisticated skills in technology and manufacturing. It has developed advanced anti-ship missiles, and the People's Liberation Army Navy (the PLAN) now has aircraft carriers. The country has developed excellent abilities in what is technically known as Anti-Access/Area Denial, A2AD – in other words, making an area like the South China Sea too dangerous for US and allied forces to operate in. In 2018, the US Navy announced a building program under which the fleet would grow to 355 ships by mid-century.

To date, no recent conflict or disagreement between China and the US has come close to provoking direct hostilities. Yet over the past decade, many observers in different nations have noted comparisons between the US/China relationship and Great Power encounters of earlier years that did in fact end in open warfare, despite the fact that neither side actually wanted war. Some pointed to the British–German rivalry before 1914, which pitted a declining imperial and industrial global power against a brash and ambitious rising state. The two came to blows in the apocalyptic First World War. Other thinkers looked to the ancient struggle between Athens and Sparta that culminated in the 30-year carnage of the Peloponnesian War. The contemporary historian of that conflict was Thucydides, who famously observed that "It was the rise of Athens, and the fear that this instilled in Sparta, that made war inevitable." In a phrase coined by political scientist Graham Allison, the two ancient powers fell into what became known as the Thucydides Trap, a phenomenon that poses worrying lessons for modern-day Sino-US relations.

War, obviously, would be a cataclysm, but other threats posed grave risks to the planet as a whole, and these too demanded extensive international cooperation – perhaps even a whole new vision of national sovereignty. It was particularly during Obama's years in office that the US devoted such a sharp focus to environmental dangers and the issue of global warming. Environmental concerns and fears achieved a striking new centrality in political debate and controversy.

10 Defending the Earth

In 2016, law enforcement agencies confronted protests on the Standing Rock Sioux reservation in North Dakota. At issue was the building of the Dakota Access pipeline, which would carry oil from the Bakken oil fields in North Dakota across the Missouri and Mississippi rivers to a terminal in Illinois. However, it was feared that the pipeline might threaten vital water supplies. Protests lasted for months, winning the support of a wide range of environmental and religious groups, both in the US and overseas. At the height of the movement, thousands joined the Native American protests and maintained an encampment, as the media regularly depicted images of fighting and alleged official brutality. The movement made clever use of social media, under the hashtag #NoDAPL (North Dakota Access Pipeline). Protesters claimed that they were not just defending their particular communities, but were protecting ancient sacred places and burial grounds. Banners carried the slogan "Defend the Sacred." The Standing Rock affair symbolized the conflict between aggressive exploitation of energy resources and the defense of community and landscape. Advocates saw resistance as a spiritual movement as much as a political one.

Awareness of environmental and ecological dangers has become widespread since the 1970s, and it has often driven protest movements and grass-roots activism. What changed in the new century was the central position that climate change acquired in the debates, and how massively that raised the stakes. Environmentalists no longer spoke of defending a particular community or landscape but literally of defending the planet, of maintaining human life in anything like the state in which it presently exists. Like the Standing Rock protests, but on a planetary scale, environmentalists used the language of the sacred. Barack Obama described trends in climate change as "terrifying."

Such apocalyptic calls raised fundamental questions about the nature and function of government, and the relationship between national sovereignty and global well-being. For activists, saving the planet demanded far-reaching official intervention difficult to reconcile with traditional views of free enterprise capitalism, or even (perhaps) of electoral democracy. These concerns shaped many controversies of the Obama years, and often forced the administration to balance its ideals with practical political realities.

CLIMATE CHANGE

Climate has often changed historically, and substantial alterations have occurred within the span of human history: particular eras have been warmer or colder. Modern discussion, though, focuses on a specific trend that emerged over the past century or so, which represents a decisive break with older patterns. At issue are gases like carbon dioxide, nitrous oxide, and methane that warm the planet's surface through the so-called greenhouse effect, and in appropriate quantities are essential to survival. Since the early nineteenth century, the rise of mass industrialization has increased levels of greenhouse gases, and already in that early era some scientists were speculating that a greenhouse effect might affect climate. Since the 1950s, global mean surface temperatures have indeed been rising, and from the 1980s a substantial scientific consensus came to believe that these changes are human-caused, or anthropogenic. Apart from smokestack factories, the main culprits are carbon-based forms of producing energy through fossil fuels, especially through petroleum and coal. The rapid rise of human populations has increased carbon emissions, as has the rise of wealthier societies in vast nations like China and India.

Projected into the near future, the prospects are alarming. By the mid-century, higher temperatures could mean rising sea levels and spreading deserts, falling supplies of food and drinkable water, and all those trends would probably mean intensified conflict and war, and forced mass migrations. In order to limit carbon emissions, in 1992 the United Nations signed a Framework Convention on Climate Change (UNFCCC), which in turn led to an international treaty in 1997, the Kyoto Protocol. In later years, outspoken warnings about potential crisis have come from the reports of the Intergovernmental Panel on Climate Change, and in 2015 Pope Francis I issued a stern warning about climate change in his encyclical *Laudato Si*. In 2015, a UNFCCC conference held in Paris agreed on a common goal of ensuring that global temperatures would not rise by more than two degrees Celsius above pre-industrial levels, and ideally by no more than 1.5 degrees.

Despite such international consensus, climate issues have been fiercely controversial within the United States, far more so than in any other advanced nation. Partly, objections are scientific, although the number of experts critiquing the general consensus represents a small minority. Some scholars offer rival interpretations of the climate change data, and especially the means by which temperatures have been measured. A number of scientists accept the reality of global warming, but challenge how far it is caused by human actions as opposed to other factors.

But political objections are also critical, especially to the proposed international framework associated with the United Nations. While calling for countries to reduce carbon emissions, any cuts would not be equally distributed, and the impact would fall much more heavily on advanced industrializing nations rather than countries in the process of modernization, above all China. As the largest producer of emissions, the US would suffer disproportionately from cuts, as would vital sectors of its economy, namely oil and, to a diminishing extent, coal. Politicians of either party representing affected areas had a strong incentive to resist the cuts called for by the proposed treaties. American conservatives also had a pronounced distaste for any solutions that involved limiting or compromising national sovereignty, and the United Nations was a long-standing cause of anger. These concerns were so important because the US Constitution required Senate ratification of any international treaty, like the Kyoto Protocol. In fact, the US was one of the handful of nations that refused to ratify Kyoto, and the Senate voted by 95–0 to reject any agreement that failed to require proportionate reductions by developing countries.

WINNING THE DEBATE?

Throughout the present century climate issues have been vigorously debated, and the theme has often surfaced in other policy debates. Environmental groups have campaigned vigorously to raise public awareness of the issue, supported by high-profile campaigners like former vice president Al Gore. In 2006, Gore's campaign was the subject of an influential documentary film, *An Inconvenient Truth*, which showed memorable depictions of prematurely melting glaciers and the effects on iconic wildlife such as polar bears. The warming theme also inspired many fictional works, both novels and films, which imagined nightmare future dystopian worlds.

Further alerting non-experts to climate dangers was the sequence of devastating storms and hurricanes that visited catastrophe on major cities and regions. Notorious examples included the hurricanes Katrina (New Orleans, 2005), Sandy (New York and New Jersey, 2012), and Harvey (Houston, 2017). Harvey alone killed over 100, and caused damage to the extent of $125 billion. Also in 2017, Hurricane Maria probably killed several hundred in Puerto Rico – some accounts place the death toll much higher – and left much of the island without power for months. Although none of these events could be wholly attributed to climate change, experts argued that global warming made such assaults far more likely and more severe, raising the possibility that future generations would live in a dangerous climatic environment. Magazines and news media offered alarming maps showing how much US coastal territory might be lost if warming proceeded as appeared likely, even threatening such key cities as New York and Miami. Reinforcing these lessons were catastrophic wildfire seasons, as occurred in California in 2018.

As these debates progressed, belief in the reality of global warming gained support. News media strongly favored the climate change cause and largely abandoned attempts to present the story as a debate between two equally valid sides. Critics of the climate consensus were marginalized. Activists denounced them as denialists, a loaded term that suggested an analogy with the neo-Nazi extremists who denied the reality of the Holocaust.

OIL WARS

Accepting the climate change narrative had multiple consequences, both in seeking to prevent future warming and in adapting to the future changes that now seemed inevitable. These issues sparked many debates in the years of Obama's presidency. The president and his advisors identified closely with environmental concerns, and Obama spoke ambitiously of his presidency as a time "when the rise of the oceans began to slow, and our planet began to heal." But political factors forced the administration to proceed cautiously.

As presently constituted, the US economy depends on oil supplies in various forms, which it uses to power automobiles, aircraft, and transport systems, and to generate electricity. There are obvious advantages to replacing foreign imports with the domestic oil in which the US is enormously rich. The problem is that much of it is difficult to access, demanding advanced technologies that are only worth using if the global price of oil is high (see Chapter 5). Other oil resources are easier or cheaper to access, but they are located in areas that are sensitive because of their environmental or ecological importance. These include undersea reserves located around much of the lengthy US coastline, both to east and west. There is also the vast Arctic Wildlife National Refuge in north-eastern Alaska, which has very large supplies of recoverable oil but in a delicate environment. Much discussed here has been the impact of drilling on local species, especially caribou. Debates about coastal drilling, and exploiting the Arctic Refuge, have continued for many years. In 2008, Republicans adopted the informal slogan "Drill, baby, drill!" to urge the full exploitation of domestic energy resources, regardless of environmental cost.

Critics meanwhile cited fears of accidents that could ruin environments of global importance. They point to the catastrophic oil spill that resulted in

2010 from an explosion at BP's Deepwater Horizon rig in the Gulf of Mexico. This resulted in the loss of 4.9 million barrels of oil, which assailed coastal lands from Louisiana through Florida. In response, the Obama administration suspended the issue of new drilling leases, and ordered a six-month moratorium on drilling (a federal court overturned the policy). But even if the oil industry could guarantee perfect safety, the unchecked emphasis on oil resources was hard to sustain given concerns about carbon emissions. Quite moderate politicians by no means committed to environmental activism argued that more thought should be given to reducing the need for oil, and shifting the emphasis of energy policy to renewable resources – to wind and solar. Nuclear reactors offer a clean and efficient means of generating energy, but these are regarded as unacceptable for safety reasons. This nervousness became still greater following the catastrophic threat to the Fukushima nuclear reactor in Japan following the 2011 tsunami.

Environmental concerns shaped attitudes to the new energy sources that now became available through fracking technologies. Fracking proved divisive for local communities who at first sight saw so much benefit from the enterprise. They rejoiced at the creation of whole new industries and substantial employment, often in rural regions that had long been poor and deprived. Individual landowners made large profits on the sale of their mineral rights, as states expanded their tax bases. But fracking threatened to pollute water supplies, endanger public health, and even to raise the risk of earthquakes. The 2010 documentary film *Gasland* publicized these dangers, and this became the bible for a grass-roots anti-fracking movement. Local activists sought to prevent fracking, either through legislation or direct action, blocking roads and trails. The resulting conflicts drew sharp lines between environmentalists and local communities. In 2014, New York state prohibited fracking, in a decision that delighted urban liberals while appalling rural communities who saw their best hopes of economic improvement lying in ruins. Some supporters of fracking threatened that whole rural areas might secede from the state, to align instead with neighboring Pennsylvania.

A still larger battle concerned the oil extracted from the tar sands of northern Alberta, in Canada. These resources are difficult and expensive to extract – and, say many, particularly troublesome in environmental terms. Once extracted, the issue then is how to transport the oil for refining and export, and pipeline networks were built in multiple phases. These connected the Canadian heartland to the US Midwest and Gulf Coast. Since 2010, several sections of the system have already been built, but rising concern about fossil fuels provoked fierce opposition to the fourth phase, Keystone XL (Export Limited). This involved building a 1,200-mile pipeline across the Great Plains states to Texas, with a daily capacity of 800,000 barrels of Canadian petroleum. The project created many thousands of jobs, although the exact number was much debated. Critics protested that, apart from increasing the supplies of fossil fuels, the pipeline would threaten water supplies in much of the region. In 2011, the administration postponed a decision, and subsequently vetoed legislation that would have approved the pipeline. In 2015, the administration explicitly rejected the fourth phase. But in this matter as in many aspects of environmental policy, the arrival of the new Trump administration in 2017 caused a reversal of Obama-era decisions, and plans were announced to complete the project. The following year, a federal judge again blocked the pipeline, berating the administration for ignoring climate change concerns.

GOING PLACES

Transportation accounts for some 71 percent of US oil consumption, and vehicles of all kinds together generate some 28 percent of US carbon emissions. Cars, trucks and buses represent the largest share of that category. This pattern could be changed in various ways: by removing or reducing people's needs to travel more extensively; to encourage them to travel in fewer vehicles and thus to reduce private transport; and to make vehicles more efficient in terms of fuel usage and gas mileage. Apart from minimizing the impact on the environment, cutting oil needs would reduce energy imports.

In terms of fuel efficiency, manufacturers have long experimented with cars that either used electricity rather than gasoline or that combined two distinct kinds of power in hybrid systems. In 2000, Toyota achieved a major commercial success when its efficient hybrid, the Prius, became available worldwide. By 2011, a million cars had been sold in the US alone. Other major manufacturers soon followed with their own hybrids. One leading name in advanced electric cars is Tesla, founded in 2003, which by 2017 was generating almost $12 billion in revenue.

In 1975, following the first oil crisis, Congress established rules for fuel efficiency standards through its Corporate Average Fuel Economy (CAFE) standards. By progressively increasing required gas mileage levels, such policies would force manufacturers to devise new technological solutions. But working against these goals was the growing popularity of larger vehicles – of light trucks and sports utility vehicles – for family and individual use. In addition, the number of miles driven had risen significantly since the 1970s. In 2007, the Democratic-controlled Congress passed an ambitious Energy Independence and Security Act, a wide-ranging measure that sought to increase the use of renewables, improve energy efficiency, and combat carbon emissions. The Act raised prescribed fuel economy standards of all vehicles, including light trucks, to 35 miles per gallon by 2020. Under the Obama administration, in 2009 government, industry, and regulators formed a National Program to implement these sweeping new standards, with a specific focus on the consequences for emissions and the impact on climate.

Any policy about transportation and vehicles involved balancing complex social needs and interests. While everyone could agree with the virtues of better fuel efficiency, the growth of regulations had serious cost consequences, and the price of entry-level cars rose significantly. This had an obvious impact on people with lower incomes, and disproportionately so in rural and suburban areas where public transportation was not a viable alternative. The gulf separating urban and non-urban populations in transportation matters grew in other ways, as younger and more educated urban residents were far less likely to consider car ownership or even learning to drive. Since the 1980s, the proportion of young people who hold driver's licenses has fallen steeply, reversing a long-established assumption about the sacrosanct role of cars and driving in American life. Between 1983 and 2014, the proportion of 16 year olds with licenses fell from 46 to 25 percent. More prosperous city residents found their needs met by public transport, and also by services like Uber. Generally, more liberal residents in large urban complexes were likely to favor the new wave of regulatory policies.

Environmental activists had high hopes for replacing motorized transport with bicycles. That shift required a significant restructuring of cities, where roads placed a strong emphasis on automobiles and trucks, and where safety issues pose a major deterrent to expanded bike use. Increasingly, cities built and enforced lanes reserved for bicycles, most fervently in progressive cities like San Francisco. Cycling activists became a visible and militant part of the environmental movement, campaigning against car use. From the 1990s, large groups of cyclists organized Critical Mass events, in which they effectively took over urban streets to the frustration of automobile drivers. However, any substantial shift to cycling was only possible in some regions, and the number of commuters regularly cycling to work remains tiny, with fewer than a million individuals nationwide compared with 120 million drivers.

Familiar fault lines – young versus old, urban versus rural – affected attitudes to another key trend emerging in the mid-2010s, namely the autonomous or self-driving car. Attractive in certain contexts and routes, any prospect of a wholesale replacement of traditional cars was alarming for many non-urban communities, and for older drivers.

OBAMA AND THE ENVIRONMENT

In an ideal society, energy would come entirely from clean renewable sources such as solar and wind power. In reality, any significant attempt to reduce US reliance on oil, gas, and coal would be a political nightmare, and very difficult to achieve in the short term. Debates over environmental policies often show little real exchange of views, as each side portrays its opponent in an extreme and unreasoning light. Environmentalists commonly assume that their opponents are ill-informed or anti-science, while critics protest that environmental policies inflict heavy financial burdens on the people least able to afford them. Issues of jobs and employment are vital, as critics portray environmentalists as elite liberals with no sense of the significance of jobs for depressed areas. This conflict emerged strongly in debates over fracking. Conscious of such sensitivities, Obama-era advocates of environmental policies framed their goals in a way that would avoid such visceral conflicts.

Instead of stressing the regulation and restriction of familiar activities, wise environmentalists spoke rather of vital new opportunities for employment and job creation. Requiring corporations to devise more efficient cars, for instance, would ideally force them to invest in new technologies with all the new employment that would result. The decline of older kinds of industry and manufacture should be seen not simply as an end but rather as a beginning, the signal for an upsurge of innovation and prosperity. New policies could be represented as optimistic and forward looking, rather than punitive or scolding. That was especially true of any shift to renewable energy sources. Sizable workforces were needed to build wind farms or install solar panels, and the new industries usually offered good pay for skilled labor. Although the outcome fell far short of expectations, new policies did indeed achieve some job growth.

Clean and renewable energy was a central part of the 2009 American Recovery and Reinvestment Act, by which the incoming administration hoped to escape from the recession. In what the administration described as "the largest single investment in clean energy in history," $90 billion was committed through investments and tax credits. This was aimed "to promote job creation and the deployment of low-carbon technologies." The announced order of priorities placed jobs first. Renewable tax credits were then extended in 2015.

These policies favored the substantial growth of renewables that has been such a marked factor of American energy policy in the present century. Wind power capacity in the United States grew from just 2.5 gigawatts (GW) in 2000 to 47 GW in 2011, and 82 GW by 2017. In 2012 alone, at the height of the Obama-era incentives, almost 12 GW of wind power was installed. By far the largest source of wind power is Texas, which is usually thought of in terms of oil and gas. Even so, by 2017 it had over 20 GW of installed capacity. Recent growth nationwide places the US ahead of all countries except China. In terms of production from wind power, the US grew from 5.6 terawatt hours (TWH) in 2000 to 254 by 2017, remarkable growth in a very few years.

Growth in solar energy has been even more dramatic. That power includes energy generated by utilities as well as that from "distributed" sources, from the rooftops of individual buildings. Taking the two together, only in 2004 did the combined figure for solar power generation reach 1 TWH. That figure then grew to 21 TWH by 2013, and to 77 by 2017. Between 2009 and 2017, the solar power produced by utilities alone grew from just 1 TWH to 52. Apart from their contributions to energy needs, renewables have indeed generated employment. The solar industry accounts for 250,000 jobs, with another 100,000 in wind, and perhaps 800,000 in the whole renewable sector combined.

This move toward renewable energy must be kept in perspective. In a typical year, the US generates about 4,000 TWH of electricity. The 2017 figure included 17 percent derived from renewable sources combined, namely hydropower (7.5 percent), wind (6.3 percent), biomass (1.6 percent) and solar (1.3 percent). That is a substantial increase from the 2000 figure, which was less than 10 percent, with wind power accounting for most of the change. The Obama administration must certainly receive due credit. But that combined total of renewables must be set aside the fossil fuels that account for 62.7 percent of electricity generation, especially natural gas (31.7 percent) and coal (30.1 percent). Even after years of decline and widespread public disapproval, nuclear power produces 20 percent of electricity generated, more than all renewables combined. Renewables would thus have to be developed a very great deal before they could hope to replace these traditional sources of energy.

OBAMA AND THE CLIMATE

The Obama administration clearly sympathized with environmental activism, but it faced severe limits on any political action requiring legislation. One telling moment came in 2009 when Congress debated a so-called cap and trade system, modeled on European practice. Under this scheme, governments would set strict limits for the overall volume of greenhouse gas emissions, but individual companies would buy or bargain for the rights to emit the gases that were permitted, in a "carbon marketplace." Such a system was proposed in the American Clean Energy and Security Act, which actually passed the House of Representatives, but it was never discussed in the US Senate although that body then had a solid Democratic majority. The issues involved in controlling emissions were simply too controversial. Making matters even harder, Republican victories in the midterm elections in 2010 and 2014 placed daunting obstacles in the way of any substantial legislative programs. When in 2016 the United States signed the historic Paris climate change agreement, the administration announced that it did not regard it as a new formal treaty of the kind that would require Congressional ratification. This approach avoided the near certainty that any attempt at a ratification vote would fail, but it did raise constitutional concerns.

Still, the federal government retained broad administrative powers that could be deployed in environmental causes, particularly through the workings of administrative and bureaucratic agencies. Such bodies had been given powers to act by Congressional action but did not face the limitation of having to receive approval for specific decisions they might make. One agency in particular had enormous potential for intervention, namely the Environmental Protection Agency (EPA) which had the duty to control pollution and limit harmful substances. The EPA had long been unpopular with conservatives for allegedly exceeding its authority, and for imposing environmentalist theories on states and local communities. Even under George W. Bush, in 2004, the agency had informed the governors of 31 states that the air pollution levels in those regions failed to meet federal standards and had to be reduced. In 2007, the US Supreme Court ruled that greenhouse gases should properly be included among dangerous air pollutants, so that the EPA was entitled and empowered to regulate their emission (*Massachusetts v. Environmental Protection Agency*, 549 U.S. 497 (2007)). Besides its direct impact on vehicle efficiency standards, this decision potentially had a critical effect on the nation's power stations, as stations run by coal or natural gas account for about 35 percent of US carbon dioxide emissions.

The agency became still more proactive under Obama. In 2014, the EPA announced a Clean Power Plan that the president formally unveiled as a signature policy the following year. The plan would reduce carbon emissions and promote renewables, requiring each state to formulate a means of reaching specified goals. If successful, American emissions would fall by 2030 by 32 percent compared to 2005 levels, helping to bring the US into line with the policies of the Paris Agreement. But the Plan was controversial. Apart from objections to the climate science, the scheme effectively enacted a sweeping new social policy by administrative fiat, rather than through Congressional debate or action. The new policy also promised to be prohibitively expensive, and the Supreme Court decided that the EPA must take account of cost factors when regulating power generation (*Michigan v. Environmental Protection Agency*, 576 U.S. (2015)).

Obama advanced environmental causes through executive orders. Environmental groups had long called for national monument status to be applied to various sites of natural beauty and historic significance. Although such designations did not necessarily involve global warming concerns, they reflected an emphasis on conservation and environmental protection rather than resource exploitation, which became much more difficult when sites received that new classification. Also, new monuments were often justified in terms of the interests and beliefs of native or indigenous communities, a rhetoric that surfaced in the Standing Rock controversy. In 2016, the president ordered the expansion of the Papahanaumokuakea marine monument in the northern Hawaiian islands. The area covered was increased from 140,000 to 583,000 square miles, or by an area larger even than the state of Alaska, thus creating the world's largest conservation area.

After the Trump victory in the 2016 election, Obama remained president for over two months. Although he was a "lame duck," his position gave him freedom of action, as he need have no concerns about the impact on an incoming administration of his own party. This allowed him to pursue policies that in other circumstances might have stirred too much opposition. In his closing months, Obama designated new national monuments on a vast scale, at the Bears Ears site in Utah and the Gold Butte National Monument in Nevada. Such a policy angered western conservatives who were already concerned about the extent of federal control over lands in their states. In all, the Obama administration created 29 national monuments.

Inevitably, the incoming Trump administration sought to check or reverse Obama's environmental agenda, just as we have seen with the Keystone Pipeline. The new president promptly announced his intention to withdraw the US from the Paris climate change framework, which he could do easily as the pact was not an officially ratified treaty. The administration announced a review of the recently designated national monuments, including Bears Ears. Nor did the Clean Power Plan meet sympathy from the new administration, particularly under EPA administrator Scott Pruitt. In 2017 the EPA began the process of dismantling and repealing the Plan. Meanwhile, the Dakota Access protesters were dispersed and evicted, as President Trump approved an expedited review of the proposed pipeline.

But the new federal hostility to environmental policies left plenty of room for activism by progressive-minded states. Liberal California especially sought to establish its own standards and policies in matters like carbon emissions, air quality, and water protection. Such moves raised delicate constitutional questions. Federalism gives states wide latitude to determine questions of internal importance, but at the same time various matters have been pre-empted by federal laws. If, for instance, California sets limits for car emissions or fuel efficiency, that places a burden on manufacturers to meet those California standards rather than limits set by the EPA, and those standards would have to be applied to cars sold anywhere in the US. In the conservative view, as stated by the Trump administration, California was thus seeking to impose its own views throughout the nation. Brushfire warfare between federal and state governments continued in the courts through the Trump years.

EVERYDAY LIFE

Media reporting about environmental issues naturally focused on protests, and on weighty public debates like that surrounding the Paris climate treaty. But quite apart from such set-piece battles, environmental concerns penetrated many aspects of everyday life, as witnessed by the bicycle lanes that now became commonplace in major cities. Critics of environmentalism found a minor but telling grievance in the gradual phasing out of incandescent light bulbs and their replacement by energy efficient models. Authorized as a tiny portion of the 2007 Energy Independence and Security Act, the new policy annoyed conservatives as a demonstration of woolly-minded elite idealists interfering with the conveniences of everyday life in order to advance their own impractical ideologies. Low-flush toilets, aimed at conserving water resources, were scarcely more popular.

In terms of the physical landscape, the most visible symbol of the new attitudes was the colossal wind turbines that became so commonplace in hitherto isolated regions. That unavoidable presence created conflicts in which the battle lines were far from obvious, and some became rather ironic. While few denied that renewable wind power was a great positive good, many residents of such areas disliked having these new objects dominating their landscape, and they organized protest movements. As the common phrase went, such things needed to be built, but "not in my back yard" – NIMBY. One such project to build turbines in Narragansett Bay off Cape Cod, in Massachusetts, stirred opposition from many traditional liberals, including members of the Kennedy family. Other environmentalists were concerned about the damage that such turbines might wreak on bird life. After 16 years of battles, the Cape Wind scheme was canceled in 2017. Such activism did raise the pressing question of just what, if any, forms of energy production might be acceptable to everyone.

New attitudes to the reuse and recycling of consumer goods changed the everyday lives of ordinary people. Activists had long raised the alarm about the constant proliferation of plastics and other materials that could not simply be left to degrade naturally back into the environment, and which became part of an ever-growing mountain of garbage, polluting both land and seas. Vastly enhancing the dangers of disposable products were the electronic products and cell phones that had become so common, and which were not expected to be used for more than a few years. Worse, such items abound with potentially toxic chemicals and heavy metals. Yet despite several decades of progress, the proportion of municipal solid waste that was recycled was still only 34 percent in 2013. Plastics became a convenient symbol of a society founded on the principle of disposability. States and local communities responded with ever-more sweeping policies limiting the use of non-biodegradable objects, prohibiting plastic bags for shopping, or requiring that consumers pay extra for bags that would once have been free. Such symbolic acts promoted awareness of larger issues, and manufacturers learned to stress how green and "environmentally friendly" their products actually were.

In other ways too, awareness of environmental issues contributed to life-style choices. Vegetarianism had gained greatly in popularity since the 1970s, partly on health grounds but also because meat production had a grave effect on the environment. Veganism, meanwhile, rejected all animal products in the name of "ethical eating" and avoiding cruelty. Moreover, cattle are a major source of the greenhouse gas methane, making dairy and meat production a significant factor in climate change. The absolute numbers of people following these choices were not large. Although the statistics are very uncertain, perhaps 2 or 3 percent of all Americans are fully vegetarian and just 0.5 percent vegan (some recent surveys describe an improbably rapid growth in vegan numbers since the mid-2010s). But particularly in major cities the proliferation of vegan shops and restaurants promoted discussions about the environmental impact of food production, not to mention the human position in the larger natural order.

Environmental issues were by no means the only area of rapid cultural change, nor the only one in which we see a powerful continuity from the radical values of earlier decades. Indeed, the Obama years witnessed a series of transformations that often recalled and echoed the tumultuous 1960s. As in environmental issues, changes driven by government and courts merged inextricably with concerns emerging from the grass roots, and with innovative social movements. That was true above all in matters of race.

11 Still the American Dilemma

In August 2014, police received reports of a convenience store robbery in Ferguson, MO, a suburb of St Louis. A white police officer, Darren Wilson, encountered two young black men whom he believed to be the offenders. As so often occurs in such situations, very different versions report what happened subsequently. The officer claims that one of the men, Michael Brown, tried to take his gun before fleeing, but a second round of violence then ensued. Wilson fired 12 shots, six of which hit Brown, killing him. Protesters claimed that Brown was shot after surrendering and raising his hands, and that his last reported words were "Don't shoot!" The incident ignited demonstrations and riots in the St Louis area, and further protests followed when Wilson was acquitted of criminal charges. Michael Brown's death attracted such passion because protesters saw it as a symbol of the violence all too often visited by police against young black men. The Ferguson events became a cause célèbre for protesters against police violence, and "Hands up! Don't shoot!" became a slogan nationwide.

Most Americans viewed the election of Barack Obama as marking a decisive change for the better in the nation's race relations, above all where African Americans were concerned. Obama could not have won without the support of a large and diverse white constituency. Many white Americans viewed the election with a powerful sense of hope – that Obama watchword – and a sense that old grievances and injustices were fading into the past. In this vision, the United States was becoming a post-racial society, which would be blessed by truly color-blind policies and attitudes. Events of the following decade sadly contradicted these early hopes, as protests highlighted continuing ills, among which police misbehavior was among the best publicized. Race-based militancy surged to levels not seen in almost 50 years.

A NEW HOPE

At first sight, the focus on black militancy was surprising. As we have seen, the US population had become much more diverse in ethnic terms in recent decades, and each group had its own specific concerns and issues. African American numbers grew only slightly, representing around 12.7 percent of the total population. During the 2010s, though, most racial activism still focused on African Americans, with black–white tensions by far the most sensitive issue in provoking protests and demonstrations. Observers could be forgiven for thinking that the massive ethnic shifts of the previous half century had never occurred. (As we will see below, those other minorities had their distinctive approaches to cultural issues.)

The revival of black activism occurred despite undoubted black progress in most aspects of American life. Besides the Obama election, other black figures occupied many political leadership roles at all levels, not to mention in private business. In the first administration of George W. Bush, Colin Powell held the office of Secretary of State, the most powerful Cabinet position, which represents the country's face in dealing with foreign countries. Succeeding Powell was another African American, Condoleezza Rice, who had already served as Bush's National Security Advisor. Under Obama, the powerful office of Attorney General was occupied by two African Americans, namely Eric Holder and Loretta Lynch. Susan Rice was Obama's National Security Advisor.

Quite apart from these political celebrities, black people held powerful and influential positions in business, public service, the judiciary, and the academic world. In everyday life, we can trace a major shift in public behavior and attitudes since the 1960s, as problems of racism were fully acknowledged in the social mainstream and black grievances achieved mass recognition and respect. In racial interactions, a revolutionary shift occurred in the manner of appropriate language and public discourse, so that "the N-word" became close to unspeakable and unprintable. One gauge of improved racial relations was the substantial migration of black families from the North and Midwest to the South, reversing a historic trend. African Americans moved to flourishing cities or suburban communities in Florida, Texas, or Georgia in pursuit of better jobs and lifestyles, without having to fear any vestiges of formal segregation. Nationally, taboos against interracial sexual behavior continued to fade.

In one sense, what did not happen matters as much as what did. Despite repeated efforts to overturn systems of racial preferences and affirmative action, the courts continued to approve those principles, although defining some limits in how they might be applied. In 2003, the US Supreme Court confirmed that racial criteria could be used in university and law school admissions in the interests of promoting a diverse student body (*Grutter v. Bollinger*, 539 U.S. 306 (2003)). That was reinforced by the 2016 decision in *Fisher v. University of Texas* (579 U.S. _____ (2016)). Variously defined, diversity remained a real goal for institutions and corporations.

CONTINUED GRIEVANCES

Despite these positives, many black Americans remained deeply disaffected. Black communities were hard hit by factors that we have already traced, both changes in technology and the transformation of the nation's ethnic composition (see Chapters 3 and 4 above). Particularly damaging was the sharp decline of old industries and the cities in which they were based. As declining inner cities became poorer and lost their sources of employment, so those areas were increasingly left to black populations, as occurred in communities like Saginaw and Flint. Detroit was the best-known example of such a ruinous urban shrinkage culminating in financial collapse. Cumulatively, these trends reversed generations of hopes for economic progress among poorer African Americans.

Most black people did not benefit from the positive changes that accompanied these social crises. Poor education left many black Americans badly equipped to participate in the high-skill tech industries that now boomed. That was a consequence of failures in public education, particularly in the fields of STEM – science, technology, engineering, and mathematics. The workforces of newer industries were by no means all white, and most included heavy representation of South and East Asians at all levels. Many corporations boasted of the strides they had made towards inclusiveness and diversity, in the sense that white people did not dominate the workforce to any greater degree than in the population at large. But "non-white" did not necessarily mean black workers, and black employees might still be confined to lower-status jobs. By some measures, US businesses today are actually as segregated as they were in the 1970s, and perhaps more so. Wage differentials between black and white are likewise comparable to the 1970s.

Growing out of that economic change, black people were poorly situated to benefit from the great restructuring that now so fundamentally changed American cities. As we have seen, gentrification reshaped cities and neighborhoods that for decades had been centers of minority culture and activism. As Detroit foundered, so Oakland, CA, flourished economically as it had not done for decades. But the new Oakland was nothing like the African American capital of earlier years. In many cities, declines in public spending gutted the public transport facilities on which poor communities relied to find work. That left many black people isolated in remote sections, and that powerfully promoted a de facto residential segregation.

Black elites actually lost some of the political power they had secured briefly in the latter years of the twentieth century. As American cities had become predominantly black, so those cities naturally elected black mayors and administrations. But that changed with both the growth of new immigration and with the gentrification that brought white residents back to center cities. In 1983, Chicago achieved a historic landmark when it elected Harold Washington as the city's first black mayor. Subsequently, Latino populations have grown alongside older white and black communities, giving the city a three-way political division and preventing any reassertion of black electoral power. Since 1989, Chicago has elected only white mayors. To date, David Dinkins (1990–1993) remains the only black mayor of New York City.

African Americans were concerned about the return of discriminatory voting practices that would reduce their political power, particularly through the use of laws demanding voters to show identification. In 2013, black leaders were shocked when the Supreme Court upheld a challenge to the 1965 Voting Rights Act. In the time of segregation, Southern states had been highly creative in devising means to prevent black people voting. Under the Voting Rights Act, Southern states or jurisdictions with a history of malpractice had to obtain Justice Department pre-approval before changing their electoral laws or policies. But in the case of *Shelby County v. Holder* (570 U.S. 529 (2013)), the Court decided that the law no longer reflected contemporary social realities, and so should no longer be upheld. In the short term the decision had few effects, but it raised the specter of future electoral manipulation. Coupled with repeated Republican successes at Congressional and state level from 2010 onward, the prospect of further black political advances was severely curtailed.

THE NEW JIM CROW

Apart from the general issues of poverty and inequality, problems associated with the criminal justice system proved explosive. African Americans suffered disproportionately from the harsh incarceration policies pursued by all governments since the late 1970s, which have made the US by far the most penal society among the advanced nations. In an influential book published in 2010, Michelle Alexander condemned these incarceration policies as a modern form of segregation and racial victimization, as "the New Jim Crow." Between 1972 and 2014, the US incarceration rate – counting both prisons and jails – has grown from 161 per 100,000 to 700 per 100,000. The actual number of inmates grew from around 400,000 in the early 1970s to 2.3 million between 2006 and 2008. Although the rate of growth then stabilized, it presently stands around 2.2 million. That does not include several million additional individuals under some other form of official control and surveillance, through probation and parole. By the peak year of 2008, that officially "controlled" population amounted to 7.3 million adults.

This upward trend was chiefly a product of the Drug War that became such a central part of government social policy from the 1980s. Through the years, legislatures had responded to the perceived drug menace by escalating sentences for drug offenses, especially in the form of mandatory sentences that gave judges no option but to impose lengthy prison terms. By 2015, some 22 percent of inmates were serving time for drug-related offenses. High incarceration rates are particularly common in those Southern states that historically were most repressive to their black populations. Of the 10 states with the highest incarceration rates, seven had been members of the former Confederacy, with Louisiana and Mississippi as the most punitive. Southern states have also been the regions most enthusiastic in the use of capital punishment. Across the nation, prisons have become wildly overcrowded, and in consequence violent and dangerous.

Mass incarceration has had devastating effects in minority communities, where so many young men are removed from society. Apart from the consequences for family life, possessing a criminal record sabotages future job prospects. Employers might look askance at felons, but even if their intentions are generous a great many trades and professions demand some form of licensing or certification; this is closed to ex-offenders. If released individuals find a job, it is usually one marked by low skills and low pay. Incarceration also has a vast political impact. Most states prohibit inmates from voting, and many extend that prohibition to some period after release, in some cases permanently. Although that disfranchisement affects felons, that serious label applies to a great many offenders whose acts would not normally be thought violent or threatening. In 2012, state disfranchisement laws prevented almost 6 million Americans from voting, a restriction that in practice placed severe limits on black voting power. In Florida alone, such laws affect 1.5 million potential voters. (In 2018, that state voted to restore voting rights to those individuals.)

Reducing the incarceration rate was a priority for the incoming Obama administration, and for his Attorney General, Eric Holder. In 2010, Holder's Justice Department instructed federal prosecutors to adopt more flexible approaches in charging and plea bargaining. In 2013, Holder announced a Smart on Crime policy, with new federal guidelines for prosecutors in drug cases. Prosecutors were encouraged to reduce the attention they paid to nonviolent trafficking cases, and to avoid seeking mandatory minimum terms. The correctional population did indeed decline somewhat, and remained at that lower level through the Obama years. The problem was that federal prisons account for only a small proportion of inmates, when set aside the vast majority confined to state prisons or local jails. Even with the most ambitious intentions, the administration could make little impact on the situation.

In 2017, incoming Attorney General Jeff Sessions announced a reversal of Holder's reforms, demanding the aggressive prosecution of drug cases.

BLACK LIVES MATTER

Besides the prisons, other parts of the criminal justice system were denounced as arms of racial oppression. In a lengthy series of widely publicized incidents, police killed black individuals, usually young men, while virtually never suffering any legal consequences themselves. Although it did not directly involve police, one deeply controversial incident involved a white civilian acting as a neighborhood watch officer, who in Florida in 2012 shot a young black man called Trayvon Martin. The killer was subsequently acquitted at trial. Such actions had of course always occurred, but the lack of eyewitness evidence made it difficult to prove official misconduct. What changed in modern times was the availability of direct visual evidence, and in 1992, a notorious video showing police beating a black motorist sparked the disastrous rioting in Los Angeles. After 2007, newly ubiquitous cell phones did much to expose police violence, and opened the way to prosecution.

Public anger fueled a loosely organized protest movement called Black Lives Matter, BLM, which often recalled the Black Power surge of the 1960s. (The original Black Panthers of that time began as a movement against perceived police aggression.) BLM reached its height in Obama's second term, between 2014 and 2016. The fact that the movement's name originated as a hashtag on Twitter says much about the changing means by which people circulated information and organized new movements, and BLM grew rapidly. The movement found many notorious cases of concern. In July 2014, New York police used a headlock or chokehold on Eric Garner, whose actual offenses were trivial and who was conspicuously not threatening any form of violence. Garner died, and his last words "I can't breathe" became another rallying cry for BLM. The Ferguson controversy ensued the following month. In Baltimore in 2015, Freddie Gray died from injuries received while being transported in a police vehicle, allegedly as officers drove wildly to terrorize their prisoner. Repeatedly, police officers charged in such deaths were acquitted, despite evidence that to many non-expert observers seemed like overwhelming evidence that grave crimes had been committed. Observers of quite moderate views asked just how blatantly illegal or unprovoked a killing by police would have to be in order to lead to conviction and punishment.

As the litany of victims grew, demonstrations and protests included the interruption of artistic and cultural events, and the blocking of busy highways. Little remarked in these incidents was the extreme reluctance of police to curb the protests or make mass arrests, even to keep key highways open; this would have been unthinkable a few decades earlier. Partly, that was a political decision intended to avoid pushing unrest to a new and more militant level, but it also reflected a much greater public sympathy for black causes and activism. Recalling the civil rights protests of the 1950s, police and politicians had no wish to see themselves demonized in future history books. Nor did they wish to provoke a response like the urban warfare of the late 1960s.

The world of sports produced one highly visible form of non-violent protest. Since the 9/11 attacks, sports events had conscientiously begun their events with the national anthem, as players and spectators stood respectfully. In 2016, footballer Colin Kaepernick of the San Francisco 49ers remained kneeling during the anthem, as a protest against police brutality and systematic oppression. Many other black players in football and other sports soon followed his lead, both at professional and collegiate levels, in what became a national movement: Take a Knee.

Demonstrations varied in seriousness and the degree of violence that ensued, but some cities were badly affected, usually when courts failed to convict police officers. Weeks of unrest in Baltimore provoked a state of emergency, and a police shooting in Milwaukee sparked days of rioting. As the potential for urban violence grew, police increasingly turned to the militarized (or explicitly military) weapons and tactics they had developed during the Drug War. Through the years, many departments had acquired surplus military weaponry and vehicles, often giving a major police presence the appearance of an occupying army in a hostile war zone. That exactly matched the rhetorical interpretation offered by the black protesters, and their many white allies and supporters, and contributed to the ongoing militancy.

A sense of racial crisis reached new heights in 2016, with guerrilla attacks against police officers. In two separate incidents, in Dallas, TX, and Baton Rouge, LA, black militants killed multiple police officers in lone-wolf shootings. Racial tensions further escalated with the election of Donald Trump in November 2016, which we will consider in Chapter 15.

DEBATING THE CAUSE

Despite its amorphous character, the Black Lives Matter movement raised many questions for both black and other Americans, and especially for those who defined themselves as centrists or liberals. Most white Americans felt that the civil rights movement had eliminated a thoroughly evil system of segregation and racism, and that since that point black Americans had generally enjoyed equal status, although with many surviving injustices. BLM suggested instead that the racism of earlier years had never gone away, and that the only solutions were in militancy, or even separatism. For these activists, post-racial America was a pernicious myth.

The "black lives" phrase was contentious, suggesting as it did to critics that these were the *only* lives that mattered. Opponents countered with the slogans Blue Lives Matter – emphasizing the danger to police officers – and the seemingly harmless and neutral All Lives Matter. To traditional liberals, that seemed inoffensive and unexceptionable, as an admirable statement of racial colorblindness. In fact, black activists and white liberal allies found this slogan intolerable, and treated it as an overt expression of racism and white supremacy. Colorblindness was no longer acceptable, and nor were once conventional assertions of anti-racist sentiment. Black activists favored assertions of racial pride and autonomy. For BLM's critics, these constituted black-oriented forms of segregation and racial supremacy.

Critics of BLM pointed to the movement's practical effects on black urban communities. In many instances, police forces and individual officers unquestionably had gravely abused their authority. Did that mean, however, that the forces themselves were wholly harmful or dangerous to the communities they aspired to serve, so that they should be excluded as far as possible? For critics of the justice system, poor and minority areas suffered from a problem of "over-policing," which meant that offenses in those areas were seriously over-recorded, and thus the inhabitants were made to look more dangerous than they really were. Other observers objected that minority areas were instead *under*-served by police, and under-protected, and that the new unrest actually made that problem far worse. Fear of riots and violent interactions made police reduce their activity in black communities, to become much less proactive, and reluctant to intervene conspicuously. The statistics are controversial, but some criminologists argue that such a hands-off approach has driven an upsurge of criminality in some cities, reversing the widespread gains in reducing crime over recent decades. By its nature, a crime spike in black areas victimizes the black and mainly poor residents of the affected communities. In this view, a Ferguson Effect actually increases black misery and deprivation. Obviously, all these rival interpretations are controversial.

Law enforcement agencies faced the dilemma of tracking extremists who were not directly connected with BLM but who shared the movement's fury with official injustice. One harrowing example was Micah Johnson, who undertook the 2016 sniper attacks that killed five Dallas officers. Although he acted alone, other militants assuredly shared his views, and several smaller-scale attacks have occurred – in New York City, Phoenix, and Baton Rouge, among other places. The customary police response to such political violence would be to identify the attacker's cause, and movements or groups sympathetic to it. Those groups would then be placed under observation and perhaps infiltrated to ensure that authorities would be able to prevent future attacks before they occurred. Such a proactive approach is effective, but it raises critical issues of civil liberties as it involves the surveillance of individuals who hold radical views but who might never commit an illegal act. In 2017, the FBI characterized the extreme margins of the militant movement as Black Identity Extremists and identified them as a significant threat to public order. Liberal politicians were troubled by any suggestion that agencies might be intervening against such a supposed movement, all the more so as this activity recalled the much-denounced COINTELPRO program that the FBI had operated in the 1960s.

WHITE SUPREMACY, WHITE PRIVILEGE

Underlying much of the new racial debate was the concept of white supremacy, a phrase that demands some unpacking. This ideology had deep historical roots in the United States, and in the early twentieth century the goal was openly espoused by segregationist politicians, mainly in the South. Advocates openly denounced racial equality, and specifically social equality, a term that implied sexual contacts across the color line.

After the collapse of segregation, ideas of white supremacy were maintained by extremists associated with the Ku Klux Klan and neo-Nazi movements, who also drew on anti-Semitic traditions. These groups were early pioneers of the internet as a means of propaganda and communication, colonizing it well before the coming of the World Wide Web in the early 1990s. In 2010, far-right leader Richard Spencer coined the phrase "alt-Right" as a label for such groups and their loose network, which became increasingly visible in following years. Racist and anti-feminist groups developed a whole eco-system of sites, bulletin boards and YouTube channels, with a special presence on 4chan. Such far-right groups viewed immigration as a sinister means to undertake a revolutionary change in the racial composition of the United States, and to destroy the power of the white race. But racial and sexual fears were inextricably connected. Alt-Right activists characterized their liberal enemies as "cucks," abbreviated from cuckold. This refers to a pornographic genre in which submissive white men passively observe while their wives have sex with (usually) dominant black men. By extension, a cuck is a white person who abandons the defense of his proper sexual or racial status, and submits to the dominance of minorities. Such racialized language had a particularly venomous tone in the era of a black president.

Alt-Right groups organized controversial demonstrations and public events with the deliberate goal of provoking confrontation and radicalizing moderates. Inspired by the rightist propaganda machine, some militants plotted acts of ethnic violence or overt terrorism. In 2018, one extremist sent pipe bombs to many liberal political and cultural leaders. Shortly afterwards, neo-Nazi terrorist Robert Bowers slaughtered 11 Jewish worshipers in a Pittsburgh synagogue.

But such overt white supremacists were numerically small and socially marginal, with nothing like the cachet and public support that the Klan had in the American South of the 1950s. Most white Americans never encountered their views directly. If they did, they wholly rejected them as an ugly vestige of Nazism, which was all but universally regarded as the most evil ideology ever devised by human beings. In no sense was white supremacism a mass movement, and it was overwhelmingly rejected by the American public, of whatever race.

In common parlance, white supremacy also had another connotation, as the term used by black activists to describe everything in American society that manifested white racial privilege or advantage. In this way, militants mobilized the popular disgust for white supremacist activism to launch a sweeping attack on US social, economic, and political arrangements, and to call for a revolutionary overthrow of the existing order. In this sense, black people themselves might even be deemed guilty of defending white supremacy if they defended the existing social order. On occasion, opponents of police violence targeted abuses committed by departments like that of Philadelphia, which at the time had an African American police chief and a high proportion of minority officers. Nevertheless, police killings of young black men were still construed as manifestations of white supremacy, rather than (for instance) as failings in police training, socialization, and culture.

That concept of white supremacy as a fundamental truth of American society also shaped, and constrained, possibilities of debate or discussion across racial lines. Since the 1980s, academic theorists had presented the concept of whiteness not as a simple biological fact but rather as an identity constructed through history and the exercise of power. Whiteness was thus problematized, presented as an issue that demanded to be resolved. In the same era, theorists likewise stressed the critical role of group identities in a deeply unequal and oppressive society. Consciousness was shaped by factors such as race, class, gender, disability, and sexual identity, and the overlaps and relationships between them (the approach known as "intersectionality"). Borrowing from Marxism, theorists held that an individual could not truly speak except in the context of their group identity, and the degree to which it represented privilege or oppression, advantage or discrimination.

From this perspective, white privilege was a potent, and virulent, aspect of that assemblage of identities. Any criticisms of black racial militancy, separatism, or extremism emanating from a white person were of their nature thoroughly tainted as manifestations of that white privilege. White speakers or writers were repeatedly told to "check your privilege." In contrast, activists denied that any statement by a black or minority person could constitute racism, which was an ideology constructed solely to defend and justify white supremacy. Again in this view, the only route to a just and equal society was to destroy whiteness, in the sense of a status holding privilege and expecting preferential treatment. In the interim, it seemed that white people could play no legitimate part in any kind of dialogue or debate.

Activist rhetoric naturally alienated many white observers, even many liberals who were well disposed to promoting racial justice. White working-class people found it bewildering, and galling, to be labeled as "privileged" when they were struggling economically. Many, moreover, were conscious of the struggles their own ancestors had encountered against social and class oppression. The new attitude was difficult for the groups known until recently as ethnics, who had immigrated at the turn of the previous century – Italians, Jews, Slavs, and others – who had suffered systematic discrimination at the hands of WASP elites. White people struggled with the new definition of racism as a structural condition afflicting all members of their society, rather than simply as malicious misbehavior.

CULTURE AND THEORY

The US has many distinguished African American academics and thinkers who study the ramifications of race, but one writer in particular earned mainstream attention in these years. This was journalist Ta-Nehisi Coates, whose influential writings included the memoir *Between the World and Me* (2015), which sold 1.5 million copies. Coates also wrote the *Black Panther* comic strip, to which we shall return shortly. Coates was influential because he expressed his ideas in such accessible and eloquent form. Particularly clear was his exposition of the view that race is a constructed phenomenon, that "race is the child of racism, not the father," and that these constructions must be destroyed in order to create a just society. In the case of killings by police, Coates minimized the actions of particular officers, and looked rather to the power of systematic racism, "the weight of an American legacy." He condemned the rhetoric of non-violence when, in practice, it so often meant "exulting non-violence for the weak and the biggest guns for the strong."

Apart from the written word, other forms of popular culture promoted racial awareness and consciousness. One landmark institution was the National Museum of African American History and Culture, part of the complex of museums within the Smithsonian Institution in Washington DC. Originally authorized in 2003, the museum was opened in 2016 by Barack Obama. The new museum – nicknamed the Blacksonian – was an enormous critical success for its architecture and exhibits, but it also attracted mass audiences and very long lines. This suggested a widespread and deeply committed interest in its contents and subject matter. Local endeavors, too, sought to reclaim the lost worlds of African American history and oppression. Civil rights museums existed in several cities, and in 2018 a new National Memorial for Peace and Justice, near Montgomery, AL, commemorated the thousands of victims of lynching.

ACTIVISM ON SCREEN

The cinema popularized new visions of African American identity. Black cinema was anything but a new phenomenon, and in the 1990s Spike Lee had regularly presented African American characters and problems. In the new militant atmosphere, activists complained just how limited had been the influence of such work in what remained an overwhelmingly white cultural mainstream. Noting the racial make-up of Oscar nominees in the 2016 Academy Awards, activists began a social media campaign under the hashtag #OscarsSoWhite, which forced the film establishment to promote and reward more works by minority directors and actors.

Several films attracted attention. In 2016, director Nate Parker released his film *The Birth of a Nation*, which focused on the celebrated 1831 slave rising led by Nat Turner. The film's title recalled the 1915 epic of that name by D. W. Griffith, which had offered a racist and neo-Confederate view of the Reconstruction era with its heroic portrayal of the Ku Klux Klan. By annexing that particular title, Parker offered a total revision of received views of American history, its heroes and villains. The film presented a favorable view of armed revolutionary violence by black people against oppression, violence that in some cases targeted white civilians. *The Birth of a Nation* received a rapturous welcome from audiences and critics.

Many other films in these years offered distinctive African American content, not necessarily with an explicitly political intent. The 2017 horror/comedy film *Get Out* depicted the white exploitation and enslavement of black bodies and souls. In terms of size of audience, the most successful production was the 2018 film *Black Panther*, one of a great many superhero films in these years. *Black Panther* differed from those counterparts in its virtually all-black cast and its settings in the fictional African kingdom of Wakanda. The film did not approach blackness as a problematic situation associated with poverty, crime, and drugs, but rather presented a richly drawn vision of a high-tech African utopia. The film was a potent cultural milestone.

The new cultural consciousness affected attitudes to other films that dealt with black topics, even in ways that would once have been seen as supportive and sympathetic. Through the decades, many Hollywood films had depicted issues of racial injustice, presenting strongly liberal conclusions. In many cases, though, the films depended on the intervention of sympathetic white characters, leaving black people as grateful recipients of benevolence from above through what is sometimes dismissed as White Savior Complex. The new environment rejected such violations of identity and authenticity, and insisted that black film-makers and actors should tell their own stories – that black people should be the heroes of their own lives. Such now-frequent protests heralded a substantial change in depictions of race and race relations in US media.

MULTIPLE MINORITIES

Black activists spoke expansively of "black and minority" groups, but those other minorities had their own interests and concerns which did not necessarily conform to that supposed common agenda. In an age of such ethnic diversification, it made little sense to present social conflicts on a traditional black–white spectrum. Latinos could readily identify with many black grievances. They too were hit hard by mass incarceration and the Drug War, and many felt excluded from the booming high-tech industries. Yet black and Latino constituencies often differed in their choice of political candidates. Asian Americans had a vital interest in opposing policies of affirmative action in which they stood to lose most dramatically.

In many cultural debates, however, those other minorities – those varied "people of color" – often shared black concerns. Both Latinos and Asians protested white privilege in areas of culture and language, and objected to demeaning media portrayals. Also sensitive across the ethnic spectrum were issues of appropriation, of white culture absorbing or imitating cultural symbols or styles, often as fashion statements. This seemed a common manifestation of white privilege. Complaints about the white stranglehold over media and film resonated.

Like Asians and Latinos too, Native peoples have declared their stake in the ongoing culture wars, and the National Museum of the American Indian (2004) was a powerful symbol of unity and progress. Indians, in fact, secured a powerful new hold over how their history was studied and retold. Since 1990, federal legislation has placed tight restrictions on how scholars could study Indian sites and remains, so that any future research could only be carried out after extensive consultation with the various tribal authorities, and with their explicit approval. (The relevant law is the Native American Graves Protection and Repatriation Act, or NAGPRA.) This constituted a minor historical revolution, and a reversal of the demeaning attitudes of earlier decades. Appropriation has been another frequent complaint for Native peoples, in the form of white people "playing Indian." Native American activists fought a long campaign to remove what they saw as disparaging names for sports teams, especially the Washington Redskins. In 2014, the Obama administration intervened forcefully in that dispute when a federal office attempted to cancel the Redskin trademark as insulting, a decision later overturned by the US Supreme Court.

Different minorities each had a powerful stake in the culture war that now raged over historical commemoration, which in turn raised basic questions over national identity. In public debate as well as in popular culture, Americans confronted the racial themes that had dominated their history, and once-radical theories about the racist character of that history now acquired mainstream status.

MEMORY WARS

For years, activists had fought against the commemoration of bygone celebrities who to modern eyes were engaged in racism or even genocide against Native peoples. The late president Andrew Jackson was an egregious example, a nightmare figure for Native activists, yet his face appeared on the $20 bill. In 2016, the US Treasury Secretary proposed replacing him on that bill with black abolitionist heroine Harriet Tubman. In progressive cities and states, the old Columbus Day steadily evolved into Indigenous People's Day. Other controversial figures who had long been respectfully commemorated included Confederate general Nathan Bedford Forrest, a brilliant soldier who was nevertheless associated with massacres of black soldiers fighting for the Union, and who later became a founder of the Ku Klux Klan. In the new century, statues and parks named for Forrest became a special target of activists.

Black activism moved far beyond protests against specific individuals to much larger historical causes. That particularly meant the cause of the Confederacy. Beyond argument, the issue of slavery had been the primary force driving Southern secession from the Union, however much it drew in such other causes such as regional identity and states' rights. In the late nineteenth century, white Southern partisans extolled the Confederacy as a noble lost cause, an idea reflected in the building of countless memorials and statues across the South. Confederate imagery thus became a focus for regional and cultural pride. In that sense, the Confederate flag was a symbol of Southernness without any necessary racist associations and, as such, it was much used by country and rock music bands. However, it was impossible to separate that commemoration from the larger issue of race and racial oppression as the main driving force of the Confederacy and its war effort.

Activism reached a new stage following the 2015 massacre of nine worshipers at an African American church in Charleston, SC, perpetrated by a young white racist. We recall that this occurred at exactly the time of BLM protests against racial oppression by the justice system. This outbreak of flagrant white supremacism provoked a potent upsurge against any and all symbols of the Confederacy. The Confederate flag was portrayed as an unacceptable symbol of slavery and racial exploitation. Confederate flags were removed from public buildings cross the South and other parts of the country, and the attack on all things Confederate extended to the many individuals whose names were commemorated in schools or streets. This proved difficult for many conservative white people, who viewed figures like Robert E. Lee or Stonewall Jackson as symbols of military valor and personal honor. But the cultural purge was difficult to halt. Colleges and other institutions were forced to re-examine the role of slavery and segregation in their own early history and development.

While this movement had its impact across the nation it was uniquely powerful in the South, where the names and structures targeted were among the most familiar and iconic. These were the statues that stood in city squares and at the heart of college campuses. It was impossible to miss the symbolic revolution in progress, and the damning judgment thus rendered on a whole structure of national history, symbolism, and identity.

Just how far the historical campaign might progress was controversial. If Nathan Bedford Forrest could generally be agreed to be a villain unworthy of respect, did a like condemnation apply to every individual who had ever expressed support for racist or segregationist views? If so, that would potentially remove monuments to virtually every leading national celebrity prior to the 1950s, and perhaps beyond. That might apply to presidents like Woodrow Wilson, who had implemented new discriminatory policies in the federal government. One of the founders of Texas was Stephen F. Austin, after whom the state capital is named. But recently, Austin's pro-slavery views and activism have led to calls to remove even his venerated name from that city.

The nation's History Wars might also extend far beyond the contested terrain of the Civil War to the still more sensitive realm of the Revolutionary War and the nation's Founding Fathers. George Washington, Thomas Jefferson, and most other Southern Patriots had been slaveholders, usually on a large scale, while some British commanders had freed and armed slaves to use them against the revolutionaries. Should that mean a similar repudiation of those national heroes? The nation's capital is Washington DC, which is named for George Washington, and it stands in the federal District of Columbia, which commemorates Columbus. How far should the rethinking of national identity go? Is any of the national heritage immune from assault?

Challenging one construction of history also implied promoting rival visions. Rediscovering the history of slavery transformed the way the past was commemorated in cities like Charleston, and especially in the plantations that are among the most beloved tourist sites of the South. Those sites have long presented a romanticized *Gone with the Wind* image of the antebellum world, but in the past two decades plantations have increasingly depicted and restored the previously all but invisible slave quarters. One dramatic change in curation was at Thomas Jefferson's house, Monticello, where visitors are now offered detailed information about the slave Sally Hemings, with whom Jefferson probably maintained a lengthy sexual relationship.

The Civil War had been followed by the Reconstruction era, in which federal governments had tried to establish black civil rights. That movement had collapsed ignominiously, and white popular memory in the South viewed Reconstruction as a disastrous time of oppression, misgovernment, and corruption. In the new re-evaluation, Reconstruction was treated much more kindly, and in one of his last acts as president in 2017 Barack Obama established a new Reconstruction Era National Monument at Beaufort, SC. Obama's proclamation declared that this long-maligned era "was in many ways the Nation's Second Founding."

Revisionism need not only reject the past and what were for so long its mainstream interpretations. Since 2015, one of the country's cultural sensations has been the musical *Hamilton*, which uses a multi-ethnic cast to present the life of Founding Father Alexander Hamilton. The show deploys a range of musical styles that are historically associated with black or Latino traditions, including hip hop. *Hamilton* retrojects modern styles to reinterpret an old story for a new generation, and that model is certain to be followed.

Re-assessing history requires rethinking its consequences. Apart from overt white supremacists, the vast majority of Americans agree that slavery was an unmitigated evil, as was the legal segregation that was its lineal off-shoot. But what should that realization mean in practice? One emerging front in recent culture wars has been the issue of reparations, the idea that the descendants of slaves should receive official compensation for the sufferings of their ancestors. The reparations theme raises multiple problems, notably in requiring a formal and official system of racial classification and labeling. And should the reparations principle be applied beyond African Americans, to Native peoples? But, however controversial, the idea is now being treated far more seriously than ever before, and it will assuredly be heard more distinctly in future Democratic administrations. For decades to come, we can expect American history to be at the heart of the nation's racial politics.

As in the 1960s, an era of upheaval in race relations was intimately linked to turmoil in matters of gender and sexuality, and there were many parallels between the various campaigns. Just as activists struggled to redefine fundamental issues of race, so the new environment challenged the most basic definitions of how gender was constituted, and rejected familiar assumptions as grounded in systematic oppression and injustice. In its way, these changes were quite as threatening to traditional concepts of "normality" as were the movements for racial change.

12 Gender and Sexuality

When Jim Obergefell married his partner John Arthur in 2013, the union was legal in Maryland, where the ceremony was conducted, but not in their home state of Ohio. As Arthur was terminally ill, Obergefell was anxious to secure proper legal recognition so that his name would appear as partner on the death certificate. A series of cases culminated in the Supreme Court, which in 2015 decided in his favor, based on the Due Process clause of the Fourteenth Amendment (*Obergefell v. Hodges*, 576 U.S. ___ (2015)). The Court effectively legalized same-sex marriage throughout all 50 states, including some that were strongly opposed to the practice. In his majority decision, Justice Anthony Kennedy spoke movingly of marriage as a fundamental right that could not be denied, and praised full equality between homosexual and heterosexual couples. Four vigorous dissents complained that the Court was de facto making itself a supreme legislature and overruling the democratically expressed will of many Americans. Dissenters pointed out the novelty of the same-sex marriage idea, which was assuredly not known to the Founding Fathers. The *Obergefell* decision highlighted many critical debates surrounding the Court, including attitudes to the Founders' original intent, and the issue of when interpreting the law should better be understood as active law-making.

These constitutional questions were weighty enough, but the decision also involved issues in the structure of society that were still more fundamental – issues of morality, concepts of sexuality and gender, individual rights and liberties, and the nature of the family. Concepts of gender especially were in rapid flux. Americans in these years were living through a heady series of cultural revolutions of a scale and rapidity unprecedented in the nation's history. Although the broad issues at stake were anything but new, the speed and thoroughness made this a startling and, for many, a troubling time. Time and again, in so many contexts, we are tempted to describe the changes with a phrase like "once unthinkable."

WOMEN AND GENDER

Progress in women's equality had been a central fact of American life since the 1960s, but those changes now accelerated mightily. The principle of gender equality became as unassailable as that of racial equality.

The central and enduring role of Hillary Clinton demonstrates major political advances for women, but that was only one example of a great many. The conservative Republican leaders most closely associated with the Tea Party movement were both women, Sarah Palin and Michele Bachmann, and we have already noted the powerful position in successive administrations of Condoleezza Rice and Loretta Lynch. After the 2016 presidential election, Senator Elizabeth Warren was among several women regarded as likely Democratic candidates in the forthcoming 2020 contest. The number of women elected to the US Congress grew from 23 in 1980 to 75 in 2000, and 118 by 2018. That current figure is less than a quarter of the overall total, but it represented a major advance on earlier years. From 2007, Democratic Party leader Nancy Pelosi served as the first woman Speaker of the House of Representatives. One of several groups backing women candidates and causes is Emily's List, the title taken from the acronym "Early Money is Like Yeast."

Future historians may well regard the 2004 presidential election as a symbolic watershed. Each party nominated two individuals, respectively for the presidency and the vice presidency, and as in every contest but one since the foundation of the republic, all four candidates were heterosexual, non-Latino, white men. The only exception to that rule had been in 1984, when the Democrats nominated Geraldine Ferraro as vice president. Few commentators remarked on the composition of the two tickets in 2004, but in retrospect that was the last time to date that all candidates were so homogeneous in race and gender, and it might well be the last of its kind for the foreseeable future.

Women occupied so many senior roles in business, media, and public institutions that it is impossible to list them. One stellar example was billionaire corporate figure Sheryl Sandberg, who serves as Chief Operating Officer of Facebook. Her bestselling 2013 book *Lean In* at once analyses the position of women in business and government, and offers women practical guidance in leadership and advancement. One of the unsuccessful candidates for the Republican presidential nomination in 2016 was Carly Fiorina, the former Chief Executive Officer of Hewlett Packard, and the first woman to serve as CEO of a Fortune Top 20 company. Throughout society, women's leadership became normal, and completely uncontroversial.

In terms of visibility to ordinary people, the rise of women in religious organizations has been singularly important. Religions of all kinds have been shaken or transformed beyond recognition by the rise of new sensibilities involving gender and sexual identity. In the mid-1970s, ordaining women was a revolutionary and deeply controversial step for most denominations.

Today, it is absolutely commonplace for many if not all traditions, Christian and Jewish, as women serve as priests, pastors, and rabbis, and at all levels of power and seniority (the Roman Catholic Church is the most conspicuous holdout). Among other milestones, in 2006 Katharine Jefferts Schori became the first woman to serve as Presiding Bishop of the Episcopal Church. In the world of higher education, women came to outnumber men as faculty in many disciplines, and many occupy very senior positions. In 2007, historian Drew Gilpin Faust became president of Harvard University. By 2017, women represented 56 percent of college students, up from 42 percent as recently as the 1970s. The scale of that shift made it ever-more controversial for scholarly gatherings to organize programs or panels with all-male participants, and those that did were roundly mocked on social media.

The struggle for full legal equality in gender matters concentrated on the US armed forces, which had been so central to the fight for racial desegregation in the 1940s. In both eras, it was a powerful argument to say that some particular group deserved full respect because its members were saving their country faithfully at the risk of their lives. Women have long served in the armed forces, but only gradually were they admitted to active combat duty. That prohibition weakened in the post-2001 wars in which women served as pilots of aircraft and helicopters, and repeatedly found themselves engaged in savage fighting. In 2005, a female sergeant won a prestigious Silver Star decoration for her actions in a battle outside Baghdad. In 2013, Defense Secretary Leon Panetta ended the formal prohibition on women serving in combat, although the process of implementation took some years. Women have subsequently passed a series of symbolic and well-publicized milestones, including graduation from the army's elite Ranger School. By 2017, the US Marine Corps admitted the first woman infantry officer in that service.

The achievements of high-profile women pioneers coexisted with fundamental shifts in the lives of ordinary women, and a major restructuring of families from the norm prevailing in the mid-twentieth century. Those changes included the sharp decline of the "standard" nuclear family unit, as mapped by the number of people living alone, cohabiting without marriage, and also bearing children outside marriage. Changes in employment patterns, as well as new sexual attitudes, led to a lengthy delay in the formation of families and households, resulting in what has been called a prolongation of adolescence far beyond anything known in earlier decades. Taken together, those shifts transformed familiar assumptions about the natural social role of women as wives and mothers. Women were not only in the workforce, but many were in positions of authority and earning high incomes.

Women's legal disabilities progressively vanished, and concepts of women's rights expanded enormously. Abortion continued to be very divisive, and conservative states passed stringent restrictions. Violence against abortion facilities and providers also continued, albeit on a much smaller scale than in the Clinton years. In 2009, a doctor was assassinated in Wichita, KS. Generally, the US Supreme Court strictly maintained the core idea of a right to abortion, and struck down laws that were felt to infringe on this by imposing an undue burden. These included so-called partial-birth abortion laws, which were overturned in 2007 (*Gonzales v. Carhart*, 550 U.S. 124 (2007)). In 2016, the Court rejected recent Texas laws in the case of *Whole Woman's Health v. Hellerstedt* in broad terms that firmly reasserted the constitutional right to abortion. If not ending controversy, the *Hellerstedt* decision ended conservative hopes of smashing liberal policies.

RETHINKING SEXUAL BEHAVIOR

Sweeping changes affected gender interactions in everyday life. Attitudes to proper sexual behavior and conduct were revolutionized, in what almost constituted a reversal of the libertarian atmosphere of the 1960s and 1970s. At that time, popular culture had reflected the widespread extolling of the freedom of sexual behavior, including casual sexual encounters, while minimizing possible harms. Any opinions to the contrary were dismissed as puritanical or Victorian.

Yet even in that era, there had been dissenting voices. Feminist protests attacked the rhetoric of the sexual revolution as justifying male sexual excess and irresponsibility while underplaying damage to women and children. A very different feminist model of sexual interactions placed much greater stress on the menace of sexual exploitation, and depicted rape and sexual abuse as integral to the maintenance of a system of patriarchal rule. Far from being rare events, acts of rape and molestation were extremely common, affecting a large proportion of the population. They were also much more harmful and destructive than had been supposed. Anti-rape campaigns popularized the term "survivor" for the victims of such assaults, stressing the life-threatening nature of the events. In interpreting such events, therapists borrowed the military concept of post-traumatic stress disorder, PTSD, suggesting the lifelong impact of involuntary sexual encounters or domestic violence. Controversial at the time, those ideas gained increasing support in the following decades, as expressed in much stricter laws concerning rape, harassment, and abuse. Since 2000, once-radical attitudes about sexual behavior became mainstreamed. Much of the older rhetoric about sexual liberation now looked like an apology for abuse and harassment.

Although rape was universally agreed to represent a severe crime, the lines defining acceptable sexual interaction were more blurred. As we have seen, the category of sexual harassment expanded following the Clarence Thomas hearings of 1991. In the new century, the scope of harassment and abuse was much more broadly defined, and seen as demanding proactive investigation and intervention. Male behaviors and propositioning that would once have been regarded as normal or, at worst, ill-mannered, came to be seen as aggressive, abusive, and subject to legal sanctions. What an earlier generation had viewed as light-hearted banter, another saw as creating a hostile climate for women and an intolerable work environment. Used in this sense, terms like "climate" and "environment" appeared in news reports at least as frequently as in their standard scientific sense. Actions were particularly likely to be seen as abusive when they occurred between individuals with different degrees of power – when, for instance, a senior male harassed a staff person or intern.

One key element in the change was Title IX, the name for a section of the US Education Amendments of 1972, which provided the basis for a revolutionary reassessment of sexual mores. Title IX was originally intended to forbid sexual discrimination in colleges and universities. Specifically, no person "shall, on the basis of sex, be excluded from participation in, be denied the benefits of, or be subjected to discrimination under any education program or activity receiving federal financial assistance." Although this sounds technical and legalistic, the scope of that clause – which initially transformed equal access to sports activity in higher education – grew mightily through the years. Soon it expanded to prohibit any behavior that might be interpreted (however broadly) as constituting harassment, discrimination, or bias. This forced universities and colleges to crack down vigorously on sexual misconduct.

The expansive approach to Title IX received vital support from the Obama administration. In 2011, a "Dear Colleague" letter instructed colleges on the duties expected under that law, which included the appointment of a Title IX coordinator with the appropriate bureaucratic structure to hear and investigate complaints. Such hearings would proceed on the civil justice system of deciding on the preponderance of the evidence, rather the criminal court standard of proof beyond a reasonable doubt. These procedures were criticized for imposing an alternative system of justice and punishment without the protections that courts conventionally granted to the accused. The Title IX system gained support from a series of notorious scandals, commonly involving heavily male-dominated institutions such as fraternities or sports teams, which had a subculture of sexual molestation and abuse. Reflecting the passionate public interest in sports, such cases attracted vast media attention and public interest. Some such cases proved unsubstantiated, and a case involving the Duke University lacrosse team in 2006 resulted in the lengthy pursuit of false charges against innocent individuals. Other scandals rested on firmer foundations, demonstrating not just the existence of "rape cultures" but the systematic misbehavior of college administrations in tolerating or trivializing abuses.

As part of the new Title IX regime, higher education institutions organized extensive training for all students and employees. In the process, the world of higher education acknowledged and enforced codes of proper sexual interaction and explicit consent that had hitherto been advocated only by militant feminists. As ever more young Americans passed through colleges and universities, Title IX reforms spread feminist definitions of proper and improper sexual behavior through the wider society. Among other things, that meant an uncompromising new emphasis on explicit sexual consent as a precondition of intimacy. Reinforcing calls for reform was the scandal surrounding the presidential candidacy of Donald Trump in 2016. As we will see in Chapter 14, his victory was almost derailed by tapes in which he boasted of aggressive sexual advances to women, framed in explicit terms.

The highly visible world of show business and entertainment helped to mainstream the new attitudes. Hollywood film-making had always been notorious for sexual exploitation, with the casting couch a well-known institution. Victims of harassment or coercion were unlikely to complain against powerful offenders, and if they did their protests would virtually never lead to official intervention. In this regard, Hollywood retained the social patterns that prevailed in conventional society some decades before. Matters changed suddenly in the Trump era. In 2017, scandal overwhelmed the powerful producer Harvey Weinstein, one of the driving forces in creating the modern US film industry. Through the years, he had often been accused of harassment and even rape, but had used his power to silence or buy off accusers. Such incidents now became public, destroying Weinstein's business, and in the process creating a new awareness of exploitation.

As the Weinstein case progressed, many other prominent celebrity women spoke out publicly about their own experiences. Women began a social media campaign under the hashtag #MeToo, inviting others to come forward. The high visibility of protesters, together with their excellent access to media events, ensured that the campaign gained national and indeed global prominence. An explosion of accusations destroyed the reputations of many celebrities, sometimes for acts committed decades previously. As on college campuses, the definition of abuse expanded from outright rape to include unwelcome propositioning and advances. The #MeToo movement spread to many other fields, including corporations, churches, and educational institutions.

In 2018, activism over abuse and harassment was further mobilized by the Supreme Court confirmation hearing of Brett Kavanaugh, who at first blush appeared to be an ideal candidate for the judicial post. But the allegation arose that at the age of 17, in 1982, he had forced unwanted sexual attentions on a woman named Christine Blasey Ford, who was then 15. Other allegations also surfaced, although some at least were determined to be false. The Kavanaugh incident ignited months of national controversy, raising critical issues of determining the real nature of long-past sexual encounters, the credibility of witnesses, and the shifting limits of sexual consent. The case was also a perfect illustration of changing sexual norms, in the sense that in earlier decades such charges would never have seen the light of day, and even if they had would have been dismissed as teenage excesses irrelevant to a public career. After extremely harsh debate, the Senate eventually confirmed Kavanaugh, but the affair left a lasting political legacy. Feminists saw Kavanaugh as a predator who escaped punishment for his crimes. Conservatives (including many women) spoke in terms of a witch hunt.

PROSTITUTION AND TRAFFICKING

Changes in attitudes to harassment and rape were revolutionary. Less sensational, but quite far-reaching, were new and much more restrictive attitudes toward prostitution. Earlier libertarian attitudes treated this offense as a harmless victimless crime, and urged decriminalization. In practice, police largely tolerated prostitution, including the quite blatant activities of "massage parlors" and frank advertising in community newspapers. In the new century, that advertising expanded successfully to the internet, where sites like Backpage.com offered an impressive variety of intimate services in communities of all sizes, especially major cities. The Craigslist site gave users the opportunity to make consensual sexual contacts, some of which were for money. If not explicitly approved, prostitution was de facto legalized, provided it did not involve underage victims. Moral conservatives were horrified, as were feminists. But as with other forms of sexual behavior, new and far more restrictive standards were soon imposed.

The new anti-vice campaign grew indirectly from the fact of mass immigration. Particularly in some nations, criminal entrepreneurs recruited women who wished to come to the US and demanded that they repay their passage through forced sexual servitude, in conditions amounting to prolonged slavery. Although police and courts received little public support when they struck at regular voluntary prostitution, the rhetoric of combatting sexual trafficking and modern-day slavery proved much more successful. Police packaged antivice campaigns as measures against human trafficking, even though the great majority of sex workers were in no sense coerced, nor did they fit the standard narrative of impoverished recent immigrants. Nevertheless, police actions achieved an impact, and a degree of public approval, not seen since the years before the sexual revolution of the 1960s and 1970s.

The new policies also effected radical changes in online behavior. The permissive atmosphere exploited by prostitutes grew out of the 1996 Communications Decency Act, which immunized online services from any civil liability growing out of acts by users. New legislation removed this protection, allowing firms like Backpage.com to face legal action for advertisements they hosted. The laws bore the emotive titles of the Stop Enabling Sex Traffickers Act (SESTA) and Allow States and Victims to Fight Online Sex Trafficking Act (FOSTA). At a stroke, in 2018, FOSTA-SESTA all but killed above-ground online advertising of the sex industry. Like many such laws, the new package had serious unintended consequences. Lacking the ability to control and screen traffic, many prostitutes were forced to find new and more perilous ways of contacting clients.

PORNOGRAPHY

In many ways, then, social changes in these years reversed the sexual libertinism of a few decades earlier. But in some areas that earlier sexual revolution achieved a surprising triumph, due entirely to technology rather than to courts or legislatures.

Through much of US history, censorship battles had been central fronts in the culture wars, and courts had agonized over the limits of censorship in sexual matters. Just what were the limits of the indecent or obscene, and when did materials become outright pornographic, and thus subject to condemnation? The boundaries of acceptable sexuality had expanded massively during the 1970s, when female nudity was commonly depicted on the cinema screen and on cable television. The new feminist consciousness placed some limits on images condemned as gratuitous exploitation. But in wider terms, the coming of the internet effectively ended the censorship wars by making what was once considered hard-core pornography available to anyone with computer access, of any age, and usually at no cost. Given their greater familiarity with new technologies, younger teenagers probably had much better access to this material than did adults. The pornography industry contemplated enthusiastically the emerging technology of virtual reality.

Restrictions were not wholly lacking, as child pornography was harshly penalized, but much of the adult material that was now easily available would have been grossly illegal in 1970, and might well have provoked attempts at prosecution as late as the mid-1980s. Significantly in light of the wider feminist victories, pornography had long been a target of women's rights activists, who had campaigned for restrictions just as fiercely as moral traditionalists and religious crusaders. They achieved their goals thoroughly in the case of prostitution, but in this other area the power of technology proved too great. America's long-running censorship wars fizzled to a conclusion early in the twenty-first century, and the sexual libertarians won.

GAY RIGHTS

In the case of gender politics, attitudes once seen as extreme became thoroughly normalized. If anything, attitudes to homosexuality changed even more swiftly and comprehensively. Again, as in the case of women's rights, the changes were not entirely new and had their origins in the upsurge of reform movements in the late 1960s. But the pace of change accelerated unimaginably, culminating fully in the Obama years.

As recently as 2000, 14 states – including most of the South – had laws on their books prohibiting homosexual conduct, usually under the general label of sodomy. These statutes were now progressively dismantled. In the 1986 case of *Bowers v. Hardwick*, the Supreme Court refused to accept that homosexual conduct was protected under the constitutional right of privacy. But that was overturned by the 2003 decision in *Lawrence v. Texas* (539 U.S. 558 (2003)), which struck down existing sodomy laws and legalized same-sex sexual activity across the nation. Over the following years, a growing range of laws went far beyond mere decriminalization to prohibiting discrimination on grounds of sexual identity.

Such changes faced real opposition. Many Americans were happy to approve legalizing private conduct between consenting adults, but that did not necessarily imply granting full legal equality. Religious groups were especially likely to oppose sweeping reforms. But gay activists skillfully drew on various strategies to legitimize their cause. Although scientific findings did not alone drive change, some proved useful rhetorically in establishing the idea that homosexuality was an unavoidable predestined condition rather than a voluntary choice or an elective lifestyle. In the 1990s, some chromosome linkage studies of families with gay members popularized misleading talk of a "gay gene."

Also influential was the language of civil rights, drawing analogies to the black struggle in earlier years. Gay groups successfully drew on that older heritage, which had struggled against multiple legal constraints, including public discrimination and the prohibition of interracial marriage. Also critical were the means by which the country had established black civil rights, through the robust exercise of federal power over the states. In some instances, judicial activism had taken decisions that legislatures were unwilling or unable to accomplish as a necessary means to achieve the larger goals of constitutional rights. Framing the gay movement as a civil rights struggle appealed to a mainstream public that was deeply sympathetic to those racial precedents. That example influenced Anthony Kennedy and other key members of the US Supreme Court, who from the mid-1990s favored gay rights in several major decisions.

As in the case of women, the issue of gay service in the US military was a crucial marker of equality. In 1993, President Bill Clinton attempted to admit openly gay personnel to the services, but the opposition he encountered was so passionate as to thwart his effort. He eventually settled on a policy of "Don't Ask, Don't Tell," a Defense Department directive under which authorities were forbidden from actively investigating or exposing gay personnel who kept their sexuality clandestine. The compromise satisfied nobody, and pressure grew until the era of Barack Obama. In 2011, the administration canceled the policy, allowing gays and lesbians to serve openly. In 2016, Obama extended the new openness to transgender personnel. The same year, Eric Fanning became the first openly gay man to serve as Secretary of the Army. Obama's administration also marked a conspicuous expansion of the gay presence in public life. In 2013, Wisconsin Democrat Tammy Baldwin became the first openly gay person elected to the US Senate, serving besides a total of six gay Representatives in the House. That House roster grew by an additional four in 2018.

Churches and religious institutions were a critical battlefield for gay rights. Since the 1970s, new attitudes to homosexuality had profoundly divided Christian churches, chiefly because the behavior was explicitly condemned in scripture, and had long been condemned as sinful. Changes in policy therefore demanded a fundamental rethinking of doctrine, and of a question as basic as the nature of proper authority in faith. Progressive views made greatest progress in the so-called mainline – the socially respectable and highly liberal bodies which still together claimed tens of millions of adherents. By the start of the century, some of these churches had gradually accepted openly gay clergy living in non-celibate relationships, although advancing such individuals to the rank of bishop remained divisive. In the Episcopal Church, the key moment occurred in 2004 with the ordination of Gene Robinson as Bishop of New Hampshire, although he was living with a male partner. That event drove some Episcopal churches into open schism, which ultimately resulted in the creation of a new alternative Anglican Church of North America. The ordination attracted protests from other churches within the worldwide Anglican Communion, which threatened to project the religious schism onto a worldwide scale. Even so, other gay ordinations followed shortly in the Episcopal Church.

Other mainline churches were not far behind. In 2010, the Evangelical Lutheran Church in America became the largest Protestant church in the US to accept non-celibate gay clergy, and in 2013 it acquired its first openly gay bishop. In 2016, the United Methodist Church consecrated as bishop Karen Oliveto, a lesbian living in a partnered relationship, although this decision was soon overturned by the church's highest court. This case demonstrates continuing dissent on gay issues, but most of the mainline churches considered the possibility of approving same-sex marriages, or at least offering blessings.

However controversial the situation in mainline churches, gay causes had made far less progress in other Christian bodies. Those included such numerous institutions as the Roman Catholics, Southern Baptists, and Mormons, all of which taught the sinfulness of homosexual behavior and were nowhere close to the formal recognition of gay clergy (Catholics were well used to the fact that many clergy were gay in orientation, although this could not be openly acknowledged). Most evangelical and Pentecostal churches were equally traditional in their teaching, although many in practice accepted gay followers. Such holdouts were so significant because they made those churches bastions of electoral support for anti-gay rights measures during political controversies.

Jews had a similar spectrum of opinion, with liberal schools of thought like Reform and Reconstructionist Judaism being much more welcoming to openly gay members and rabbis, while other traditions were more reluctant. Even so, openly gay and lesbian rabbis became a familiar phenomenon in the first decade of the century. In 2014, a lesbian became president of the Reconstructionist Rabbinical College and Jewish Reconstructionist Communities. The following year, a lesbian rabbi from the Reform tradition became president of the prestigious and old-established Central Conference of American Rabbis.

GAY PEOPLE IN MEDIA

While these reforms and advances were widely covered in national news, cinema and television disseminated new attitudes to a mass audience. Gay characters had long been a feature of films, although portrayals prior to the 1980s tended to be a sensitive matter. Gay activists frequently complained that even when gay characters or environments appeared in film, they were often depicted as pathological and violent, and an old cliché demanded that gay characters tended to die at the end of films. One startling breakthrough occurred in 2005 with the Western, *Brokeback Mountain*. Beyond its explicit gay romance, the film was notable as a major production starring two heart-throb stars, Heath Ledger and Jake Gyllenhaal. The film was both a critical and a popular hit, winning three Academy Awards as well as many lesser prizes. Over the following decade, gay and transgender themes proliferated in cinema, while openly gay film-makers and technical figures were prominent prizewinners. The 2016 film *Moonlight* told the story of a gay African American coming of age, and the film won three Academy Awards. The range of gay-themed films nominated for, or awarded, Oscars in 2018 led to that year's ceremony being characterized as "the gayest Oscars ever."

Television contributed to changing the social climate. As in film, gay characters featured sporadically from the 1970s onwards, but usually in marginal or token roles. As we have seen previously, cable television was crucial to pushing the boundaries of taste and expectations and offering material that at the time seemed truly daring. One factor was the import of British material, from a country far more liberated on gay issues. The pioneering British show *Queer as Folk* appeared on the US Showtime network from 2000 through 2005, and Showtime also offered the lesbian-themed *The L Word* (2004–2009). Even more significant in terms of reaching a mass audience were network shows, following the pathbreaking situation comedy *Will and Grace* (NBC 1998–2006), and since 2010 the number of shows and characters has simply proliferated too much for individual comments or listings. Through these years, too, one of the most popular live shows played across the country was the musical *Rent*, which premiered in 1996. The show focused on bohemian and gay life in the ramshackle New York City of the AIDS era. No less striking than the use of gay characters in these various productions was the portrayal of anyone who expressed any anti-gay views, and who were depicted as boorish, ignorant, or violent. The media offer zero tolerance to homophobia.

The normalization of gay themes and characters provoked remarkably little public protest. That transformation both reflected a shift in public attitudes and supplied further arguments for the removal of any remaining prejudices. The mainstreaming of homosexual behavior, and its attendant cultures, was well symbolized by the immense popularity of Gay Pride events in cities across the nation. Shorn of their more revolutionary implications, and often with a corporate and even family-friendly aspect, such events became a standard part of the urban year. One negative consequence of the new toleration was a near-collapse of many aspects of the old gay subculture. Lacking the requirement to supply the needs of what was once a despised or marginalized subculture, many historic gay institutions faded or vanished, including most avowedly gay bookstores and cinemas. Meanwhile, gay themes entered the commonplace historical narrative. In 2016, with virtually no controversy, President Obama declared New York's Stonewall Inn a National Historical Site. The US Navy proposed to name a ship after assassinated gay activist Harvey Milk.

SAME-SEX MARRIAGE

In the present century, same-sex marriage has been the most contentious issue in the gay rights struggle. So broadly accepted is the idea today that its incendiary quality requires some explanation. For gay activists, moves to true equality could never be complete without that step, as achieving full "equality" became an effective index of social and sexual liberalization. Opposition to that idea was portrayed as a form of homophobia or prejudice, comparable to the racism that in earlier generations had tried to ban interracial marriages.

But the reality was more complex. Many Americans, whether religious believers or not, favored removing all civil and criminal disabilities suffered by homosexuals, but they placed marriage in a special category. Marriage, in that view, was fundamentally and essentially connected to the male–female bond, and to the begetting and support of children. Many heterosexual marriages, of course, did not involve childbearing, but they still fell within that general framework. Those ideas were held still more absolutely by many religious believers, Christian and Jewish, on the basis of clear scriptural authority as well as long tradition. Marriage was a heterosexual institution, and even to speak of "same-sex marriage" was inappropriate, even a parody of the real institution. As the debate progressed, opponents of same-sex marriage showed themselves ever-more willing to contemplate forms of civil union that offered all the legal advantages of matrimony but resisted being drawn into that ultimate territory.

Prior to the late 1990s, same-sex marriage scarcely even existed on the agenda of radical activists, and certainly not of most politicians. Al Gore had supported the Defense of Marriage Act (DOMA) which limited the concepts of "marriage" and "spouse" to heterosexual couples, and he reiterated that view in the 2000 debates between presidential candidates. Marriage, he said, "is a sacred institution between a man and a woman." George W. Bush agreed, though he supported some kinds of civil union. Even so, the fact that the candidates even faced a question on the topic would have stunned observers of any previous election. As late as 2008, Obama said, "I believe marriage is between a man and a woman. I am not in favor of gay marriage," although that contradicted some earlier statements of his. Not until 2013 did Hillary Clinton speak out in favor of same-sex marriage.

In 2003, the Supreme Judicial Court of Massachusetts ruled that the state was required to grant full rights to gay marriage (*Goodridge v. Dept. of Public Health*, 798 N.E.2d 941). Thereafter, legalized same-sex marriage spread quickly across the nation. Overwhelmingly, this occurred through decisions by courts rather than legislators, and when the issue was out to the electorate responses were mixed. Even in liberal California, voters in 2000 approved a proposition banning same-sex marriage, and by an overwhelming margin of 61–39. A subsequent vote in 2008 rejected same-sex unions by a smaller, but still convincing, 52–48 majority. Through the first decade of the century, opinion surveys generally showed majorities of Americans opposed to same-sex marriage, usually by 20 points or more. That hostile proportion shrank steadily until 2011, when supporters began to constitute a majority. By 2015, support was running around 60 percent. This opinion was of course unequally distributed, and major portions of the South remained strongly opposed.

Matters then changed fast, as courts moved into the vanguard. In 2013, in *US v. Windsor*, the US Supreme Court overturned key portions of DOMA, so that the federal government would have to recognize gay marriages approved by particular states (*United States v. Windsor*, 570 U.S. 744 (2013)). The *Obergefell* decision marked the culmination of this story, granting same-sex couples the right to marry anywhere in the country, and overturning all state laws to the contrary. Arguably even more revolutionary in its implications, although rarely acknowledged in public debate, same-sex couples also gained the right to adopt children. Further Supreme Court decisions in 2016–2017 removed the final obstacles to LGBT adoptions and to discrimination in issuing birth certificates.

"Marriage equality" has become part of the social landscape. By 2017, 62 percent of Americans approved of same-sex marriage, and the figure is far higher among young adults. Social conservatives acknowledged that reversing the process was hopeless, and the focus of their activity then shifted to protecting the rights of those who dissented from the new normality – for instance, bakers who for religious reasons refused to provide cakes for same-sex weddings. Although such cases raised acute issues of religious freedom, the larger question of same-sex unions was settled. Churches and religious institutions began the process of debating whether and how to accept the new reality in their practices, through solemnizing same-sex marriages.

TRANSGENDER FRONTIERS

So accepted was the principle of gay equality that activists felt free to advance another cause that again was once on the far fringes of radical thought, namely that of transgendered people.

Concepts of gender change assumed that gender identity was constructed, rather than a simple natural biological phenomenon. "Sex change" surgery – gender reassignment – had become more commonplace since the 1960s, and famous cases publicized the idea that some individuals overwhelmingly felt themselves to belong to a different gender to that which they were assigned at birth. In the 2010s the rights of transgendered people became a frontier of sexual liberalism, as part of the larger LGBTQ cause. (That acronym has morphed and expanded its name through the years, and currently denotes Lesbian, Gay, Bisexual, Transgender, and Queer and/or Questioning.) In 2014, the federal Justice Department determined that the prohibition on sex discrimination in Title VII of the 1964 Civil Rights Act extended protection to transgendered workers. The transgender issue reached a mass audience through the intense media attention devoted to the case of former athlete Bruce Jenner, who had been a heroic figure in the athletic world of the 1970s. In 2015, Bruce Jenner came out publicly as a "trans woman" under the name Caitlyn Jenner.

Although statistics are uncertain, one commonly cited estimate suggests that 1.4 million Americans identify as transgender, but that is an extreme maximum figure, and does not mean that all have undergone a full surgical transition. But the issue went far beyond the rights of a tiny minority, raising as it did fundamental questions about the definition of gender. Gender, in this progressive view, was not just a simple male–female binary, but rather represented a spectrum. According to the emerging approach, a person's true gender identity was an absolute and unquestionable fact that the individual came to recognize, likely from an early age. And if gender was constructed, then it could be remolded by appropriate changes in social structures and arrangements. From a progressive viewpoint, this raised the possibility of fundamental shifts in concepts of human nature. That in turn appalled conservatives.

The transgender worldview was deeply counter-intuitive to a mainstream audience that had only recently come to accept the view that gay people were not mentally ill. Large sections of that mainstream did not accept that gender was so fluid or indeterminate, or that a person's impression of "true" identity should be taken so absolutely. That was especially true when activists spoke of young children identifying with some other gender, and requiring the highly interventionist treatment and surgery necessary to "transition." Most upsetting was the speed with which this ideology was achieving orthodox status. What seemed to many ordinary people to be obvious ideas of human nature were now scorned as the dated ideology of "gender binarism." Around 2006, activists imported the word "cisgender" into English to denote those who unquestioningly accepted their given gender identity.

New ideas had policy consequences. If a man originally named John Doe transitioned to become a woman named Jane, the progressive view was that this was her true and authentic identity and she should be acknowledged as Jane in all respects, including gaining access to the appropriate bathroom facilities. She should also be described by the female pronoun, or else by another descriptor of her choice, without external compulsion. In 2016, these approaches received powerful official sanction from the federal government, when the Education and Justice Departments issued a joint letter prescribing the proper treatment of transgender pupils in public schools. Among other things, this required schools to allow students to use the bathroom facilities of their choice. The letter grounded this policy in Title IX regulations, although that original law had never envisaged providing for transgendered people. Local jurisdictions offered further legal support for the cause. In 2016, New York City demanded that employers "use an individual's preferred name, pronoun and title (e.g., Ms./Mrs.) regardless of the individual's sex assigned at birth, anatomy, gender, medical history, appearance, or the sex indicated on the individual's identification."

Having lost the war over the basic gay rights struggles, conservative efforts shifted to seeking to prevent the seemingly inexorable march of transgender issues. As in so many earlier morality campaigns, the critical opportunity came with perceived threats to children. Conservative critics raised the prospect of men asserting a female identity in order to gain access to girls' toilets or showers for purposes of voyeurism or sexual assault. Responding to such fears, conservative state legislatures passed measures focused on the bathroom access issue. In the process they encountered fierce opposition from liberal critics who presented the safeguards as blatant homophobia and "transphobia," a wholly new concept to most Americans. (Only in 2013 did the word appear in the *Oxford English Dictionary*.) Intense battle raged over a "bathroom bill" passed in 2017 in North Carolina, which faced potentially disastrous boycott threats from conference planners, business organizations, and sports teams. The US Justice Department intervened to invoke federal civil rights law in order to prevent discrimination against transgendered people. North Carolina was forced to repeal its law, and other attempts to pass similar measures failed elsewhere, notably in Texas.

A widespread media consensus presented the offending bills as harshly homophobic. By presenting conservatives as obsessed with bathrooms and toilet functions, activists successfully discredited and mocked their objections. The affair suggests the thorough acceptance of quite radical agendas about sexual orientation, both by the media and by a substantial majority of educated opinion.

In 1996, the US Congress passed its Defense of Marriage Act by crushing majorities – 342 to 67 in the House, 85 to 14 in the Senate. Just two decades later, anyone in public life who reasserted the basic principles of that law would place themselves at the extreme fringes of conservative opinion, and would likely exclude themselves altogether from political life. That is a gauge of the revolution in concepts of sexuality and gender that had occurred in that time. Key debates of the culture wars ended as the liberal or progressive side gained such a decisive victory that its opponents could scarcely even mount a credible last stand. Meanwhile, Barack Obama ended his presidential term with extraordinarily high approval ratings. In so many matters, the heart of American cultural politics had moved dramatically to the cultural and progressive Left. But that did not mark the end of the nation's long-running culture wars, which now raged on multiple fronts both new and familiar. Those wars had not ended: rather the battle lines were reshaped and rethought.

13 Culture Wars and Campus Wars

As Halloween approached in 2015, Yale was one of many universities that advised its students how to avoid choosing costumes that might offend anyone's sensitivities, for instance by exploiting racial or sexual stereotypes. In response, the academic couple in charge of one of Yale's residential undergraduate colleges issued a thoughtful email justifying the legitimacy and even usefulness of acts or symbols that some might find offensive, when presented as parody or satire. Erika Christakis urged that potential conflicts should be dealt with through rational discussion, and might actually serve as effective teaching moments. This call for tolerance sparked an uproar, as students *en masse* confronted and harangued her husband, Nicholas Christakis, shrieking abuse in ugly moments that circulated widely on video. Protesters aggressively scorned any suggestion that the matters at issue should be the subject of intellectual disagreement, demanding instead that colleges should offer their students emotional comfort and security. The couple was forced to resign from Yale. Together with many similar incidents in these years, the Yale affair demonstrated how very radical views had become entrenched on many liberal or progressive college campuses. In other events, speakers who were deemed controversial or insensitive were silenced by what critics denounced as the state of mob rule that appeared to exist on many campuses.

But the passionate reaction against such outbreaks also demonstrated the vigorous opposition to extremism from traditional-minded liberals and centrists as well as conservatives. Such cases detonated national controversies over rights to free speech on campuses. They also focused a familiar and influential conservative theme, namely the gulf that separated elites from the values of ordinary patriotic Americans, who rejected the hare-brained excesses emanating from the ivory tower as much as from the federal government. Those anti-elite and anti-establishment beliefs would become starkly apparent during the election year of 2016, and in the new stress on populism. In the much-quoted words of Andrew Breitbart, "Politics is downstream from culture." On the surface, the headlong changes in social and cultural attitudes occurred with so little opposition as to suggest that the culture wars had ended with the effective surrender of the conservative side. But as campus battles suggest, such struggles still raged, and commonly focused on the balance between majoritarian demands and individual rights.

CONSERVATISM REDEFINED

The story of conservatism in these years is paradoxical. In electoral terms, the midterm contests of 2010 and 2014 marked historic triumphs for a Republican Party strongly identified with cultural conservatism, and in 2016 the party won the presidency in addition to both Houses of Congress. Republican hegemony was still firmer at state level. Yet any assessment of the culture wars would declare a near-total liberal victory. When Pat Buchanan declared that conflict in 1992, he delineated the key battles to which he summoned conservative activism, and in subsequent years conservatives lost virtually all these battles. Buchanan's speech at the Republican National Convention had not even mentioned same-sex marriage, which in 1992 was nowhere on the horizon, yet by 2015 it was the law of the land. From a traditionalist perspective this was not just the slippery slope to some worse horror, it was in itself the foot of the mountain. The sudden and triumphant war against Confederate symbols was little less stunning, and the effective legalization of hard-core pornography was painful. In light of the multiple social revolutions in progress, it is startling to see how little impact those issues made at any level during the election year of 2016. No serious candidate urged banning same-sex marriage or returning Confederate symbolism to public places, while only extreme diehards contemplated attacking pornography as a public health danger.

The absence of effective opposition demands explanation. Partly, conservatives found it difficult to oppose policies established by the courts, which overruled even the vigorous protests of legislatures. More broadly, activists successfully framed causes like same-sex marriage in terms of individual rights and libertarianism, the rights of ordinary people to pursue their own lives and lifestyles without dictates from the state or the larger community. Such rhetoric was particularly appealing given the rise of individualism in a society in which technology so actively favored decentralization, autonomy, and choice. Such trends boded ill for conservatives who had once defined themselves as the "moral majority."

Religious changes also had their impact, as conservatives suffered from the systematic weakening of morality arguments grounded in religious belief.

Since their heyday in the 1980s, religious-based political campaigns had inspired growing revulsion at the worldly and cynical nature of some churches and leaders. That trend has been aggravated by repeated scandals, commonly involving sexual misbehavior. By far the most important and numerous religious institution in the United States is the Roman Catholic Church, which still in the 1980s exercised potent political influence in many regions and in many areas of life. It was gravely weakened by the progressive exposure of sexual abuse scandals involving clergy, which reached critical new intensity in 2002. Thereafter, many dioceses had to devote their primary efforts to fighting litigation, which was financially ruinous. Even if Catholic leaders had the resources to engage in cultural warfare, liberals could easily denounce them for their hypocrisy in speaking out on sexual matters, especially where children were concerned.

Although the United States is still far removed from secularization on a European scale, there has been a sizable growth of people declaring themselves as professing no religion, of being "Nones." That especially affects millennials, the generation born between 1980 and 2000. Between 1986 and 2016, the proportion of young adults (aged 18–29 years) claiming no religious affiliation grew from 10 to 39 percent. Together with outright atheists and secularists, the Nones have been consistent supporters of liberal-left causes, especially in matters of sexuality and gender.

LIBERTY AND MORALITY

But conservatives did not simply fade away, ceding all ground to a new progressive consensus. Rather, they reformulated their fundamental arguments, especially by stressing the rights of individuals and families who dissented from such views – people who might actually form a very numerous part of the population. Those dissenters were presented as victims of an aggressive state apparatus which was supported by a monochrome liberal media. Together, this political and cultural establishment constructed a rigid set of social orthodoxies that could only be withstood by heroic resisters. As such, victims needed to be celebrated and aided. That had the effect of deploying libertarian and anti-elitist rhetoric against progressive causes.

Lacking any consensus for traditional morality, conservatives argued instead that apparent victories for one particular group actively harmed the rights and liberties of some other population. Such arguments were persuasive when the victims were children and other groups who could not properly give their consent to being harmed. In transgender issues, bathroom battles were framed in terms of the protection of vulnerable children in schools and public places.

One major exception to sweeping liberal victories in these years involved abortion, where libertarian arguments about women's rights could never erase concerns about the distinct rights of the unborn child. Even in their most pronounced decisions in favor of the right to abortion, the courts always accepted the need to balance the rights of mother and child. Anti-abortion sentiment remained strong. Also, a distinction can be made between approving the existence of a practice and supporting it through the spending of public money, using taxes paid by citizens whose religious and moral beliefs were strongly opposed to it. For many years, conservative politicians have opposed any funding of the organization Planned Parenthood, which among its other functions is a major provider of legal abortions. Following a number of actions by state governments, in 2016 the Obama administration forbade states from withholding funding from agencies that supplied abortions, with Planned Parenthood the obvious focus of concern. This measure was, however, overturned in court.

Asserting the rights of dissenters commonly took the form of defending freedom of religion, especially when the issues at stake involved sensitive matters of gender and sexuality. Conservative religious believers faced many difficulties when ideas they found abhorrent were institutionalized in law, and some thinkers advocated forms of withdrawal from a society that in effect had turned from Judeo-Christian principles to state-worshiping paganism. Rod Dreher attracted much attention for his 2017 book *The Benedict Option*, which imagined believers forming communities of their own from which they might withstand the new Dark Age.

Conservative legal activists defended faithful believers from the new consensus. The Obamacare law had required that employers provide female employees with free access to contraception, an idea that offended the religious beliefs of some corporate leaders. In 2014, the US Supreme Court accepted the religious freedom arguments made in one case by the evangelical Christian owners of the firm Hobby Lobby. The religious freedom approach was rhetorically important in issues involving gay rights, where gay activists portrayed their opponents as motivated by hatred and homophobia. Conservatives resisted such a taint by stressing the legitimate moral and religious objections of those who refused to accept the principle of same-sex marriage. This included the local officials who refused to sign same-sex wedding licenses or the bakers who declined to serve same-sex weddings. Conservatives thus invoked powerful First

Amendment rights of freedom of speech and religious practice, and they achieved some successes. In 2018, the US Supreme Court decided in favor of a Colorado baker in such a case, criticizing the state agency that accused him of bigotry rather than respecting his sincere religious beliefs (*Masterpiece Cakeshop Ltd. v. Colorado Civil Rights Commission*, 584 U.S. 138 S. Ct. 1719 (2018)). Several conservative states passed "religious refusal" laws to support objectors.

The stress on individual rights meant that conservatives were surprisingly silent on other issues that in earlier years would assuredly have played a central role in culture war issues. In the 1960s, recreational drug use had been a vital marker dividing generations and cultures, and calls for drug legalization had been violently contested, with marijuana the center of debate. In 1970, the federal government institutionalized the harshest possible view of the question by classifying marijuana as a schedule I drug, deemed highly dangerous. Campaigns to legalize marijuana had followed ever since, and these finally bore fruit at the start of the century. Some states favored legalizing the drug for medicinal purposes, while in 2012 Colorado and Washington became the first states to legalize it explicitly for recreational use. But those state reforms ran up against rigid federal prohibition. This was relaxed somewhat under Eric Holder, but then reimposed under the Trump administration. Conservatives were deeply divided about the issue. Some opposed drug legalization of any kind, using the old law and order rhetoric, while others accepted libertarian arguments. The flagship conservative magazine *National Review* favored the latter approach, and supported decriminalization. That such a once bitterly divisive issue should come to occupy such a marginal position in culture war debates demonstrates how far the rhetoric of individual rights had come to replace public morality claims in conservative approaches.

GUN RIGHTS

On other issues, those individual rights approaches produced some of the bitterest battles in the new culture wars. That was true above all in struggles over private gun ownership, as guns became a potent symbol of resistance to the liberal consensus. Indeed, this represented the biggest area in which progressive activism failed to make any headway, and indeed actively lost ground.

The Second Amendment of the US Constitution famously (and confusingly) declares that "A well regulated militia, being necessary to the security of a free state, the right of the people to keep and bear arms, shall not be infringed." But does this assert an absolute individual right to bear arms, or must that right be exercised only in the organized context of a state militia? In the 1960s, politicians had discussed various forms of gun regulation, and the National Rifle Association (NRA) had been open to compromise, especially on handguns. Individual states and liberal cities passed quite severe restrictions on gun ownership. Matters changed following the conservative victories in 1994, when the NRA abandoned its long-standing attempts to remain bipartisan and adhered to the Republican Party and to the political Right. (Other organizations representing gun owners were still more explicitly political, and hard line.) The gun rights movement now demanded strict adherence to "the right to bear arms." Over the next two decades, pro-gun activists expanded the rights they claimed, as many states passed laws to help citizens carry weapons for their protection (right-to-carry and concealed-carry laws) and made it easier to justify self-defense against intruders and criminals (so-called stand-your-ground laws).

The courts largely accepted and defended the constitutional arguments for private gun ownership. One pivotal case focused on a law in Washington DC that prohibited private gun ownership for self-defense, unconnected with a state militia. In the 2008 case of *District of Columbia v. Heller* (554 U.S. 570 (2008)), the US Supreme Court reasserted the individual right to bear arms for self-defense, and that decision was further reinforced by the 2010 case of *McDonald v. Chicago* (561 U.S. 742 (2010)).

Meanwhile, the actual number of guns being manufactured and owned grew sharply. The number of guns of all kinds manufactured annually in the US grew from 3 million in 2004 to 10.9 million in 2013. By 2016, some 300 million guns were in circulation in the US, double the per capita rate of the 1960s. By 2016, 16 million Americans had permits allowing them to carry concealed firearms. Ironically, this profusion of firearms actually served as a potent argument in favor of the pro-gun cause, as the expansion coincided with the sharp decline in crime rates that we have already witnessed. That did not mean that a proliferation of guns of itself meant less crime, but rather that gun ownership of itself was evidently not directly correlated with violence. Matters might have been different if violent crime rates were in fact spiraling upward, but they were not. One curiosity about the gun figures was that as the number of weapons grew, so the number of households owning a gun actually fell. Partly, this change reflected a decline in the popularity of hunting among the young. But the consequence was that the households that did own guns were far more committed to defending their rights, and invested in gun ownership as a core constitutional right.

MASS KILLINGS

The best arguments that advocates of gun control could muster were the notorious outbreaks of gun violence that did occur, including acts like the assassination attempt on US Congressional Representative Gabrielle Giffords in 2011. Giffords herself later became a prominent activist for gun control. Demands for gun control peaked following the repeated incidents of mass murder in these years, in which an individual (virtually always a man) used semi-automatic weaponry to kill many innocent people at random. Settings and targets included college campuses (Virginia Tech University, 2007) and a crowded cinema (Aurora, CO, 2012). At a country music concert in Las Vegas in 2017, a strikingly well-armed sniper killed 58 victims and injured several hundred more. Although all these incidents were horrific in their particular ways, the most appalling was the assault in Sandy Hook, CT, in 2012, when a shooter killed 20 children aged six or seven years old, besides several staff and teachers. These randomly directed cases were over and above acts of explicit terrorism like the shootings at Orlando and San Bernardino.

Every one of these instances was followed by calls for tighter controls over firearms, a linkage that seemed obvious to liberal or progressive opinion. In a much-quoted story, the satirical magazine *The Onion* headlined a story "'No Way To Prevent This,' Says Only Nation Where This Regularly Happens." From that point of view, the lesson was too straightforward to require discussion: mass murders occurred because access to deadly firearms was far too easy and must be curtailed. As every other advanced country in the world knew, there simply were no good reasons to justify the private possession of lethal military firearms. In response, gun rights activists countered that, however tragic, mass murders were extremely rare acts, accounting for far less than 1 percent of all homicides in the US. Moreover, argued these believers, gun ownership actually deterred crime, and by far the worst violent crime occurred in politically liberal cities with strict gun control laws. Chicago had seven hundred homicides in 2016 alone, a number of victims larger than the combined total for all mass murder episodes nationwide for the previous decade. From this perspective, what was required was not the passing of new laws but the enforcement of existing ones.

The gun control debate focused most of the key themes of earlier culture wars, including proper gender roles and masculine behavior which were both seen as threatened by an overreaching liberal state. Just how entangled gun ownership became with larger cultural issues was epitomized by Sarah Palin's response to Obama's dismissal of rural reactionaries: "The president says small Americans – small-town Americans – we bitterly cling to our religion and our guns. . . . We say keep your change; we'll keep our God, our guns, our Constitution!" From the gun rights standpoint, citizens should be able to rely on their own resources to defend their families. Also pivotal was the defense of what activists took to be the explicit provisions of the Constitution, which should not be trampled because of emotive and usually inaccurate media coverage. Liberals differed on matters on constitutional interpretation, but also argued for the necessity of regulation and government power to promote the public welfare – in this case, the reduction of savage violence. Even if the Constitution did justify a right to bear arms, that document had been written for a very different society, and its provisions should no longer be seen as sacrosanct.

The debate proceeded with little real exchange of views, but with one serious unintended consequence. The more pronounced and explicit gun control arguments became, the more they provoked individuals to buy more guns before those items were prohibited. Each liberal victory in politics, and each furor over a mass murder case, has in practice been followed by yet another upward spiral in gun ownership, creating an ever-more determined body of resisters to change.

Some recent events have perhaps suggested a break in the long-standing impasse. In 2018, 17 were killed in a shooting at the Marjory Stoneman Douglas High School in Parkland, FL. This atrocity inspired a national movement of young people committed to a radical reform of gun laws, using the hashtag #NeverAgain, and the slogan March for our Lives. Liberals were galvanized by the vision of teenagers organizing and demonstrating for progressive causes, recalling the idealism associated with the 1960s. It remains to be seen how or whether such a new coalition might change rigid attitudes.

CAMPUS WARS

Although not raising such literal life or death issues, debates over campus free speech likewise revolved around similar themes of rights and responsibilities, of the individual and the collective, and the ability of a majority to limit minority rights in the name of social defense. Beyond the ethical issue of tolerating dissenting views, such clashes raised vital constitutional questions.

As interpreted by American courts, traditional liberal approaches to free speech assumed an individual's right to present unpopular or hurtful speech, provided that speech did not reach the stage of actively inciting or directly provoking criminality. That understanding has been transformed and upended in recent years by changes that we have already witnessed in concepts of privilege and oppression, and the politics of identity. From the point of view of a progressive campus activist, consciousness and identity are both determined by the history and interests of a group, as conditioned by factors of race, gender, sexuality, or disability. This theory of intersectionality developed in universities and academic settings from the 1990s, and it increasingly dominated the rhetoric of radical movements. Those ideas were prominent in large cities with many institutions of higher education – as was the case in virtually all major metropolitan areas.

Of necessity, a white heterosexual man (like Nicholas Christakis) speaks from a position of privilege, which can and must be limited if that harms or offends the historically oppressed or underprivileged. Escalating the force of that argument are claims that mere exposure to hostile ideologies such as racism or homophobia might inflict acute psychological damage and might even leave a legacy of post-traumatic stress disorder, PTSD. To that extent, the classical ideology of free speech is itself a tool of oppression, inequality, and white privilege. Activists warned of the baneful effects of micro-aggressions, seemingly minor types of speech and interpersonal behavior that actually involved subtle forms of bias and discrimination, and which thereby inflicted harm on victims.

Campus protests focused on issues of race and racism, areas in which progressives did not grant the validity of any competing perspective: these were moral and political absolutes. As protests mounted, so did conservative criticisms of extreme leftist and progressive orthodoxy prevailing on campuses. Militant activists had for some years been known as "social justice warriors," but from 2011 that term occurred increasingly and negatively in conservative diatribes, commonly abbreviated to the mocking label of "SJWs." Particularly loathed were leftist professors who propagandized their students. Such "tenured radicals" became central to conservative rhetoric and publications, and some became demon figures. In 2015, one University of Missouri professor was filmed not only attempting to remove a journalist investigating a protest, but calling for assistance with the ominous words "I need some muscle over here!" Horror stories about campus extremism became a mainstay of media outlets, and generally presented a stereotype of ranting fanaticism, characterized by hatred of men, of white people, and of the United States past and present. Leftist opposition to Israeli policies produced multiple accounts of anti-Semitic statements and propaganda on campuses. Usually, such stories focused on conservative individuals or groups who were persecuted or victimized by far-left extremism. Alt-Right groups delighted not just in reporting outrages, but in creating incidents that would foment strife, by "triggering SJWs."

College campuses became the setting for fierce battles over the rights of conservative speakers, detonating national debates over free speech rights and the legitimate limits of protest. Protests focused not just on outspoken provocateurs like libertarian Milo Yiannopoulos or far-rightist Richard Spencer but on academics whose views were seen as unacceptable, with varying degrees of plausibility. Adding to the effectiveness of protest, militants made extensive use of new technologies and social media, especially Twitter, as a means of galvanizing actions. Conservative media portrayed American campuses as in the throes of a free speech crisis, and such incidents acquired legal dimensions. In many cases, these colleges were publicly funded, putting pressure on legislatures to investigate or to reduce funding. Although universities like Yale are private institutions, their involvement with government money and support places them within the scope of federal policy, for instance in matters like the enforcement of Title IX codes. Arguably, that positions those colleges within the scope of federal laws and courts. At the same time, the principle of academic tenure prevented the dismissal of faculty for even the most egregious violations.

WOKE AND SNOWFLAKES

Illustrating the battle lines of the new culture wars are several slang words that emerged to describe or (often) stigmatize new kinds of consciousness and sensitivity. On the progressive side, activists commonly used the word "woke" for someone who had come to acknowledge structural injustice and who recognized the need for sweeping change. Originating in the black slang of the 1960s, the word was popularized by singer Eryakh Badu in 2008. In 2014, the rise of Black Lives Matter spread the word across racial lines, with the call to "Stay Woke!" By definition, someone who was not woke was still asleep to injustice.

Conservatives had very different views of the new campus radicals, whom they termed "snowflakes" as well as SJWs. From this perspective, "snowflake" referred to activists who were hypersensitive to anything that could be construed, however improbably, as offending sensibilities about race, gender, or disability. By their nature, snowflakes melted in the slightest heat. The notorious campus confrontation at Yale in 2015 led to scornful denunciations of Generation Snowflake, and the word became widespread the following year. The fact that each snowflake in nature is unique implies, by extension, that militants were "special snowflakes" with a wildly exaggerated sense of entitlement and privilege. That gave them a tendency to childish tantrums, and (for men) the word suggested a lack of manhood, or effeminacy. Conservatives mocked student demands for "trigger warnings" that would precede discussions of controversial issues in classroom materials which might otherwise trigger the kind of flashbacks associated with PTSD. Conservatives were also scornful of the "safe spaces" that colleges created for their students, where they could be immune from troubling speech or actions in the unfriendly world at large.

Beyond the name-calling, the fault lines in campus controversies closely paralleled national political battles. The sins for which campus revolutionaries were increasingly pilloried were exactly those for which conservatives attacked liberals, and specifically leaders like Barack Obama and Hillary Clinton. Like the "woke" campus militants, those Democrats were portrayed as unreasoningly hostile to conventional American ideas and norms, and determined to impose their wild and impractical views on an unwilling public. For conservatives, the hothouse world of the campus offered a nightmare vision of the whole country in miniature. It supported the populist vision of a world in which those who thought of themselves as "normal" or conventional were under permanent threat from extremism. For working- and middle-class white people – and especially for men – this was an alarming picture. The cultural gulf powerfully recalled the conflicts of the late 1960s when radicals had infuriated social conservatives, encouraging Republicans to target their appeal (successfully) to "the un-black, un-poor and un-young." In the context of the 2010s, culture war clashes opened the way for nostalgic political campaigns to restore an imagined old order, to make America great again.

As Obama's second term drew to its close, liberals could claim far-reaching political victories, but at least as important were the underlying social shifts which had called forth sizable popular movements. A new public consciousness had emerged in such fundamental matters as confronting historical racism, appreciating environmental threats, and acknowledging gay equality. The nation seemed to have accepted critical portions of the progressive agenda, of ideas of social justice. From a liberal perspective, the epic scale of these changes would be amply symbolized when, as seemed all but certain, the nation's first black president was succeeded by the first woman incumbent. But as became increasingly apparent in 2016, older struggles and conflicts – grievances over economic change, immigration, globalization, and the culture war – had by no means vanished. Shortly after that year's election, a troubled Barack Obama mused whether his agenda had been over-ambitious: "Maybe we pushed too far….Maybe people just want to fall back into their tribe." But the fact that the president was so dismissive of opposition indicates a more general failure to comprehend the resentment that social changes – and administration policies – were stirring.

14 The 2016 Election

On November 8, 2016, the US held its presidential election. Although the polls showed a close race, the final consensus was that Hillary Clinton would comfortably defeat Republican Donald Trump by a national margin of around 2 or 3 percent in the popular vote. Some Democratic partisans ventured the hope that the polls were being too modest, and that Clinton would actually achieve a landslide victory, winning traditionally Republican states that had always seemed beyond their grasp. Very few observers challenged this consensus. By far the most accurate prediction of the actual outcome came in a comic cartoon published in the liberal magazine *The New Yorker* to coincide with Halloween on that October 31. Cartoonist David Sipress portrayed a child dressed in the most terrifying costume then imaginable, namely an electoral map that showed Republican red sweeping over the battleground states and conquering most of the Midwest. If not quite perfect in detail, Sipress's map was the most accurate prophecy of the actual outcome.

That a cartoonist's nightmare triumphed over all the projections of political experts suggests what an extraordinarily unusual year this was. The election illustrated and focused long-standing grievances and discontents, and demonstrated that national divisions were much starker than most observers had ever supposed. After years of national debate about issues of race and gender, the election served as a potent reminder that themes of class and economic interest were by no means extinct.

CLINTON'S DEMOCRATS

As the year began, the electoral story seemed thoroughly predictable. It was commonly accepted that Hillary Clinton would be the Democratic standard-bearer, while the Republican candidacy would be contested by a number of well-known figures, one of whom would surely take the lead as the process developed. In the aftermath of a still-popular President Obama, the Democrats should have commanded a strong advantage, especially as the economy was generally in good shape. As in 2008, the election seemed to be Hillary Clinton's to lose, and as time would tell that historical analogy proved all too accurate.

215

The Clinton campaign soon faced unexpected difficulties and a vigorous challenge from Vermont senator Bernie Sanders. Sanders was in many ways an unlikely rival who represented an earlier political era. Apart from his age (he would be 75 on election day) he remained an unabashed advocate of socialist policies, which won support from left and liberal voters. Young people committed to social justice were attracted by the sense that this was a sincere and honest politician not connected to machines or party establishments, and free of the sordid world of campaign finance. Sanders spoke with a passion that was in marked contrast to Hillary Clinton's stilted delivery, which was more appropriate to policy professionals – to "wonks." As the slogan claimed, followers would "Feel the Bern." (Others, controversially, denounced Clinton with a call to "Bern the Witch".) Sanders came very close to defeating Clinton in the Iowa caucuses in February, and he took a sweeping lead in the New Hampshire primary. He won further primary victories in many different regions, commonly with margins far larger than opinion polls predicted.

His insurgency continued through May, even though Clinton was now receiving covert backing from the Democratic Party apparatus. What made her victory inevitable was the heavy support she received from the so-called super-delegates, elected officials and party activists representing a variety of interest groups. As the Sanders campaign complained, he was defeated less by the voters than by a party machine. Only by early July was the Clinton victory unambiguous, far later in the year than might have been expected. Her rocky path should have been a warning about what to expect in the coming national election, particularly if a wild card candidate mobilized mass support from the disaffected.

As a candidate, Hillary Clinton had significant advantages, in terms of a long and distinguished public career, not to mention strong if not uncritical support from much of the media. Yet her hopes for election depended on reproducing something like the coalition that had favored Barack Obama in 2008. Democrat strategists were attracted to the theory of the coalition of the ascendant, which journalist Ron Brownstein had formulated based on the 2008 experience. This coalition would combine immigrants, racial minorities, millennials, and highly educated white people – all groups projected to grow steadily in numbers. In that vision, the party could easily achieve repeated victories, provided it held on to enough traditional working-class support in old Democrat heartlands.

But Hillary Clinton lacked many of the qualities that had allowed Obama to mobilize those diverse constituencies. If the Obama of 2008 was a vigorous young (47) African American man commonly regarded as a charismatic speaker, the Hillary of 2016 was much older (69), and had health issues. She lacked her husband's easy ability to communicate with working- and middle-class audiences, whose values he apparently shared. Hillary Clinton was an establishment figure par excellence, who was closely identified with policies from her husband's administration, particularly in matters of free trade and globalization. Her success depended on mobilizing a large black and minority vote, but Bill Clinton's administration was identified with the Drug War and policies of mass incarceration. She exemplified so much that many people loathed and distrusted about the political and social status quo. Worse, she had little sense of how unpopular that situation might be, and nor did her later post-election comments demonstrate any greater awareness of those realities. She rarely acknowledged the legitimacy of any objections to herself or her policies, and framed opposition in terms of unreasoning hatred of herself, her family, or her gender.

She also faced some scandals. One arose from the 2012 terrorist attack in Benghazi, when as Secretary of State she had allegedly been too slow to take action that might have saved American lives. But in 2016 that seemingly endless investigation produced a genuinely damaging domestic exposé. While holding her Cabinet office, she had channeled official email through a private non-secure server, which could easily have been penetrated by outside countries or agencies. Her remarks on the matter suggested a striking lack of concern with the affair, and ignorance of technical aspects. She affected not to understand the idea of "wiping" a server, except by using a cloth. The security violation might have broken criminal laws, and the affair duly sparked an investigation by the FBI. The scandal was potentially damaging among people with any experience of military service, who knew the dire penalties that awaited low-level personnel guilty of far smaller breaches of security protocols. Although this was not the only factor driving veteran support away from Clinton, in the November election veterans favored Trump over Clinton by a margin of 60 to 34.

TRUMP'S REPUBLICANS

When the year began, the Republicans faced the luxury of a wide range of plausible candidates, reflecting the party's recent successes in winning elections at national and state level. Among a large field, several candidates stood out, including two US senators of Latino origin, namely Ted Cruz of Texas and Florida's Marco Rubio. Other plausible figures included John Kasich of Ohio and Jeb Bush, brother of the former president George W. Bush.

But the early primaries and caucuses favored none of the predicted candidates. Instead, they demonstrated startling support for Donald Trump, a buccaneering businessman and property developer, whose main attraction for the public seemed to be his absolute lack of association with the political mainstream. Trump appalled establishment Republicans by his abrasive personal style and populist manner, and his total disconnect with any traditional sense of the party's constituencies or positions. Despite this – or because of it – he scored a solid victory in the New Hampshire primary, and continued to rack up victories through early May. As his rivals withdrew he became the party's presumptive nominee, long before Clinton secured any such position on her side of the partisan divide. Those early Republican voters eliminated any and every candidate associated with the party's establishment, or the political elite generally.

Knowing as we do the outcome of the eventual contest, it is difficult to convey the utter lack of seriousness with which informed observers and journalists took the Trump campaign, which was depicted as a political prank or media stunt. The Clinton camp actively promoted Trump's cause as a means of discrediting other "serious" Republican candidates, whom they regarded as a much graver threat. Giving added credence to that approach was the extreme amateurism that marked the Trump camp throughout the year, right up to its eventual victory.

DONALD TRUMP

Trump himself had long been a celebrity public figure whose properties were generally marked by ostentatious displays of wealth that critics mocked as excess and vulgarity. But his financial enterprises had ventured far beyond office blocks and hotels. Commonly accused of egomania (or megalomania), he had applied the Trump brand to various products, including steaks, a casino resort, and even a Trump University, although few of these had enjoyed anything like the success he hoped. But his greatest product was himself and his public image as a triumphant tycoon, which reached a mass public through his appearances on the reality show *The Apprentice*. Married three times, his personal life had been a regular feature of the gossip columns and tabloids. If critics mocked his image as cartoonish, he had the virtue of instant name recognition.

In his public persona, Trump presented himself as a man so wealthy and powerful in his own right that he had no need to make concessions to orthodoxies or forms of political correctness. Owing nobody, he could say the things that needed to be said. Although often inconsistent, he repeatedly made outrageous statements that combined nativism and anti-immigrant sentiment with economic protectionism. His anti-immigrant tone was directed particularly against Muslims, an effective gambit at the time of jihadi attacks. In this as in other matters, his views reflected those of a somewhat earlier America, the time of his young adulthood. (He would be 70 on election day.) His slogan Make America Great Again (MAGA) could be interpreted in many possible ways according to individual taste, but it recalled an era free of contemporary complexities and nuances. Trump preached a doctrine of America First, a phrase that critics attacked for its association with pre-World War II policies of appeasing Nazi Germany. Remarkably, given his wealth and background, Trump successfully portrayed himself as the champion of the common man and woman, whom the elites had forgotten. He promised to "drain the swamp" of conventional Washington politics, its lobbying and systematic corruption.

To the media, and to other politicians, Trump's message seemed extreme and even farcical. On immigration from Mexico, he promised to build a huge wall and have Mexico pay for it. As serious politics, this was ludicrous. But as observers noted, Trump's audiences drew a clear distinction between hearing his message literally and taking it seriously. Whether or not such a wall could ever be built, Trump was at least trying to address concerns about the border, in a way that mainstream politicians were not. On this and other issues, the breadth of his support indicates the near despair with the existing order experienced by many groups, especially working-class white people. Trump was ideally placed to capitalize on the widespread popular disillusion with the political and cultural establishment. This was particularly potent in rural and old industrial areas that felt themselves neglected by government and savaged by the effects of successive free trade agreements.

The ensuing election campaign reached depths of malice and provocative rhetoric scarcely precedented in modern times. At one point, Trump openly threatened to prosecute and imprison his opponent on the scandal arising from the email and the private server. Enthusiastic Trump followers chanted "Lock her up!"

As a candidate, Trump inspired a kind of bipartisan terror. Republicans worried desperately that such an unpopular candidate might cost the party their treasured fortresses in both Houses of Congress. Trump's campaign could also taint the party irrevocably in the eyes of non-white groups who would be so pivotal to the electoral future. Republican leaders recalled with horror how its anti-immigrant policies in the 1990s had virtually destroyed the party in California, which in effect became a one-party Democratic state.

Virtually no prominent Republican newspapers or media outlets endorsed Trump, and many Republican candidates maintained their distance from the would-be president. Some principled conservatives assumed an uncompromising stance of "Never Trump!" At various points, establishment Republicans privately debated the means by which Trump could be replaced by a conventional candidate, such as future vice president Mike Pence.

Democrats in turn expressed alarm that Trump authentically did portend something like an American fascism, or at least the outbreak of a kind of Latin American dictator syndrome. Liberals commonly explained Trump's appeal in terms of raw racism, and media outlets highlighted pro-Trump activism by white supremacist and extremist sects, including the remnants of the Ku Klux Klan.

TWO CAMPAIGNS

The Trump campaign faced its worst danger in October 2016, when a tape surfaced of the candidate speaking off the record while en route to tape a show called *Access Hollywood*. He discussed techniques of seducing women, and in the process he boasted of harassment and sexual assaults that arguably violated criminal laws. Immune from the threat of consequences, he claimed, a star or celebrity could just "grab them by the pussy." These revelations supplied ammunition to public debate about women's rights and safety in a patriarchal society. In electoral terms, the tape affair was far more serious than scandals that have irrevocably destroyed the candidacy of other figures, and it threatened the already weak hold that the Republican Party had on women's votes. This was already an issue because of Trump's perceived bullying of Hillary Clinton during the presidential debates. Yet Trump survived. Particularly effective as a response was a press conference that his camp called in which women reported being harassed, molested or even raped by Bill Clinton. Those charges had long been known, yet through the years they had been scorned or minimized by his wife, Hillary. This sent the message that the Clinton campaign in practice cared little about sexual violence or women victims.

Meanwhile, several missteps and misfortunes undermined Hillary Clinton's position. Following a commemoration of the September 11 attacks, pneumonia caused her to collapse publicly, confirming rumors that she was concealing health issues and that the media were colluding in this effort. Clinton could scarcely be blamed for this episode, but she was certainly responsible for another blow she suffered at this time. Seeking to account for the support for Donald Trump, she described half his following as racists and nativists, a "basket of deplorables." As the remark was reported, it was suggested that the "deplorable" label applied to anyone who failed to support the leftist/liberal Democratic agenda in its entirety, and that Clinton was expressing her contempt for the whole white middle and working class. Her speech was a gift to her populist enemies, who proudly declared themselves deplorables. Nor was her characterization accidental, as she had often used this term in private conversation. That indicated a real lack of understanding of the forces and concerns driving support for Trump, especially in troubled working-class areas, and that in turn caused her campaign to make serious errors in how it deployed its resources.

Still more stinging was a statement by FBI director James Comey, only 11 days before the actual election. Although earlier statements had suggested that the email server investigation had been laid to rest, Comey now informed Congress of newly discovered evidence that would demand further investigation, and the fact that the affair was being reopened was promptly leaked to the media. Reopening this affair was damaging to the Clinton campaign, which had for some months regarded the case as closed and forgotten.

THE ELECTION

Despite these drawbacks, Democrats remained thoroughly confident of victory, to the point of preparing flamboyant celebrations to welcome the first woman president. The reasons for that belief are important in understanding both the eventual result and the popular response to that outcome. In most major cities and in some key regions, support for Clinton was so strong and uniform that there was little reason to suppose that Trump followers even existed, except perhaps in the most remote parts of Appalachia. Democrats found no difficulty in recruiting media stars and A-list celebrities to campaign for Clinton, while the Trump campaign struggled to find well-known faces. Generally, the Clinton campaign assumed that older industrial areas would remain true to the Democratic loyalty they had traditionally held, and which had been revived by Obama. In one telling episode in the days immediately before the election, Trump staged major campaign rallies in Michigan, where he attracted large and enthusiastic support. The media saw this effort as a classic illustration of his incompetence, as it was so obvious that Michigan was faithful Democratic territory, part of the "blue wall" of reliable industrial states. Instead, they advised condescendingly, Trump should concentrate on marginal battleground states where he might have some faint hope of affecting the result. In fact, Trump would take Michigan.

Trump's campaign took not just states in the South but also most of the Midwest and the historic Rustbelt. He won all the main battleground states where the two parties had long been in contention – Ohio, Florida, and North Carolina. He smashed the blue wall, taking such states as Wisconsin and Pennsylvania, besides Michigan. Trump took all 20 of the Congressional districts with the highest share of manufacturing jobs. Far from tainting Republican Congressional candidates, the Trump victory actually assisted many to retain tightly contested seats, ensuring a Republican majority in both Houses in the new Congress. To the astonishment of most observers, the 2016 election left the Republican Party in charge of the White House and Congress, and in a position to shape the future of the Supreme Court.

This presidential election is often cited, wrongly, as marking a catastrophic failure of opinion polling. In fact, the consensus estimate of what Clinton's final lead would be in the popular vote – around 3 percent – was impressively close to the final reality, of 2.1 percent, or almost 3 million votes. But the US does not decide elections on the basis of popular numbers but rather relies on electoral votes, so the exact distribution of those popular votes matters enormously. Clinton massively outpolled Trump in heavily Democratic California, while Trump eked out thin popular majorities in states like Wisconsin and Pennsylvania. Nevertheless, that gave Trump an overwhelming position in the Electoral College, with 304 votes to Clinton's 227. To oversimplify, the result of the 2016 election can be summarized easily: Democrats won California by 4 million votes, and lost the rest of the country by 1 million.

In explaining the final result, factors of race, class, and culture all played their part. The central reality in 2016 was that white people favored Trump over Clinton by a margin of 21 percent, and white people still constitute around 70 percent of the electorate. Despite the rapid growth of immigrant and minority populations in recent years, prophecies of a majority–minority nation remain some decades in the future, and that fact was crucial for both parties. The prospect of such a shift had encouraged Democrats to underplay the significance of traditional white working-class support. Complicating the story, a surprising number of people of ethnic minority background actually voted for Trump. That included 29 percent of Hispanics and a comparable proportion of Asians. Besides racial groups, Trump attracted the support of a surprising number of women, 41 percent of the whole, confounding expectations that he would be utterly condemned as a symbol of sexism as much as racism.

Class also mattered. As journalists belatedly examined the centers of Trump strength around the country, they repeatedly found a common pattern of formerly prosperous areas where industries had declined or vanished, and where older cultural assumptions had been thrown into confusion. Education proved a good predictor of electoral loyalties. College graduates favored Clinton over Trump by a four-point margin, while people without a college degree leaned to Trump by eight points. Among voters with postgraduate education, Clinton led by a 58–37 majority. This points to the role of education in determining attitudes to new technologies and to globalization.

THE MORNING AFTER

No election outcome is ever an easy matter for the losing side, but the 2016 contest was uniquely traumatic for Democrats and liberals who had begun that evening with near-total confidence of victory. Popular responses on the internet, on YouTube, were extreme to the point of hysteria, with participants openly weeping and indulging in the darkest speculations as to what the coming months might bring. (Conservatives delighted in showing these productions for their unintentionally humorous qualities.) Immigrant groups particularly were alarmed by Trump's success. So were academics and college students.

In trying to understand the outcome, liberals consistently stressed the racial motives driving Trump voters, rarely acknowledging economic or cultural concerns. Ta-Nehisi Coates argued simply that "whiteness brought us Donald Trump," and scorned competing arguments, for instance about class, as forms of denial – as "escapism" or "theater." (Complicating his argument was that many of the Trump voters in old industrial areas had cast their previous two votes for Barack Obama.) The victory was thus portrayed as a vicious white backlash, as liberals presented their rivals as hard-core racists, nativists, and white supremacists. Others viewed Clinton's defeat in scarcely more creditable terms, as the triumph of misogyny.

Particularly in college towns, some popular demonstrations turned to violence, most notoriously with a serious outbreak in Berkeley, CA, by so-called Antifa (Anti-Fascist) militants. As anti-Trump groups developed and coalesced into a national movement, they adopted the name "the Resistance," harking back to the militants who struggled against Nazi rule in the Second World War. These responses – and especially the "Nazi/Fascist" analogies – both illustrated the political and cultural divisions that the election had revealed and aggravated them.

Many liberals responded to the outcome with a pattern of denial, as they found multiple ways of challenging the election's legitimacy. In the process, they postulated many conspiracy theories, of varying degrees of plausibility. Even after the November contest, diehard Democrats continued to hope that Trump might still be defeated. Under the Constitution, the formal decision to choose a president occurs at the meeting of the Electoral College in mid-December, when the electors reflect the choices made by their states. Normally, there is no doubt that electors would simply follow the November ballot, but protesters now put heavy pressure on the college to ignore those results and become "faithless electors," choosing someone other than Trump. Petitions encouraging such a defection attracted millions of signatures.

A lawsuit by Green Party leader Jill Stein raised concerns that the Trump victories in Wisconsin, Pennsylvania, and possibly elsewhere might have been decided by external interference in the system of electronic voting. Accordingly, the suit demanded a total recount of those results by hand, although the time taken for such a process would force a serious delay in the Electoral College vote. The courts rejected all such efforts, but the idea that Trump owed his victory to electoral fraud remains an article of faith for many liberals. In fact, no plausible evidence has ever been produced to show any successful interference with the voting process in this election, in any state. Ultimately, all efforts to overturn the November election result failed, but they demonstrated a degree of last-ditch desperation not witnessed in modern American electoral history.

These challenges contributed to denying the legitimacy of the whole Trump presidency, and the new administration. Such attitudes set a disturbing precedent for future elections, encouraging other defeated parties to question results, however convincing they might appear on the surface. Beyond undermining national unity, this was a worrying prospect for the future of democracy.

RUSSIA

Conspiracy theories about the campaign focused on possible activity by Russia under the guidance of Vladimir Putin. Beyond question, Putin's government had long pursued efforts to destabilize and discredit rival regimes, and the Russians were experts in cyber-warfare and propaganda. That the Russians did seek to intervene in the US election is certain, but the degree of their activity – and its possible success – remains deeply controversial. Any discussion of these activities is difficult, because so much of the evidence derives from the murky world of clandestine intelligence. Also, as the theories and investigations developed over the following years, very different charges tended to become confused, so that well-documented Russian attempts at propaganda have been treated alongside speculative and wholly unsubstantiated allegations of direct involvement in the voting process, such as hacking voting machines.

The gravest charge was that Donald Trump himself was a Russian agent of influence, controlled by that country's intelligence service. Trump through the years had many business dealings with Russia, and according to some allegations his sexual activities had exposed him to blackmail and control. But again, everything depends on the reliability of the sources on which such claims are based. The main source for these "Russian agent" charges was Christopher Steele, a former officer of the respected British intelligence service, MI6. In 2016, Steele developed a damning dossier on the Trump allegations which was circulated to the US media. Despite Steele's credible background, the charges suffered from two critical weaknesses, namely that much of the work was compiled while he was working for an agency under contract to the Democratic Party and the Clinton campaign; and that the charges remain wholly unverified. Critics protested that they might well be disinformation or black propaganda of the kind that circulates so freely in the intelligence world, and which was possibly being used to discredit the US electoral process as a whole. After years of intense investigation, the well-informed investigative journalist Bob Woodward reported finding no direct evidence of collusion or espionage between Trump and Russia.

More plausible were allegations that senior members of the Trump campaign (or of the Trump family), in pursuit of materials to discredit Hillary Clinton, had dealt directly with groups or individuals connected to the Russian intelligence apparatus. During the whole campaign at least a dozen Trump-connected figures met with Russians, including people connected with the Kremlin or Russian intelligence agencies, although it is not clear that the Americans had any notion they were dealing with representatives of the Russian state. Later inquiries particularly focused on a June 2016 meeting at New York City's Trump Tower, at which several Trump associates met Russian representatives following a Russian offer to produce material harmful to Hillary Clinton. Charges of colluding with the Russians were the original justifications for the 2017 appointment of Robert Mueller as a special prosecutor to investigate possible Trump/Russia collaboration during the election. But "collusion" is a vague term which need not have any criminal content, and as the investigation proceeded evidence of collusion became ever harder to assess or prove. Of course, fresh evidence might yet come to light. (As we will see, Mueller did vigorously pursue other related matters.)

Where the Russians enjoyed most success was in the realm of electronic interference and hacking. In June and July 2016, Russians hacked the computers of the Democratic National Committee, finding a rich trove of embarrassing material that helped discredit Hillary Clinton and aggravated the already tense relations between her followers and those of Bernie Sanders. Russia was heavily involved in flooding social media with fake news, a phrase that first became famous during this period. At least 100 million Americans received some such content, stemming from Russian web brigades or "troll farms." Technically, most of the stories that the Russians circulated were not fake in the sense of being wholly fabricated, but rather they highlighted embarrassing themes in American life with a goal of sowing dissension and exploiting tensions and grievances. Yet the "fake news" term has become useful shorthand for such a campaign. Making all this possible was the extremely detailed information that the firm Cambridge Analytica had obtained through exploiting Facebook data, a scandal that I described in Chapter 4. This allowed not just micro-advertising aimed at particular individuals in electorally crucial areas but also the spread of false stories and rumors. That such activity occurred is beyond doubt, but its impact on the actual outcome of the vote is unknown.

Investigations of real and alleged Russian misdeeds continued through the Trump presidency. Rarely noticed in the furor was the historical irony that these concerns precisely reproduced the nightmares of the Cold War years in the 1950s, although with the political labels reversed. Then as today, Americans were alarmed about the extent of Russian espionage and meddling in the United States, and the threat of highly placed deep penetration agents in powerful positions. To combat this menace, full trust had to be placed in the FBI and other law enforcement agencies. That closely describes attitudes in the Trump years, although in the modern era it is liberals rather than conservatives who most passionately fear and magnify the Russian threat which conservatives minimize or mock. Liberals even return to a sensational Cold War thriller when they label Trump with the Cold War title of "Manchurian Candidate." Meanwhile, Trump's most prominent nemesis figures, Robert Mueller and James Comey, were successive directors of the FBI. It is a strange reversal.

AN OLD/NEW POLITICS

The 2016 election stunned informed observers, in politics, the media, and the academic world. Yet even the alignments and issues that seemed most stunning were anything but novel, and in fact they represented long-term trends that we have repeatedly described in previous chapters. The changes were already there: now they were obvious.

That is most apparent in the acute divisions that now emerged between sections of the country that had either benefited or suffered from rapid economic change and globalization. Economic concerns were inextricably bound up with attitudes to social change, as it affected matters as basic as morality and family cohesion. The association of new sexual and family attitudes with Hollywood and celebrity culture meant that Clinton's campaign gained far less advantage than it expected from deploying such a stellar array of celebrities on her behalf, and might even have damaged her cause.

Those social shifts had vital implications for the two parties. For half a century following the New Deal of the 1930s, Democrats had found a firm base in the industrial working class and the unions. They forfeited that support in the Reagan years, but most believed they had regained it under Obama, to the extent that they could afford to take working-class voters for granted. What was missing in this view was the extent to which the Democratic Party since the 1990s had become associated with globalization in all its forms, including mass immigration as well as over-large government. This lesson should have been brought home by the successive disasters that Democrats had suffered through the years at all levels of government except the presidency. The party thus lacked the generation of experienced governors or younger Congressional figures who should properly have emerged as its next generation of leadership. That point was amply demonstrated as the party sought new standard bearers to take the place of Hillary Clinton, but among the early contenders they found few potential leaders who would by the time of the next presidential contest be significantly younger than her. In 2020, Elizabeth Warren will be 71, Joe Biden 77, Bernie Sanders 79. All would thus be older than Ronald Reagan was at the time of his first presidential victory in 1980. Against such a background, younger figures like Kamala Harris stood out conspicuously.

Republicans faced very different problems and had many recent victories to report. Like Democrats, though, they were scarcely less tainted as representatives of the status quo. If in fact Republicans stood for sweeping changes, why had they achieved so little since their triumph in taking Congress in 2010? Trump owed his emergence as the party's presidential candidate less to his own virtues than to the systematic rejection of any other prominent Republican associated with that established political and economic order – with the "swamp." Again, this dissidence was nothing new, although earlier manifestations had received little media coverage. As early as 2008, vice-presidential candidate Sarah Palin had offered an ideological mix of hard-right anti-establishment populism together with an appeal to evangelicals and social conservatives. Well-established traditions of anti-elite dissidence were only awaiting the appropriate figurehead.

In matters of technology, too, the election was less surprising than it should have been, and served as a wake-up call to trends that had been long in evidence. For decades, American states had moved in a gradual and patchy way towards electronic voting, but without paying sufficient concern to possible hacking or manipulation. Few jurisdictions recorded results in both electronic and paper form, which remains the best way to ensure safety. The lack of safeguards permitted the upsurge of conspiracy theories and claims that simply could not be tested or verified. Moreover, election campaigns had for years employed social media and the information derived from that, but had not envisaged the potential of a vast data breach that could supply so much precious personal information to propagandists. The election showed the critical need for democratic systems to catch up with the challenges and opportunities of the social media age.

No less evident was the radically different environment of news. Long past was the age in which most Americans could be presumed to rely on a common range of sources of news and opinion, in what was slightingly referred to as the "mainstream media" (often abbreviated to MSM). Many people relied on internet sources or social media, permitting instant access to news but also posing the danger of manipulation and allowing the rapid spread of conspiracy theories. Social media encouraged users to remain within a given part of the political spectrum, with little exposure to rival views. To use a popular analogy, they remained within a particular silo not connected to the silos familiar to their neighbors or fellow citizens. Lacking knowledge of rival political currents also made it easy for observers to be surprised or shocked when those foes achieved an unexpected success, as occurred in November 2016.

Although such changes are difficult to quantify, the overwhelming popularity of social media contributed to a general coarsening of debate and discussion, encouraging exchanges in which anonymous participants denounce adversaries in harsh and even obscene terms with little fear of check or reprimand. That toxic all-or-nothing environment seriously undermined concepts of legitimate disagreement or opposition. Even if it was not the major cause of rigid national polarization, social media contributed mightily to the process.

Donald Trump took office in January 2017, after one of the most tumultuous electoral years in US history, a result that had been utterly unexpected a year previously. But at every stage of his administration he had to confront a new political and cultural environment that made effective government difficult. His own personal decisions made that process harder.

15 Trump

In August 2017, far-right protesters gathered in Charlottesville, VA, to oppose the removal of statues of Confederate leaders. This Unite the Right rally attracted white supremacist and neo-Nazi groups, as well as many left-wing counter-protesters. In the clashes that ensued, a far-rightist drove a car into a crowd of protesters, killing a young woman. Reacting to the events, President Trump declared that "I think there is blame on both sides. You had some very bad people in that group. You also had some very fine people on both sides." As his remarks were reported and interpreted, Trump was condemned for describing Nazis and Klansmen as "very fine people," justifying the liberal attacks on him as a white supremacist. At the same time, he seemed to be condemning those people who protested against the extreme Right. Many conservatives joined in that reaction, finding his words utterly unacceptable.

That incident exemplified the extreme passions that now characterized political debate, and the widespread rejection of the legitimacy of the Trump administration. At the same time, ironically, the affair demonstrated not the aggressive power of a would-be dictator, but rather the president's startling weakness. The Trump years were an era of chaos and confrontation.

TRUMP AS PRESIDENT

American historians sometimes exaggerate the part played by individual leaders in shaping particular eras. In the Trump case, though, such a focus on personality and mindset is inevitable, even if it does run the risk of attempting amateur psychological analysis. To illustrate the critical role of personality, we might imagine a counter-factual in which the new president had a determined vision rooted in a hard-right populist ideology, and he was surrounded by a dedicated corps of advisors who were equally committed, and moreover experienced in the ways of Washington politics. With the support of both Houses of Congress, such a president could have achieved a far-reaching political transformation of the kind dreaded by liberals, and even a shift to a more authoritarian regime. Hypothetically, such an administration could rapidly fulfill many of the goals long sought by the Republican Right, including the prompt abolition of Obamacare, strict limitations on abortion, and a drastic revision of immigration policy, even a closing of the borders. Such successes would have recast the Republican Party itself firmly in the mold of the charismatic transformative leader.

Even to imagine such a scenario – which differed so radically from what actually occurred – serves to underline the significance of Donald Trump's personal failings as a leader and administrator, and the degree to which he squandered the potential advantages he possessed as he began his administration. His style of leadership was erratic and capricious, and prized personal loyalty over virtually any other feature. From the first days, Trump found it difficult to find reliable subordinates with an understanding of political realities, and those he did find he swiftly alienated. Senior political offices experienced transitions and personnel turnover at an unprecedented rate. Many offices and ambassadorships remained vacant years into an administration that was increasingly dysfunctional.

Donald Trump's opinions proved changeable, even mercurial, and depended largely on particular individuals with whom he had recently had exchanges. His remarks on major political issues, such as gun control, often demanded swift exposition, revision, and even outright withdrawal. Senior officials frequently found their statements and explanations contradicted by rivals, or by the president himself. One early advisor and chief strategist was Steve Bannon, a convinced and highly ideological rightist and nationalist, but Bannon lost office in mid-2017. Together, these constant changes and new directions created an atmosphere of endemic instability, both political and personal. Trump offered no clear vision of change.

As president, Donald Trump's behavior repeatedly indicated a heavy emphasis on his own ego, with an acute sensitivity to perceived slights or criticisms. Such attitudes were appropriate for a show business celebrity, but they were difficult to reconcile with the presidential office. Rather than being guided by ideology, one of his major concerns was in establishing his superiority to his predecessor, Barack Obama, which involved the point-by-point reversal or dismantling of everything that president had done. Trump's first official controversy began at his inauguration in January 2017, an event he claimed (wrongly) to have been far larger than those of his predecessors. Closely related to the question of ego was Trump's stringent demand for unquestioning personal loyalty in political officers, an issue that precipitated a break with FBI director James Comey, and which provoked Comey's sensational dismissal in May 2017.

Some of Trump's actions raised real questions about the president's knowledge or grasp of fundamental constitutional matters, and the limits of his own power. In 2018, he challenged the principle that being born in the United States qualified an individual for US citizenship, and suggested instead that citizenship should only be granted to the children of parents who were themselves citizens. He therefore intended to issue an executive order establishing this new and narrower principle. One might take differing views of the merits of Trump's proposal, but his suggested reform ran contrary to the explicit language of the US Constitution, which firmly establishes the birthright principle. Even the most reactionary judge would immediately over-turn any executive order such as Trump proposed. The question then arises why the president would even waste time considering such an impossible thing. Perhaps he intended a cynical political ploy by which he would issue an executive order knowing it would be overturned, so that the courts would be blamed for failing to defend what his loyal supporters might regard as a proper view of US citizenship. But the more troubling possibility is that the elected president genuinely neither knew nor understood the basic workings of the Constitution, the separation of powers, or the capacity of the courts to overrule the executive. Nor was the birthright issue the only instance to arouse such concerns. Time and again, Trump launched into legal and consti-tutional battles that he could never win.

THE UNFILTERED VOICE

Adding to the president's difficulties was his enthusiasm about presenting his views directly and immediately, commonly through the instant medium of Twitter. This was historically unprecedented. Political figures, like ordinary citizens, might wish to express views based on instant reactions to situations, but usually they have been restrained both by the limitations of technology and by the advice of their subordinates and associates. Trump experienced no such restraints, and spoke his views directly and without concern for conse-quences. Such impromptu remarks were damaging in themselves, and under-mined delicate political stances or endangered policy decisions. On occasion, as scandals arose, rash words threatened to expose the president personally to legal repercussions. Trump's tweets and off-the-cuff statements gave constant ammunition to his critics, and repeatedly revealed his ignorance of constitu-tional matters and the limits of the presidential office he occupied. To borrow a familiar cliché, as a political leader Donald Trump really was his own worst enemy.

Even some of Trump's most criticized comments could have been defen-sible if phrased more diplomatically. To take the example mentioned earlier, he could easily have responded to the Charlottesville violence with a balanced statement formulated in consultation with experienced advisors and speech-writers. He might have flatly condemned white supremacist extremism and the violence that it provoked, while understanding and defending the legiti-mate motives of moderate conservatives and traditionalists who feared an over-swift removal of precious historical monuments. The same hypotheti-cal statement could have paid all respect to the admirable motives of liberal protesters yet at the same time denouncing the extremism of violent leftist Antifa groups. Both sides thus had "very fine people." Even if such a judicious pronouncement would not have satisfied all sides, it would have avoided the near-universal condemnation that greeted his actual unfiltered words. In real-ity, effective advisors were not available, and even if they had been he would not have listened to them.

Trump's main problem was that he stood so far outside the conven-tions of the political establishment, and showed no willingness to make concessions or compromises that might have changed that situation. On the other hand, if he had been part of the establishment loop then he never would have been elected president in the circumstances of 2016. The very strengths that secured his election became the weaknesses that so benighted his presidency.

SENATE AND COURTS

Despite the controversial circumstances of his election, Trump began his presidency with some major advantages, especially in terms of economic conditions. Unemployment remained historically low, a fact for which the president insisted on claiming full credit. Moreover, the Republican Party held both Houses of Congress from 2017 to 2019, and they secured some important victories. They were helped in this by the precedent established by Democratic Senate leader Harry Reid who had eliminated the need for a super-majority to confirm Cabinet officers and judges. Without this "nuclear option" Republicans would not have been able to confirm most of Trump's Cabinet nominees. The new setting also permitted them to approve many new judicial appointments, pushing the federal judiciary in conservative directions. New judges were likely to be originalists; that is, they applied the Constitution according to their understandings of the original intent of the Founding Fathers. In modern times, this intellectual movement found its prophet in conservative hero Antonin Scalia.

The new system of simple majority voting in the Senate acquired a vital new importance in Supreme Court nominations. In 2017, Republicans extended the principle to approve the nomination of Neil Gorsuch, a strong social conservative. In 2018, the resignation of moderate Justice Anthony Kennedy gave Trump another nomination, allowing him to choose another conservative, Brett Kavanaugh. As we have seen, what appeared to be a straightforward choice provoked a poisonous controversy when Kavanaugh was accused of sexual misconduct dating back to his high school years. But despite intense national divisions, the Senate approved the nomination by 50–48.

In retrospect, these changes in the Supreme Court underscore once again the extraordinary significance of the 2016 election. If Hillary Clinton had indeed won, and moreover secured a Democratic Senate majority, she would have been able to make those two nominations, and almost certainly more. The fact of a Democratic president would likely have persuaded Ruth Bader Ginsburg to accept retirement, and perhaps other older Justices as well. In that situation, Hillary Clinton would have set her (liberal) mark on the Supreme Court for a generation to come, besides remaking the federal judiciary at all levels.

REVERSALS

Among the administration's early senior members, two in particular stand out both for visibility and impact. These were Jeff Sessions, the Attorney General, and EPA administrator Scott Pruitt (both of whom eventually resigned in 2018). Together, they attempted a wide-ranging reversal of the liberal policies of the Obama years, and in the process became demon figures for left and liberal critics. Pruitt proved a dedicated foe of liberal environmental attitudes and policies. As we have seen, Trump scored some early victories in halting or reversing environmental policies that Obama had implemented through executive order, while beginning a longer-term rollback in related areas. Instead of combatting emissions, Trump sought a new emphasis on carbon-based fuels, on oil and even coal, and rejected attempts to improve gas mileage on automobiles. In criminal justice matters, too, Sessions tried to reverse the reforms of his Obama-era predecessor, Eric Holder, by insisting on more severe sentencing policies and rejecting any efforts to legalize marijuana.

But such attempts at setting the clock back characterized many aspects of the administration. Trump's Education Department tried to limit or undermine affirmative action policies and the workings of Title IX in higher education. The Health and Human Services Department reversed the Obama era's progressive stance on transgender matters, preferring to define gender as a status biologically conditioned at birth. In finance, a special target of resentment was the 2010 Dodd–Frank Wall Street Reform and Consumer Protection Act, originally passed to prevent a recurrence of the 2008 meltdown. Although the law could not be repealed in its entirety, specific aspects of its work have been modified or weakened. The administration also subverted the Obamacare framework, chipping away at specific provisions. In 2017, Congress repealed the individual mandate that was a fundamental component of the original vision.

The president's most ambitious initiatives involved immigration reform, an area of passionate concern to his most devoted followers. In his first two years, those efforts most prominently included an attempt to prevent immigrants arriving from a series of countries in the Middle East and North Africa. Although not framed in religious terms, this was generally termed the "Muslim Ban." (Ironically, the measure also made life much harder for persecuted Christian refugees from those countries.) The administration cut back dramatically on the number of refugees and asylum seekers that the US admitted. Of special concern was the issue of the Dreamers, those who had arrived in the US illegally as children but who had grown up knowing little other than American life. In 2017, the administration tried to end the generous Obama-era policy of Deferred Action for Childhood Arrivals (DACA), using both the president's executive powers and calling for Congressional action. Such attempts repeatedly encountered fierce opposition from the federal courts, leaving the present status of DACA unclear.

Immigrant communities, especially Latinos, were hard hit by the threat of forced removal faced by undocumented families. In 2018, hard-line administration policies detonated a major crisis with a decision to treat undocumented newcomers with zero tolerance. Among other things, this meant putting families into detention and separating children from parents – in some cases, so they could not be returned. This generated widespread protests in the US and internationally, and provoked heated rhetoric about the US operating "concentration camps." So fierce was popular reaction on the Left as to raise significant questions about the enforcement of immigration law, and some liberals urged the wholesale abolition of the immigration service, ICE (Immigration and Customs Enforcement).

Besides such measures, the president made sporadic efforts to build the border wall to which he had drawn such attention in his campaign. As predicted, that project proved extremely difficult on both financial and practical grounds, quite apart from its desirability. In late 2018, the wall issue provoked a battle with the incoming Democratic House of Representatives over the federal budget, and the ensuing conflict resulted in a disastrous shutdown of the US government. Such shutdowns had occurred before, but this example was by far the longest, at 35 days, and the most damaging. Although the president's faithful followers remained firm on the necessity of immigration restrictions, the shutdown gravely undermined his popular support.

Despite many failures and defeats, the administration achieved some successes on immigration, more than might have been thought from media coverage. Commonly, liberal groups sued to prevent the implementation of some new initiative, such as the Muslim Ban, and a lower level federal court would agree with their protest. But while the media were reporting a serious defeat for the administration, that case would then proceed through higher levels of appeal and even to the Supreme Court, which on occasion upheld the president's constitutional right to enact such a policy.

BUDGETS AND DEFICITS

In some matters, the administration adopted strong right-wing policies, and many conservatives enthusiastically echoed Trump's hostility to the administrative state. To them, the EPA (for instance) was an over-mighty agency that properly needed to be defanged, if not eliminated. But Trump often veered far from familiar conservatism. This was apparent in the federal budget approved for fiscal year 2018, under the Trumpian title *America First: A Budget Blueprint to Make America Great Again*. The law approved substantial tax cuts, which benefited a large cross section of Americans, but better-off citizens did particularly well. Even so, the law achieved little by way of the program cuts that conservatives had long sought, not even symbolic acts such as eliminating the public broadcasting system. Trump achieved political consensus by agreeing with liberal Democrats on ambitious spending plans that appalled those alarmed by spiraling budget deficits. This was Big Government writ large, and it threatened dire long-term consequences.

So starkly did such a fiscal approach differ from Republican rhetoric in recent years as to raise serious questions about what (if anything) the party actually stood for. It was not hard to imagine how the party would have responded if the Obama administration had presented such a spendthrift budget. A like question about core values faced conservative Christians and particularly evangelicals, who had for four decades been such a vital constituency of the Republican cause. The fact that evangelicals voted so overwhelmingly for Trump in 2016 caused much soul searching among the movement's followers, given the candidate's flagrant violations of traditional sexual morality, his multiple marriages and admitted adulteries, and his administration's indifference to the issues cherished by Christian voters. At worst, this seemingly cynical willingness to compromise values suggested that evangelicals were acting less out of belief than from a kind of tribalism, rooted in racial and regional values, and in white identity.

From many different perspectives, Republicans had to confront fundamental debates over values. How far should the party adopt Trumpism? Could it survive without?

AMERICA FIRST

Ideological divides were no less apparent in foreign affairs. Since the Clinton years, Republicans had been deeply split over questions of US intervention abroad, and particularly in the exercise of military power. After many setbacks, neo-conservatives advocated direct intervention against rising powers that sought weapons of mass destruction, with Iran as a special target. Isolationists, in contrast, were encouraged by Trump's adoption of the America First slogan, and hoped to avoid foreign entanglements. In practice, both factions would face repeated disappointments. Partly, this was because President Trump pursued his own idiosyncratic course, with all its inconsistencies, but there are also legitimate grounds to ask how far he actually understood global issues. This was the message of the bestselling exposé book *Fear*, published in 2018 by Bob Woodward, who demonstrated the turbulent disarray among the administration's officials and advisors, who desperately tried to cope with the president's capricious moods. In practice, "America First" seemed to mean whatever the president understood it to mean on particular days.

Trump's conduct of foreign policy represented a signal rejection of long-standing liberal assumptions, especially about international consensus. Trump was repeatedly at odds with US allies, generally on economic grounds: he denounced the European Union and Canada for unfair trading practices with the US. He threatened to tear up the NAFTA pact, which he replaced by a new USMCA, or US–Mexico–Canada Agreement. In practice, this differed little from the older NAFTA, and was mainly a symbolic rebranding. But his economic nationalism led him to launch trade wars against Europe and China, which inflicted real harm in some US regions that had strongly supported the president. The US even contemplated withdrawal from the World Trade Organization, which had long been viewed as a sacrosanct part of the global trading order. That was in addition to US withdrawal from the Paris climate change pact.

Most perilous was Trump's attempt to cut US contributions to NATO. These actions placed NATO under greater strains than it had known for many years, and raised European fears about the US commitment to transatlantic defense. In itself, complaints about European allies failing to bear their proper share of the defense burden were nothing new, and Obama in 2016 had won media praise for ridiculing the Europeans as "free riders." In Trump's case, the attack was so sensitive when contextualized alongside so many other barbs. Through all such disputes he often deployed aggressive and even threatening rhetoric in his tweets and statements, and personally insulted key Western leaders. He threatened a vision of the US detached from all its key allies and agreements.

In another departure from the foreign policy consensus, Trump downplayed concerns about human rights in several other countries and spoke warmly of authoritarian or dictatorial leaders, with whom he seemed to feel a kinship. Trump spoke admiringly of Philippine leader Rodrigo Duterte, and even China's Xi Jinping. Such attitudes meshed with an America First approach that treated the internal affairs of other nations as outside the proper concern of American policymakers, unless and until they impinged directly on US interests. The United Nations provided an arena for such competing views. For decades, conservatives had resented UN activism on human rights issues that regularly targeted Western powers while ignoring the far worse abuses of Islamic or socialist countries. Trump's UN ambassador, Nikki Haley, spoke out forcefully against such perceived double standards. In 2018, the US withdrew from the Human Rights Council of the United Nations, long a bugbear for conservatives.

In light of charges about Russian collusion with his election campaign, Trump's relations with Vladimir Putin were ambiguous. One low point of the presidency occurred in July 2018 when the two leaders met in Finland, where Trump explicitly accepted Putin's denials of interference in the recent US election, thus running against the forceful opinion of US intelligence and law enforcement. This announcement provoked political and media reaction at least as severe as to his intervention in the Charlottesville affair, to the point that some liberal observers accused the president of treason. Republicans, too, were harshly critical. Yet suggestions that Trump was over-friendly to Russia – if not a Russian puppet – looked implausible when just a few months later the president announced US withdrawal from the INF Treaty – the Intermediate-Range Nuclear Forces Treaty – originally signed in 1987 as a cornerstone of Reagan-era arms control policy. Trump's announced view was that the Russian violations of the Treaty demanded that it be abrogated – although it was not clear whether the President had the power to undertake such a step without

Senate approval. The Russians were as outraged by this decision as they had been delighted by earlier Trump statements. The contrast between the two Trump pronouncements makes it difficult to see much consistency in his attitudes or policies, beyond his inbuilt tendency to make snap decisions and to respond to impulse – to shoot from the hip.

Ideological and personal concerns came together in shaping Trump's response to the increasingly dangerous situation in North Korea, which was making such progress in its nuclear ambitions. Apart from obvious concerns for US security, Trump also had a powerful ambition to succeed in an area where his predecessors had achieved so little. Like Obama, though, Trump faced few viable options. Trump initially seemed to be leaning to intervention, and in one televised statement, he threatened North Korea with "fire and fury." It remains open to question what impact this had on the North Korean regime, but not long afterwards the country's leadership showed a surprising openness to negotiation. In 2018, Trump held personal talks with North Korean leader Kim Jong Un, as the latter agreed publicly to abandon nuclear weapons. The reality of such an outcome remains uncertain, and it is highly unlikely that Kim intended anything other than a rhetorical flourish. Although Trump hailed the agreement as a mighty victory, it was less substantial than the deal that Obama had made with Iran, the pact that Trump himself had so often condemned as profoundly flawed. In 2018, in fact, Trump abrogated that Iranian deal, to the horror of the US's European allies.

The president also had to deal with other unfinished business from the Obama years, in the form of the war in Syria. Initially, Trump appalled isolationist supporters by his willingness to maintain the US military presence in Syria. He was even prepared to punish Syrian chemical warfare attacks against that country's rebels with US and Allied air raids. On multiple occasions, US forces faced the risk of direct conflict with Russian surrogate forces in the country, and that even escalated to direct combat against Russian mercenaries. In this area, Trump's conduct of foreign affairs was surprisingly close to what had for several years been the consensus in Washington. In late 2018, however, the president then reversed himself to announce the withdrawal of US forces in Syria, causing general puzzlement as much as shock.

In practice, Trump-era policy did not depart too much from Obama's in dealings with China, which was so heavily engaged in the illegal development and fortification of the South China Sea. Despite Trump's rhetoric of a strong America that would once more be respected on the global stage, the US showed little interest in curbing or reversing that expansionist policy, which represented an incalculable victory for Chinese military strength. In these years, Xi Jinping successfully made China great again.

SCANDALS

From the first days of his presidency, Donald Trump faced the threat of multiple scandals and investigations, and liberals were enthusiastically advocating impeachment from the day that they had failed to prevent him taking office. Several critical issues threatened damaging consequences. One was financial, in that Trump had refused to separate his personal economic enterprises from official business in ways that were expected by the ethics code and probably by criminal law. Arguably, he violated the constitutional prohibition on accepting "foreign emoluments." Trump was the first major politician in 40 years who had simply refused to publish his income tax returns, raising suspicions about what he might be concealing. In this matter as in so much else, Trump treated his political life much as he pursued his business activities, and through the years he had made frequent use of legal non-disclosure agreements (NDAs) that required associates and contacts to maintain strict secrecy about transactions, at the cost of exorbitant fines or penalties.

Much more serious were the alleged Trump ties to the Russian government and intelligence services, and to their efforts in the 2016 election. In May 2017, the Justice Department appointed Robert Mueller as Special Counsel, and he pursued his investigations throughout the president's first term. Liberal critics of the administration had high hopes of the Mueller probe. At best, they expected some direct evidence that Trump officials (or Trump himself) had worked directly and knowingly with Russian intelligence in an effort to steal the election. Seeming to confirm that the administration had much to hide, Trump repeatedly threatened to close the investigation, an act that would have caused a constitutional crisis. But although the Russia investigation ventured into delicate areas, its results were far from clear-cut. It became increasingly clear that there was no smoking gun in the sense of a direct connection with the Russian government or its agencies. That was quite different from negotiating or holding conversations with individuals whose Russian official connections were not known.

Still, the Mueller investigation had its effects, with the prosecution of Trump advisors and associates who might otherwise have served as presidential advisors and aides. That contributed to the president's isolation. Moreover, it raised the specter of witnesses whom the prosecution might "turn" to testify against Trump personally. Principal targets in such legal maneuvrings included Trump's close advisor Roger Stone, and his campaign chair, Paul Manafort. Another central player in these events was Michael Flynn, who served as Trump's National Security Advisor in 2017, and who pled guilty to relatively minor charges in the Mueller investigation.

The suggestion was that he did so as part of a bargain that would require him to testify against Trump. As in previous investigations, the Special Counsel's attention also moved to other matters not directly concerned with the collusion issue. As noted earlier, Trump dismissed FBI chief Comey in circumstances that are disputed. According to one account, Trump made this decision after requesting Comey to close or restrict an investigation relating to the Russia inquiry, and thus to give Michael Flynn a break. If this sequence was in fact proven – that Comey's refusal directly caused his dismissal – then Trump might have committed the offense of obstruction of justice, which could form the basis of impeachment proceedings. Also perilous would be any false statements that Trump or his advisors gave under oath, which would constitute the criminal offense of perjury.

One peril facing the presidency involved an issue intrinsically far less serious than the grim charges of foreign espionage and manipulation of the US electoral system. Through the years, Donald Trump had had a series of sexual affairs, one of which in 2006 involved the pornography star Stormy Daniels. Reportedly, the Trump camp was concerned that this story might surface before the 2016 election, and the then-candidate's attorney Michael Cohen paid hush money to Daniels, requiring her to sign a NDA. Subsequent exposés have indicated that at least one other woman was likewise paid off. The circumstances surrounding these payments were potentially damaging if the funds stemmed from the presidential campaign, or were intended to influence an election, which raised the prospect of campaign finance violations. Matters became doubly dangerous when Cohen cooperated with investigators, and presumably undertook to implicate Trump and to testify against him.

Despite the abundant talk of impeachment, any such action would face severe obstacles. A majority of the House of Representatives must agree that a president has committed "high crimes and misdemeanors," a notoriously vague term. But once the House has passed articles of impeachment, the president must be tried by the Senate, where conviction requires a vote of two-thirds of those present. That would mean 67 Senators from the total complement of 100. Absent some extremely clear and incontestable evidence of outright criminality, it is highly likely that a Trump impeachment would be seen as a purely partisan action, which would be decided on straight party lines. The odds against achieving that two-thirds majority would be high. When the House impeached Bill Clinton in 1998–1999, only 50 Senate votes could be found to support his removal from office, leaving him acquitted. In the aftermath, Clinton successfully presented himself as the victim of partisan extremism, and the whole affair damaged Republican electoral chances. That precedent undoubtedly concerns modern-day Democratic leaders.

RESISTANCE

Few presidents have met such sustained and bitter domestic opposition as Trump did from the "Resistance," a term that expanded beyond Democrats resenting Hillary Clinton's defeat to a wide range of social movements. Trump's inauguration in 2017 was greeted by the Women's March, an enormous gathering in Washington, claiming several hundred thousand participants. Many chose the emblem of the pink "pussy hat." This core event was coordinated with other like events across the United States, which together claimed millions of participants in all. That feminist upsurge later merged into the #MeToo outcry against sexual harassment and assault, which was further fueled by the Kavanaugh confirmation hearings. Feminist authors like Rebecca Traister urged the necessity of anger and rage in driving women's activism, in mobilizing "the revolutionary power of women's anger." Educated and liberal women in particular placed their hopes in sweeping electoral change, as women came forward in unprecedented numbers as potential political candidates. Although Democrats hoped for a blue wave favoring their party in the 2018 midterms, the resulting election should more accurately be seen as a pink wave, as women were galvanized. Multiple other causes provoked large public demonstrations, including the rising anti-gun movement.

A wave of activism caused an efflorescence of activist movements within the Democratic coalition: the Working Families Party, Justice Democrats, the Progressive Change Campaign, and Our Revolution. The old Democratic Socialists of America, DSA, tried valiantly to bring the socialist cause back to the heart of US politics. Through 2017 and 2018, DSA membership swelled, mainly among young adults: between 2013 and 2018, the group's median age plummeted from 68 to 33. The DSA upsurge was over and above the rise of movements like Black Lives Matter and #MeToo. Even the venerable American Civil Liberties Union acquired a new lease of life as a core organizing element in the Resistance. In 2017 and 2018, its membership swelled from 450,000 to 1.8 million.

The most visible public faces of Resistance were celebrities and stars of film and television. Few visible personalities resisted the larger liberal trend as entertainment events became regular manifestations of anti-Trump sentiment. Particularly active were the comedians who fronted late-night television talk shows, such as Jimmy Kimmel, John Oliver, Stephen Colbert, and Trevor Noah. The long-running comedy show *Saturday Night Live* became a dependable platform for anti-Trump commentary and satire. Reflecting shifts in the consumption of media, such shows played a core role in public opposition that major newspapers might have done in an earlier generation. In the process, celebrities often used coarse and obscene language that would have been far beyond the pale in previous years but which now became mainstreamed. Also in the realm of popular culture, the television series of *The Handmaid's Tale* gave feminists ammunition in their attacks on what they denounced as a sexist and reactionary government which (they claimed) was seeking to turn the US into a nightmare patriarchal dystopia like the "Gilead" of that program. Michael Moore offered a blistering attack on Trump in his film *11/9*, which refers to the date that the 2016 election result was declared. The title recalls the other date of 9/11 as, in Moore's view, the Trump election was a comparable act of devastating violence and sabotage committed against the United States.

As in the 1960s, activists combined calls for legislative action with mass protests and street demonstrations. Beyond questions of legality, such direct action ventured into politically uncharted territory. In 2018, activists called for personal protests against conservative leaders and Trump associates in public places or even at their homes, a hazardous policy that threatened to incite violence. The previous year, a leftist militant had shot two senior Republican politicians at baseball practice in Alexandria, VA. Obviously such a crime could in no sense be blamed on liberal causes, any more than the shooting of Representative Giffords in 2011 was the work of the Tea Party. But intense political partisanship does tend to provoke individuals already prone to violence, who could now find specific targets for their grievances and obsessions. What the Resistance saw as the expression of legitimate outrage against tainted political malefactors could easily be viewed by less committed voters as incitement to mob rule and vigilantism.

In addition to mounting rhetorical opposition to the administration, many city and state governments resisted the implementation of policies they found unacceptable. Such tactics raised grave constitutional issues which dated back to the earliest years of the republic. At various times, states had challenged or threatened to ignore federal policies through a theory of nullification. This had on occasion provoked federal threats of armed force and even civil war. In the modern context, such local dissidence was complicated by its association not so much with states as with cities, which had no formal place in the constitutional system. Even so, cities determined to resist federal policies especially on the key issue of immigration, stressing their status as sanctuaries and forbidding employees to cooperate with the unpopular ICE. Some states practiced political dissidence on a scale that threatened significant legal conflicts. By far the most important was California, which occupies an economic role comparable to the largest European nations. This was a "sanctuary state," and as we have seen California sought an independent role in environmental issues.

THE 2018 MIDTERMS

The midterm elections in 2018 attracted partisan interest and commitment far exceeding many presidential contests in earlier years. Many media accounts reported voter fury, and told of normally tranquil individuals uninterested in politics who now acquired a passionate dedication to challenging or removing Trump. This dedication, which was obvious on Twitter and social media, naturally led to heavy turnout in the midterms – perhaps 114 million voters, compared to 83 million as recently as 2014. Election-related spending exceeded $5 billion. Democrats hoped not only to make major advances in both houses of Congress, but for a liberal blue wave, a fundamental reorientation of national politics and parties.

As predicted, Democrats did in fact win back the House of Representatives, with a strong gain of 40 seats. Particularly gratifying were a series of victories in marginal districts in the swing states that had given Trump his victory in 2016. Democrats defeated some of the leading Republican advocates of anti-union and right-to-work laws. The party won many successes at state level, where the competition in this year was unusually fierce, and seven governorships. Such state victories are so important because they supply the rising politicians who will almost certainly play a role in national politics some years later. For a party with such an aging leadership, this was a significant step forward. Also heartening was the revival of Democratic support in Sunbelt and formerly Red Republican states, which now became competitive – Purple, if not yet Blue. Even in Texas, Democrat Beto O'Rourke made a respectable showing in the Senate race, raising high hopes for future victories. Nationally, Democrats cemented their support among the coalition of the ascendant. As the *Washington Post* observed about the new House of Representatives that took office in 2019, 90 percent of the Republican caucus were white men, compared to only a third of Democratic members. The coalition of forces behind the Democratic victory was symbolized by Alexandra Ocasio-Cortez, a 29-year-old Latina of Puerto Rican descent, a former waitress and a DSA member, who won election to the House of Representatives from New York City's 14th District. Young, millennial, female, Latina, and urban, she perfectly epitomizes the "ascendant," and she emerged overnight as a potential political superstar. Her use of social media contributed to her popular celebrity.

But talk of a historic realignment was debatable. The scale of the Democrat victory in the House was significantly smaller than the midterm Republican triumphs of 1994 or 2010. Instead of marking a new political direction, 2018 rather looked like a standard pattern in which all incoming presidents face heavy losses in their first midterms. That is what happened to Reagan in 1982, Clinton in 1994, and Obama in 2010, all of whom managed to recover and win re-election. Significantly, the Republicans of 2018 not only held on to control of the Senate but slightly increased their majority. Given the worst-case scenario that Republicans had imagined before the midterms, these results were a relief.

However we interpret the results, the consequences are far-reaching. Losing the House meant that the administration would find it very difficult to pass legislation, and Democratic Representatives declared a firm commitment to investigating possible wrongdoing by the administration, and by the President personally. Taken together, these changes promised an era of political gridlock reminiscent of the later Obama years. But at the same time, the Republican hold on the Senate limited many of the worst consequences of Democratic anger, including possible impeachment.

DEMOCRATIC DEBATES

The Trump phenomenon posed agonizing dilemmas for Republicans, who feared for the long-term future of their party. But Democrats too were conflicted. If Democrats could agree completely in their loathing for Trump and his administration, they were far from unified on their course of future action, and the impeachment issue epitomized the divisions. While activists favored a swift move to impeach, more moderate Democrats nervously recalled how the Republican campaign against Bill Clinton had collapsed in the late 1990s. Scarcely less thorny was the proposal to seek to impeach Supreme Court Justices, notably Brett Kavanaugh. Any such action would certainly be seen as nakedly partisan, and it would invite retaliation against liberal Justices in future years.

The extreme frustration among liberals was also directed at other causes that would hitherto have been considered unacceptably extreme but which were now discussed with surprising frankness. Some of the proposals that now surfaced were quite revolutionary in their nature. If the Supreme Court was now under solid conservative domination, then perhaps the time had come to dilute that conservative majority by expanding the overall size of the court and adding new liberal Justices – by "court-packing." The problem with this ultra-liberal approach was that future Republican administrations would retaliate in kind, adding new conservative Justices when they had the power, and creating chaos in the judicial branch.

Repeatedly, Democrats faced the dilemma that Republicans had encountered in earlier times, namely that enthusiastic party loyalists demand policies that might well be unacceptably extreme to ordinary voters. That conflict had been at the heart of debates over the nature of the Democratic Party from Bill Clinton's time onward. After the 2016 debacle, some Democrats had urged outreach to the disaffected white working-class voters who had favored Obama, but who then turned to Trump. That would mean the party accepting moderate policies aimed at building consensus on social issues like abortion and guns, and acknowledging concerns about immigration. Other activists regarded any such effort as futile and counter-productive, and demanded a sharper focus on something like the coalition of the ascendant, with explicitly radical policies.

On many issues, calls for moderation confronted ideals of purity. In immigration matters, activists found no difficulty in demanding not just the extensive reform of ICE but its total abolition. But if Democrats adopted that cause as a platform issue, that left them in the position of seemingly calling for the complete opening of the nation's borders to all immigration. And if most Democrats could agree on the virtues of more stringent gun control laws, many younger activists were calling for restrictions that would be deeply unpopular in many regions of the country. Other issues were no less sensitive. Although Alexandra Ocasio-Cortez attracted widespread support, her personal appeal was combined with political beliefs that placed her at odds with the party establishment, and which would be potentially explosive for any national party platform. Ocasio-Cortez and like-minded progressives favored the defense of Palestinian rights, which threatened to ignite concerns over relations with Israel and to alienate Jewish voters.

The new progressives also made climate activism central to the social justice cause, calling for a program of unprecedented government intervention and spending that was termed a "Green New Deal." That might be attractive to many, especially when framed in terms of mass job creation, but Ocasio-Cortez advocated a total US conversion to renewable energy resources as early as 2030, which even quite radical experts in the field of energy regard as impractical and utopian. Citing the imminent peril posed by climate change, other young activists called for campaigns of direct action and civil disobedience, which again raised questions of legality. It was a perennial dilemma: how far should activism go, and how fast?

Donald Trump faced severe difficulties that repeatedly threatened to destroy his presidency and wreck the Republican Party. But the same crises that challenged the Right also posed other quite different challenges for Democrats. Both national parties faced years of traumatic inter-party conflict, threatening to divide generations and genders, as much as ideologies.

Conclusion: Only Tomorrow

In discussing changing ethnic attitudes in recent history, I mentioned the case of the character Apu in *The Simpsons*, suggesting that it would be unimaginable for media today to portray such a figure (see above, Chapter 3). In many other areas too, a modern audience must look with astonishment at media depictions of just a quarter century past; that gulf of comprehension indicates the speed of changes in this era. So swiftly have these transformations occurred – and are continuing to occur – that only with difficulty can we imagine how they might develop in the near future, say over the next two decades. Can we even contemplate the world of 2040?

Besides ethnic changes, revolutionary new attitudes to sexual behavior make it difficult for contemporary younger audiences to watch films or television programs of a few decades back without defining the interactions depicted as harassment, stalking, or worse. In the 1990s, popular television series like *Friends* and *Seinfeld* appealed to young audiences of liberal disposition, but today those series' attitudes to issues of sexism and homophobia make them extremely problematic for many. So does their un-diverse casting. Such a sea change forces us to ask what aspects of contemporary life will baffle and appall audiences in 20 years' time. We can reasonably make some predictions about the US of the 2040s, in terms of its ethnic balance, its majority–minority composition, but such social currents and grievances are quite beyond us. We can project that transgender concerns, and matters of gender fluidity, will be a likely focus of broad social evolution, but other trends will yet surprise us.

Going further, what are the behaviors and attitudes that today are quite mainstream and acceptable that in 20 years will appear shocking, and possibly subject to legal action or criminal prosecution? Think of the range of concerns in 2019 that were beyond imagining in 1999. We should also think how those multiple shifts have affected everyday speech and linguistic usage. What might we be saying casually now that in 20 years would be viewed as stunningly insensitive or offensive?

Recent experience suggests that one critical arena of future change will be the American past, or rather our constructions of that past, based on evolving forms of racial and ethnic consciousness. It would be illuminating to see how Americans of 2040 will retell the national story, identify its great episodes, its heroes and villains. How will those new perceptions be reflected in something as basic as the names given to cities and states? Literally, what will the map of the United States look like by that time?

Nowhere are social transformations more apparent than in matters of technology and the impact of high tech on everyday life. Countless fictional portrayals from as recently as the 1990s make little sense to younger audiences today because the plots depend on a degree of ignorance that is now scarcely imaginable. Looking backward, contemporary audiences are bemused that characters in a film fail to check the background of a suspicious character, or why those characters can get lost, or why they do not check the reviews of an attraction. Are no search engines readily available? Why do those characters not just use their smartphones? If we look back today at the depictions of computers or cellphones 20 or 30 years ago, they seem unbelievably primitive.

We might debate whether any era of American history has witnessed such sweeping technological changes in such a short time. Some inventions have of course had their impact, such as the telegraph, or the internal combustion engine, or television, but the accumulated nature of recent innovations is unprecedented, as is the time frame. Nor is there any suggestion that the rate of advances is slowing – in biology as much as electronics or robotics – and only a daring futurologist would dare to project their combined impacts by 2040.

Predictions of America's near future have a very mixed record of accuracy, although some seemingly wild prophecies have turned out far more accurately than their authors dared believe. As early as 2000, *The Simpsons* (again) set a story in a near future in which a Trump presidency has shattered the US economy. Also in 2000, I wrote a satirically intended commentary on a forthcoming US invasion of Afghanistan, an event that I absolutely did not foresee as a literal prospect. In March 2001, the conspiracy-oriented television series *The Lone Gunmen* depicted a plot to fly an airliner into the World Trade Center, with the goal of starting a war to enrich profiteers. In retrospect, one of the most powerful of these wholly accidental triumphs was Billy Joel's 1976 song "Miami 2017 (Seen The Lights Go Out On Broadway)." It portrayed a Manhattan devastated by violence and terrorism, as its skyscrapers tumble. After September 2001, that vision seemed eerily prophetic, and as in the song the catastrophe really did force authorities to "sen[d] a carrier up from Norfolk [Virginia]." By raw chance, seers can achieve real successes.

Referring to the September 11 attacks also makes us realize how unwise we are simply to extrapolate contemporary realities into the future, to extend graphs of contemporary trends. In fact, history can be reshaped by sudden events foreseen by few at the time, and certainly not by the political establishment. Only in their aftermath can we trace the stages leading up to such unexpected and crucial developments, what are termed Black Swan events. September 11 was one instance, and so in its way was the 2008 crash: if many expected a financial reckoning around that time, few foresaw its catastrophic scale. Some writers use the acronym GUBU for such epic happenings, which are "grotesque, unbelievable, bizarre, and unprecedented." Of their nature, we simply cannot predict the Black Swans of the next 20 years – the wars, or epidemics, or insurrections, or sneak attacks, or natural disasters, or economic crises – although we should assume that one or more such GUBUs will occur. They are simply beyond our reckoning.

But it is in matters of technology that predictions so conspicuously fail to foresee reality, and virtually always because those attempted prophecies are far too timid, too conservative. Another popular vision of more or less our own time appeared in the 1973 dystopian film *Soylent Green*, which portrays the world of 2022. In imagining how the super-rich and sophisticated of that era would while away their leisure time, the film-makers plausibly foresaw them playing video games. But the specific game in vogue is Computer Space, an extremely simple video tennis activity comparable to Pong, and one that would already appear embarrassingly childish by 1980. That example should serve as a sobering warning to anyone seeking to describe the likely technological worlds of 2040. However daring we may believe we are being, we are not going far enough.

So extensive, so dizzying, have been the developments of the past 20 years as to make us dubious about trying to project the future with any confidence. The future has arrived far faster than anyone could have expected.

Suggestions for Further Reading

The resources available for studying contemporary history are vast, and that abundance is both their strength and their weakness. Instead of drawing on history books narrowly defined, we often look to works of journalism or biography, or of political or social commentary, much of which is avowedly partisan. As I have often noted, partisanship in the political realm is so intense that it is all but impossible to imagine a sober and objective account of Hillary Clinton or Donald Trump that might satisfy all readers. That comment should serve as a caveat in many of the suggestions that follow. These books are instructive and often valuable, but many make no claim to objectivity. The following listing is, of course, highly selective.

General surveys of the era include H. W. Brands, *American Dreams* (Penguin, 2010). In *Restless Giant* (Oxford University Press, 2005) James T. Patterson surveys US history from 1974 through 2000, "from Watergate to Bush v. Gore."

On the "unsettled accounts" inherited from the 1990s, useful surveys include Haynes Johnson, *The Best of Times* (Harcourt, 2001) and Gil Troy, *The Age of Clinton* (Thomas Dunne Books, 2015). Steve Kornacki, *The Red and the Blue* (HarperCollins, 2018) studies the party politics of that era, "the birth of political tribalism," and the impact of that trend in later decades. In *A Bubble in Time* (Ivan R. Dee, 2009), William L. O'Neill describes the "interwar years" of 1989–2001, from the end of the Cold War through 9/11. Bill Clinton's own (sprawling) autobiography is titled *My Life* (Alfred A. Knopf, 2004). For conservative movements, see David Farber, *The Rise and Fall of Modern American Conservatism* (Princeton University Press, 2012). Despite its title, Sean Wilentz, *The Age of Reagan* (HarperCollins, 2008) explores that political inheritance up to 2008. For cultural history in this era, see Phillip E. Wegner, *Life Between Two Deaths, 1989–2001* (Duke University Press, 2009) and Telly Davidson, *Culture War* (McFarland & Company, Inc., 2016). Andrew Hartman, *A War for the Soul of America* (The University of Chicago Press, 2015) traces the evolution of the culture wars.

The origins of the internet have attracted a vast literature. One useful entry point is Brian McCullough, *How the Internet Happened* (Liveright, 2018).

Suggesting the excitement of that early era is the title of W. Joseph Campbell's *1995: The Year the Future Began* (University of California Press, 2015). Adam Fisher's *Valley of Genius* (Twelve, 2018) is a substantial history of Silicon Valley and the rise of the tech industry. For the world of video games in the 1990s, see Blake J. Harris's semi-fictionalized *Console Wars: Sega, Nintendo, and the Battle That Defined a Generation* (HarperCollins, 2014).

The events surrounding 9/11 and the wars that followed are described in works by Lawrence Wright – in *The Looming Tower* (Alfred A. Knopf, 2006) – and Steve Coll, author of *Ghost Wars* (Penguin, 2004) and *Directorate S* (Penguin, 2018). Peter Bergen described the struggle between the US and al-Qaeda in his *The Longest War* (Free Press, 2011), and covered the quest to find Osama bin Laden in *Manhunt* (Bodley Head, 2012). In *Against All Enemies* (Simon & Schuster, 2004), former US advisor Richard Clarke presented a critical analysis of recent administration debates over responses to terrorism and Middle Eastern threats. For first-hand accounts of Iraq, see Thomas E. Ricks, *Fiasco* (Penguin, 2006); Rajiv Chandrasekaran, *Imperial Life in the Emerald City* (Alfred A. Knopf, 2006); and Dexter Filkins, *The Forever War* (Alfred A. Knopf, 2008). The twin wars are discussed in J. Kael Weston's polemical *The Mirror Test* (Alfred A. Knopf, 2016).

On the presidency of George W. Bush, see Robert Draper, *Dead Certain* (Simon & Schuster, 2007). There is much of value in Bob Woodward's trilogy *Bush at War*; *Plan of Attack*; and *State of Denial* (Simon & Schuster, 2002–2006). Chris Edelson, *Power Without Constraint* (University of Wisconsin Press, 2016) describes the impact of 9/11 and the subsequent wars on the role of the presidency. For Bush's most significant advisors, see Stephen F. Hayes, *Cheney* (HarperCollins, 2007) and (on Donald Rumsfeld) Bradley Graham, *By His Own Rules* (PublicAffairs, 2009).

One rich source on recent immigration history is Tom Gjelten, *A Nation of Nations* (Simon & Schuster, 2016). In his *Amexica* (Penguin, 2010), Ed Vulliamy describes the nation's southern borderlands with a special focus on immigration issues. Joel Kotkin's *The Next Hundred Million* (Penguin, 2010) explores near-future trends in ethnicity, migration, and urban growth. William H. Frey, *Diversity Explosion* (new edition, Brookings Institution Press, 2018) describes the impact of changing demographics.

The number of recent titles on the high-tech world is close to endless. Some important contributions include John Battelle, *The Search* (Portfolio, 2005), on Google and the search engine firms; and Scott Galloway, *The Four* (Portfolio, 2017) on the world of the goliath corporations, Amazon, Apple, Facebook, and Google. The long and influential rivalry between Apple and Google is the subject of Fred Vogelstein's *Dogfight* (Sarah Crichton Books, 2013).

José van Dijck surveys the topic of social media in *The Culture of Connectivity* (Oxford University Press, 2013). Some of the most accessible writing about the high-tech boom can be found in biographies, such as Walter Isaacson's *Steve Jobs* (Little, Brown, 2011), or memoirs, like Satya Nadella's *Hit Refresh* (HarperCollins, 2017). In *Chaos Monkeys* (HarperCollins, 2016), Antonio Garcia Martinez has much to say about the culture of Silicon Valley. Critical and even apocalyptic books about this culture abound. Emily Chang's *Brotopia* (Portfolio, 2018) analyses the powerful and deeply embedded sexist biases in Silicon Valley life. John Carreyrou's *Bad Blood* (Alfred A. Knopf, 2018) is a revealing case study of Silicon Valley malfeasance. Jamie Bartlett's *The People vs Tech* (Ebury Press, 2018) argues that the growth of the internet gravely undermines democracy.

On advances in biological technology, and gene editing, see Jennifer Doudna and Samuel Sternberg, *A Crack in Creation* (Vintage, 2017). Through a case study of one company, Barry Werth's *The Antidote* (Simon & Schuster, 2014) tells us much about the larger New Pharma industry. Although not concerned with the tech world, Ken Auletta's *Frenemies* (Penguin, 2018) uses the advertising world as a case study of the epic disruption of the corporate world in this era.

Conditions in declining cities and industries have also attracted many writers. One much-quoted contribution is J. D. Vance's *Hillbilly Elegy* (HarperCollins, 2016), in which the story of one family serves as an epitome for the larger crisis of the white working class. In *Steeltown U.S.A.* (University Press of Kansas, 2002) Sherry Lee Linkon and John Russo use Youngstown, OH, to explore the role of memory and history in a declining industrial city. Chloe E. Taft, *From Steel to Slots* (Harvard University Press, 2016) studies a former industrial city that attempted to restore its fortunes through casino gambling. Also useful is Mark Binelli, *Detroit City is the Place To Be* (Metropolitan Books, 2012). The water crisis in Flint, MI, is described in Anna Clark, *The Poisoned City* (Metropolitan Books, 2018).

On a broader scale, Matt Taibbi explores ideas of inequality and the wealth gap in *The Divide* (Spiegel & Grau, 2014), as does George Packer in his kaleidoscopic book *The Unwinding* (Faber & Faber, 2014). Charles Murray's *Coming Apart* (Crown Publishing, 2012) traces "The State of White America 1960–2010." Nancy Isenberg's *White Trash* (Viking, 2016) examines the intersection of race and class in US history, with many implications for contemporary realities; and see Nell Irvin Painter, *The History of White People* (W. W. Norton & Company Ltd., 2011). For labor, see Raymond L. Hogler, *The End of American Labor Unions* (Praeger, 2015) and Sarah Kessler, *Gigged: The End of the Job and the Future of Work* (Random House, 2018). For the decline of permanent employment and "real jobs," see also Louis Hyman, *Temp* (Viking, 2018). In her *Dopesick* (Little, Brown, 2018), Beth Macy offers a wide-ranging perspective on the opioid crisis, for which see also Barry Meier, *Pain Killer* (revised edition, Random House, 2018).

Paul Taylor's *The Next America* (PublicAffairs, 2014) addresses generational divides and tensions.

For "the American Energy Revolution," see Charles R. Morris, *Comeback* (PublicAffairs, 2013); Russell Gold, *The Boom* (Simon & Schuster, 2014); and Gary Sernovitz, *The Green and the Black* (St. Martin's Press, 2016). Bethany McLean offers a sweeping account of fracking and other recent changes in the US energy world in her memorably titled *Saudi America* (Columbia Global Reports, 2018). The local impact of fracking is described in Tom Wilber, *Under the Surface* (Cornell University Press, 2012) and in Eliza Griswold, *Amity and Prosperity* (Farrar, Straus and Giroux, 2018). Richard Heinberg harshly critiques the new oil boom on environmental grounds in *Snake Oil* (Post Carbon Institute, 2013).

On long-term trends in urban development and growth, see Alan Ehrenhalt, *The Great Inversion and the Future of the American City* (Alfred A. Knopf, 2012). As we have seen, one of the most influential theorists on contemporary cities is Richard Florida, whose views are expressed in *The Rise of the Creative Class* (expanded edition, Basic Books, 2014) and *The New Urban Crisis* (Basic Books, 2017). Patrick Sharkey addresses "the great crime decline" in *Uneasy Peace* (W. W. Norton & Company Ltd., 2018). For new forms of urban poverty, see Matthew Desmond, *Evicted* (Penguin, 2016). Randy Shaw, *Generation Priced Out* (University of California Press, 2018) discusses the impact of inequality on the urban middle classes and poor.

Among the many contributions on the crisis of 2008, see Andrew Ross Sorkin, *Too Big to Fail* (Viking, 2009); William Cohan, *House of Cards* (Doubleday Books, 2009); Michael Lewis, *The Big Short* (W. W. Norton & Company Ltd., 2010); and Bethany McLean and Joseph Nocera, *All the Devils Are Here* (Portfolio, 2010). Adam Tooze offers a global perspective in *Crashed* (Viking, 2018). Barry Eichengreen, *Hall of Mirrors* (Oxford University Press, 2015) is an innovative comparison of the twin economic crises of the 1930s and 2007–2008. Former Treasury Secretary Henry M. Paulson offers his personal view of the crisis in *On the Brink* (Business Plus, 2010).

For the 2008 presidential campaign, see John Heilemann and Mark Halperin, *Game Change* (Harper Perennial, 2010), and Jeffrey C. Alexander, *The Performance of Politics* (Oxford University Press, 2010). Halperin and Heilemann also studied the 2012 election in *Double Down* (Penguin, 2014). Obama's presidency is assessed in adulatory terms in Michael D'Antonio,

A Consequential President (Thomas Dunne Books, 2017). Ben Rhodes, *The World as It Is* (Penguin, 2018) is a memoir of the Obama White House. For health care reform and Obamacare, see Steven Brill, *America's Bitter Pill* (Random House, 2015).

One significant analysis of electoral politics is found in Thomas Frank's *What's the Matter with Kansas?* (Metropolitan Books, 2004), which addresses the question of why working- and middle-class people so often vote against what appears to be their economic self-interest. The book has much to say about the roots of conservative populism. Changes in electoral structures and party funding are discussed in Martin Gilens' manifesto *Affluence and Influence* (Princeton University Press, 2012). Kate Zernike discusses the Tea Party in *Boiling Mad* (Times Books, 2010). On Occupy, see Todd Gitlin, *Occupy Nation* (HarperCollins, 2012), and for related radical protests, Sarah Jaffe's *Necessary Trouble* (Nation Books, 2016). Dan Kaufman describes partisan conflict and protests in one key state in his *The Fall of Wisconsin* (W. W. Norton & Company Ltd., 2018). In *The Great Alignment* (Yale University Press, 2018), Alan I. Abramowitz presents an ambitious discussion of shifts in parties and partisanship in providing the context for the Trump years.

For Obama's national security policy, see Charlie Savage, *Power Wars* (Little, Brown, 2015). Lawrence Wright, *The Terror Years* (Alfred A. Knopf, 2016) traces the origins of ISIS and Islamic State. Obama's Iran policy is described in Trita Parsi, *Losing an Enemy* (Yale University Press, 2017). Sung Chull Kim and Michael D. Cohen describe another enduring nightmare in *North Korea and Nuclear Weapons* (Georgetown University Press, 2017). For a groundbreaking study of cyber-warfare, see John P. Carlin, with Garrett M. Graff, *Dawn of the Code War* (Public Affairs, 2018).

Among many books on environmentalism and climate issues, see especially Patrick Allitt, *A Climate of Crisis* (Penguin, 2014). We also find ambitious manifestos like Jedediah Purdy's *After Nature* (Harvard University Press, 2015). In *This Changes Everything* (Alfred A. Knopf, 2014), Naomi Klein presents a revolutionary manifesto for fighting climate change. Thomas L. Friedman popularized green themes in his 2008 book *Hot, Flat and Crowded* (Farrar, Straus and Giroux). Dan Egan offers a local case study of ongoing environmental crisis in *The Life and Death of the Great Lakes* (W. W. Norton & Company Ltd., 2018).

For racial issues in the Obama era, see Michael Tesler, *Post-Racial or Most-Racial?* (University of Chicago Press, 2016) and Michael Eric Dyson, *The Black Presidency* (Houghton Mifflin Harcourt, 2016). Michelle Alexander, *The New Jim Crow* (New Press, 2010) describes mass incarceration and the racial aspects of criminal justice. For the conditions that produced Black

Lives Matter, see Wesley Lowery, *They Can't Kill Us All* (Little, Brown, 2016). Howard Bryant, *The Heritage* (Beacon Press, 2018) discusses political protest activities by black athletes. In *Between the World and Me* (Spiegel & Grau, 2015), Ta-Nehisi Coates offers a highly personal (and influential) view of American racial history. See also his *We Were Eight Years in Power* (One World, 2017).

Former New Orleans Mayor Mitch Landrieu addresses white responses to the new movements in *In the Shadow of Statues* (Viking, 2018). For white supremacism see George Hawley, *Making Sense of the Alt-Right* (Columbia University Press, 2017) and Kathleen Belew's *Bring the War Home* (Harvard University Press, 2018).

On the gay rights movement, see Lillian Faderman, *The Gay Revolution* (Simon & Schuster, 2015), while Jo Becker, *Forcing the Spring* (Penguin, 2014) describes the arrival of same-sex marriage.

The 2016 election has already attracted many authors, few of whom on either side offer much pretense of balance, and some are unapologetically angry about the outcome. That partisan quality is inevitable in Hillary Clinton's *What Happened* (Simon & Schuster, 2017). Her "doomed campaign" is the subject of *Shattered* (Crown Publishing, 2017) by Jonathan Allen and Amie Parnes. Amy Chozick supplies a pro-Hillary analysis in *Chasing Hillary* (HarperCollins, 2018). Katy Tur offers a first-hand account of the campaign in the aptly titled *Unbelievable* (Dey Street Books, 2017). For the new president's background, see Marc Fisher and Michael Kranish, *Trump Revealed* (Simon & Schuster, 2016).

In the aftermath of the election, many writers struggled to understand Trump's appeal, and in the process they generated several works on the state of white conservative America – which was here viewed almost as a distant primitive land. Caitríona Perry surveys "Trump Country" in her *In America* (Gill Books, 2017), and Trump's appeal is also the subject of *The People Are Going to Rise Like the Waters Upon Your Shore* (Counterpoint, 2017) by Jared Yates Sexton. Working-class Louisiana is the subject of Arlie Russell Hochschild's *Strangers in Their Own Land* (The New Press, 2016), while Ben Bradlee, Jr., offers a Pennsylvania case study in *The Forgotten* (Little, Brown, 2018). John Judis, *The Populist Explosion* (Columbia Global Reports, 2016) puts populism in a longer historical framework, and John L. Campbell seeks the roots of Trumpism in *American Discontent* (Oxford University Press, 2018). For Trump's populist base, see Selena Zito and Brad Todd, *The Great Revolt* (Crown, 2018).

That earlier comment about partisanship applies to most of the early books about the Trump presidency, some of which verge on the apocalyptic. One sober exception is Michael Nelson's *Trump's First Year* (University of Virginia Press, 2018). Much angrier is David Frum's *Trumpocracy* (HarperCollins, 2018). Even more than usual, personal memoirs of political life tend to be apologetic and self-justifying. See for instance Michael Wolff's *Fire and Fury* (Little, Brown, 2018). Bob Woodward's *Fear* (Simon & Schuster, 2018) is a major study of the factions and divisions in the Trump White House, in a book that became a major news event in its own right.

As I have often remarked in these chapters, the US Supreme Court has been critical to political and social development. Major authors on this topic include Jeffrey Toobin, in his books *The Nine* (Anchor, 2008) and *The Oath* (Doubleday, 2012), which describes the Court in the Obama years. Laurence Tribe focuses on the Court under the leadership of John Roberts in *Uncertain Justice* (Henry Holt and Co., 2014). The crucial and controversial figure of Justice Antonin Scalia is the subject of Joan Biskupic, *American Original* (Sarah Crichton Books, 2009), and Richard L. Hasen, *The Justice of Contradictions* (Yale University Press, 2018). See also Jane S. de Hart, *Ruth Bader Ginsburg* (Alfred A. Knopf, 2018).

State studies offer valuable information. For California in this era, see Kevin Starr, *Coast of Dreams* (Alfred A. Knopf, 2004), and Manuel Pastor, *State of Resistance* (The New Press, 2018). For Texas, see Lawrence Wright, *God Save Texas* (Alfred A. Knopf, 2018).

When we look at any period of US history, some of the best resources are found in popular media, in novels, films, magazines, and television. In this era above all, the internet provides perhaps the most direct reflections of changing public attitudes.

Index